WINDOWS
NT4
Administrator's
Black Book

WINDOWS
NT4
Administrator's
Black Book

Paul Taylor

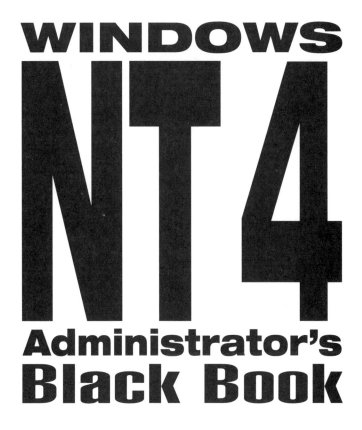 THE CORIOLIS GROUP

Publisher	*Keith Weiskamp*
Editorial Project Leader	*Toni Zuccarini*
Developmental Editor	*Joanne Slike*
Copy Editor	*Marisa Pena*
Cover Artist and Cover Design	*Anthony Stock*
Interior Design	*Nicole Birney*
Layout Production	*Rob Mauhar*
Proofreader	*Mary Millhollon*
Indexer	*Richard Evans*

The Coriolis Group, Inc.
14455 N. Hayden Road, Suite 220
Scottsdale, AZ 85260
Phone: (602) 483-0192
Fax: (602) 483-0193
Web address: http://www.coriolis.com

ISBN 1-57610-114-2 : $39.99

Printed in the United States of America

10 9 8 7 6 5 4 3 2 1

To Alyson

Contents

Chapter 8   Event And System
Monitoring Tools 299

Introduction

This book is aimed at both novice and experienced Windows NT system administratorswho work with either Windows NT Workstation or Server. Both are covered in this book. For the novice administrator, *Windows NT 4 System Administrator's Black Book* guides you through the steps needed to perform day-to-day administration tasks and gives useful background technical details on how and why Windows NT functions as it does. For the experienced administrator, this book is designed to be the one you reach for when you need to get a job done fast and right.

Each chapter of this book is divided into three sections: the first section provides technical information on the topics covered in the chapter. The next, and usually largest, section of each chapter provides a practical guide on how to perform the administrative tasks required to configure and maintain Windows NT. The last section of each chapter contains "Quick Reference Specifications" and the "Utilities To Use"—both of these can be used by the system administrator as a memory aid to quickly locate information.

The practical guides have examples based on real-life situations, many of which you may well have already encountered or will encounter in the future. The humor encountered in these examples is the result of my own years of experience as a busy system administrator.

The book is broken down into the following chapters:

Chapter 1 provides an overview of the key components of Windows NT. The practical guide provides examples on administrating these key components.

Chapter 2 introduces and explains system security. The practical guide provides examples on configuring system security.

Chapter 3 provides details of the system startup and shutdown procedure. The practical guide provides examples on changing and interpreting the startup and shutdown procedure.

Chapter 4 introduces the disk and file systems, paying particular attention to NTFS, and includes details on NTFS security. The practical guide provides examples on configuring and using both the file and disk systems.

Chapter 5 provides details on the User Environment and covers both User and Group rights and account setup, as well as configuring the user's working environment. The practical guide provides examples on both account and environment configuration.

Chapter 6 introduces the Windows NT print system, starting with Microsoft terminology for printing and covering the problems of printing in multiarchitecture environments. The practical guide provides examples on all aspects of the print system.

Chapter 7 covers networking and the roles servers play in the Windows NT environment. Details on each of the supported protocols are provided. The practical guide covers both networking and network integration.

Chapter 8 covers the Event and System monitoring tools, including system performance and network monitoring. The practical guide provides examples on configuring and using the monitoring tools.

Chapter 9 provides details on troubleshooting Windows NT, including details on common boot problems and fixes. The practical guide provides details on system recovery techniques and fault finding.

Chapter 10 provides details of the hardware and licensing requirements for Wind ows NT. The practical guide covers both installations and upgrades.

Chapter 11 provides hints and tips that cover various aspects of the operating system. The practical guide provide step-by-step instructions on implementing the hints and tips.

Appendix A provides an administrative tools reference guide that can be used to locate the correct tool for a particular administrative task.

Appendix B covers the changes and enhancements introduced with Windows NT 4.

Appendix C provides details on each of the Windows NT user rights.

Appendix D covers basic networking technologies, aimed at providing a grounding in networking for system administrators.

Chapter 1

Windows NT Overview

Administrator's Notes...

Chapter

1

This chapter introduces the key core components of Windows NT and provides examples on how to make changes to them. An in-depth technical description of each component has been avoided, because this information is not needed in the day-to-day management of a Windows NT system.

Windows NT Architecture

Windows NT has been designed in a modular form; the operating system as a whole is made up of separate software components, with each component managing a separate function of the operating system. This modular configuration ensures that future upgrades and extensions to the operating system can be made without having to change the entire operating system. The separate modules of the operating system do not share any program code, and all communication between the modules is done via system calls.

The Windows NT architecture is further divided into two separate sections: kernel mode and user mode. *Kernel mode* permits direct access to the computer hardware and is the mode that key components of the operating system run in. *User mode* has no direct access to the computer hardware and is a less-privileged mode than kernel mode. Applications and some Windows NT subsystems run in user mode.

Hardware Abstraction Layer

To enable Windows NT to run on computer systems with different architectures, a hardware abstraction layer (HAL) is used at the lowest level of the operating system. The HAL hides the actual physical characteristics of the computer hardware and presents a uniform interface to the high-level components of Windows NT.

Different HALs are provided by either Microsoft or the computer hardware manufacturer. The HAL operates in kernel mode.

Microkernel

The microkernel can be considered the core component of Windows NT. The microkernel is responsible for scheduling all jobs on the processor and controls all processors in a multiprocessor system. Because the microkernel is responsible for scheduling all activity, it cannot be removed from main memory; in other words, the microkernel cannot be paged out.

Several other software components make up the basic operating system. More details on these and the whole Windows NT architecture can be found in the Windows NT Resource Kit.

Windows NT Workstation And Server

Both Windows NT Workstation and Server share the same core operating system code. In fact, during the startup of a Windows NT system, the Registry configuration is checked by the operating system to determine if the system is to be run as a workstation or a server.

Windows NT Workstation is designed to be used as a powerful, secure, multitasking desktop client. Windows NT Server, on the other hand, is aimed at providing a network operating system and is supplied with enhanced administration tools to accomplish this. More details about the differences between Windows NT Workstation and Server can be found with the documentation and licenses that ship with the products.

Virtual Memory System

Windows NT uses a 32-bit, demand-paging virtual memory system to manage the available memory. This provides each process with 4 GB of virtual memory; of this, 2 GB is reserved for the operating system, and 2 GB is available for use by the process.

The memory is defined as *virtual* because, by using disk space, the operating system allocates more memory to a process than is physically available. In other words, 32 MB of physical memory may be installed in your computer, but the virtual memory system will allow the full 2 GB of virtual memory to be used by your process.

The virtual memory system is based on a demand-paging technique, where data is moved from main memory to disk when not in use and paged back into physical memory when required by the process. The removal of memory pages to the paging file is only done when the Virtual Memory Manager needs to free memory for other processes to use, so if the system never runs short of memory, paging will never occur.

The temporary area of disk space that is used to hold the data moved from main memory is known as the *paging file*. The paging file is created at an initial size and will grow as required up to the maximum size set. However, whenever the paging file grows, a small performance penalty is incurred. The preferred setup is to have the initial size of the paging file configured so that it doesn't need to grow.

Multiple paging files can be created on separate physical disks to increase the performance of the memory management system.

Process Priorities

Windows NT uses 31 process priorities to schedule processes to run. The priorities range from 1, which is the lowest priority, to 31, which is the highest. The actual priority at which a process runs is not static but is dynamically adjusted by Windows NT, to ensure optimum response. The dynamic adjustment of the process priority can be ± 2 from the process's base priority class. The base priority class is established when the process is started and can be changed once a process is running by using the Task Manager.

Four base priorities are available, which cover the 31 priority levels. These are shown in Table 1.1, along with the priority ranges they cover. At the extreme ends of the priority ranges, such as priority 6, you'll notice an overlap. By default, processes are started at the normal priority class—priority 7.

Care must be taken when running applications at the realtime priority class. Because the application would then be running at the same priority as the operating system, the operating system could be inhibited from functioning properly.

Priority Class	Priority Range
Idle	1–6
Normal	6–10
High	11–15
Realtime	16–31

Table 1.1   Base priorities.

The Registry

The Registry acts as a configuration database and contains virtually all of the Windows NT user and system configuration data. The data contained in the Registry is organized in a tree format, similar to how folders and files are stored on a disk.

The Registry is split into five subtrees, which contain keys and subkeys. These keys can contain data items known as *value entries*. The value entries are constructed in three parts: the value name, the data type of the value, and the actual value data. For example, you can see these parts in the Registry entry ServiceName:REG_SZ:Browser. Table 1.2 lists the data types used by the Registry.

Data Type	Description
REG_BINARY	Contains binary data. Hardware configuration data is stored in this format. Windows NT Diagnostics provides an easy-to-understand display of data stored in this way.
REG_DWORD	Contains data that is represented by a 4-byte number. Service values and interrupt levels are stored in this format.
REG_EXPAND_SZ	An expandable data string containing a logical assignment that is evaluated when the Registry value is accessed by an application.
REG_MULTI_SZ	Contains multiple strings in plaintext. Entries are separated by null characters.
REG_SZ	Contains a plaintext string. These are often the values changed manually by the system administrator.

Table 1.2   Registry data types.

In addition, the Registry has collections of keys, subkeys, and value entries called *hives* that start at the root of the Registry. The HKEY_LOCAL_MACHINE\System hive is shown in Figure 1.1. A hive is contained in a single file contained in the %SYSTEMROOT%\SYSTEM32\CONFIG folder. Table 1.3 provides an overview of each Registry subtree.

The administrator usually manages the Registry indirectly by using the system administration tools that automatically perform the necessary configuration changes to the Registry. If the change you require can't be achieved with the administration tools, you can use the Registry Editor REGEDT32 to make manual changes. Great care should be taken when using the Registry Editor; Windows NT can be rendered inoperative by incorrect changes to the Registry.

Because of the importance of the Registry to Windows NT, all changes to the Registry are either completed or not made. In other words, should the system fail for any reason while several Registry entries are being changed (often an administration tool must change several Registry entries for a new configuration to be implemented), the Registry would ensure that all the required entries are changed or that no changes are made, thus leaving the Registry in a known state.

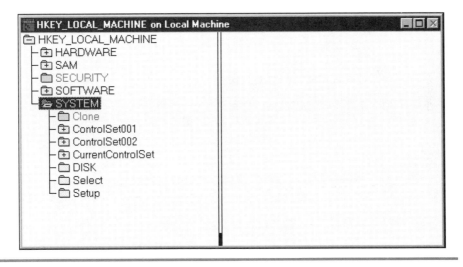

The system hive.
Figure 1.1

Subtree	Description
HKEY_LOCAL_MACHINE	Holds the local computer information, including the hardware configuration data, the Security Account Manager database, and the software configuration. The information held in this subtree is the same no matter who is actually logged on to the computer system.
HKEY_CLASSES_ROOT	Holds the associations between file types and applications. This subtree is an alias from HKEY_LOCAL_MACHINE\ SOFTWARE\Classes; the associations held here can be defined by using the Windows NT Explorer Options menu.
HKEY_CURRENT_CONFIG	Holds the configuration information for the hardware profile currently in use.
HKEY_CURRENT_USER	Holds the user profile for the user who is currently logged on, and contains data on the user's desktop and network share configuration.
HKEY_USERS	Holds all loaded user profiles, including the profile for the user who is currently logged on. The default profile held here will be used as a template for users who don't have a profile the first time they log on.

Table 1.3   Registry subtrees.

Workgroups And Domains

Windows NT can be used in either a workgroup or domain configuration. The main points of both configurations are pointed out in the following sections.

Workgroup

Each computer participating in a workgroup is considered to be equal. A Security Account Manager (SAM) database is held on each computer in the workgroup. The workgroup is defined as functioning on a peer-to-peer basis.

Because each computer holds its own SAM, the administration of the workgroup must be performed locally on each computer in the workgroup. The security policies are set on a system-wide basis. A workgroup configuration is usually only suitable for small numbers of users and computers.

Domain

All computers participating in a domain use a central domain SAM. The domain database is managed by Windows NT servers. (Details of the roles played by Windows NT servers in a domain can be found in Chapter 7.) Because a central domain database is used, the administration of the domain is also centralized, making the domain model suitable for larger numbers of computers and users. The security policies are set on a domain-wide basis.

Practical

Guide To

Windows NT

The following section provides real-life examples and step-by-step instructions on how to change some of the key components of Windows NT. As with any configuration changes to a working system, make sure you know what you're changing and why.

Using The Registry Editor In Read-Only Mode

Due to an unfortunate accident last week that left a Windows NT workstation clinically diagnosed as brain-dead, you have decided to take more care when poking about in the Registry (not that you're exactly holding your hand up to take the blame on this one). To spare future sleepless nights, you decide to leave the Registry Editor in read-only mode until you really need to make a change.

1. Choose Start|Run. The Run dialog box appears.

2. Click Browse, and use the Browse dialog box to select the Registry Editor REGEDT32, located in the SYSTEM32 subfolder. Click OK. The Registry Editor window is displayed.

3. Choose Options|Read-Only Mode. No changes made to the Registry while using the Registry Editor in read-only mode will be saved.

Finding A Registry Key

You have been tasked with making some changes to the Registry. You have one small problem, though: You can't quite remember where the key is located in the Registry that you need to change. Having to say "I can't find it" won't do your credibility any good at all. Luckily, the Find function can be pressed into action.

1. Choose Start|Run. The Run dialog box appears.

2. Click Browse, and use the Browse dialog box to select the Registry Editor REGEDT32, located in the SYSTEM32 subfolder. Click OK. The Registry Editor window is displayed.

3. Select the required subtree, for example, HKEY_LOCAL_MACHINE. Choose View|Find Key. The Find dialog box appears. Enter the key you want to search for, as shown in Figure 1.2. Click Find Next, and the subtree is searched.

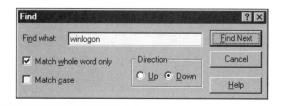

The Find dialog box.
Figure 1.2

Managing A Remote Computer's Registry

One of the users in the manufacturing plant has a problem with his computer that you must sort out. You need to look at the Registry to get an idea of the current configuration, but it's stifling out there in the plant, and you don't want to leave the air-conditioned comfort of your office. You decide to use the Remote Computer option to access the Registry.

1. Choose Start|Run. The Run dialog box appears.

2. Click Browse, and use the Browse dialog box to select the Registry Editor REGEDT32, located in the SYSTEM32 subfolder. Click OK. The Registry Editor is displayed.

3. Choose Registry|Select Computer. The Select Computer dialog box appears, as shown in Figure 1.3.

4. From the Select Computer list, select the computer whose Registry you want to manage, and click OK. The Registry Editor connects to the remote computer, and a warning dialog box appears, advising that auto-refresh will not be available for the remote Registry. The HKEY_LOCAL_MACHINE and HKEY_USERS subtrees are displayed.

5. To exit from the remote computer Registry, choose Registry|Close while one of the remote subtrees is selected.

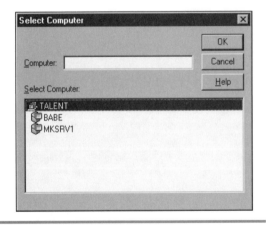

The Select Computer dialog box.
Figure 1.3

Saving A Registry Subkey

You have decided to make copies of the Registry subkeys on several computers so you can compare their configurations and also have a record of the current configuration.

1. Choose Start|Run. The Run dialog box appears.

2. Click Browse, and use the Browse dialog box to select the Registry Editor REGEDT32, located in the SYSTEM32 subfolder. Click OK. The Registry Editor appears.

3. Select the subtree you want to save. Choose Registry|Save Subtree As. The Save As dialog box appears, as shown in Figure 1.4.

The subtree will be saved as a plaintext file and can be used for future reference.

note

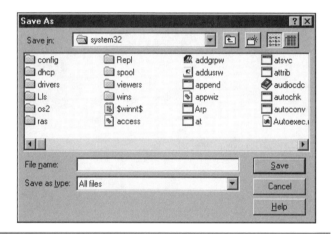

The Save As dialog box.
Figure 1.4

Changing The Size Of The Paging File

You have just increased your computer system memory from 32 MB to 64 MB, and, having a full grasp of the way the Windows NT virtual memory system works, you realize you should increase the size of your paging file. Here's how you do it:

1. Choose Start|Settings|Control Panel. The Control Panel window appears.

2. Double click the System icon. The System Properties sheet appears.

3. Click the Performance tab. The Performance page is displayed, as shown in Figure 1.5.

4. The current total size of the paging file is shown. Click Change. The Virtual Memory dialog box is displayed, as shown in Figure 1.6.

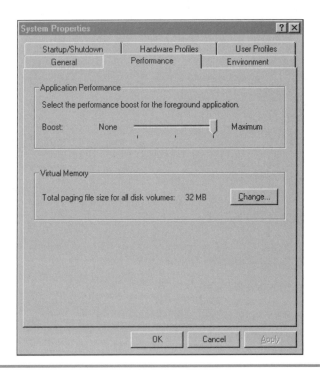

The Performance page.
Figure 1.5

5. The current size of the paging file is shown in the Total Paging File Size For All Drives pane. As shown in Figure 1.6, the current allocated size for the paging file is less than the recommended size. It's a good idea to increase the paging file to be at least equal to the recommended size.

6. Enter the size you require into the Initial Size box, and choose Set. Click OK, and you are returned to the Performance page. Click Close. You need to restart the computer before the increased paging file can be used. Click Yes to restart now.

The algorithm for working out the initial size of the paging file is the memory size + 12 MB. So for 64 MB of memory, you should set an initial paging file size of 74 MB.

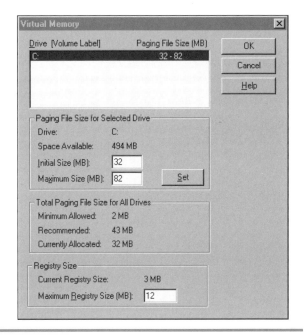

The Virtual Memory dialog box.
Figure 1.6

Creating Multiple Paging Files On Separate Disks

While having one of your rare flashes of inspiration, you decide to create the initial paging files you require on separate physical disks (you can check if the drive letter is mapped to a separate physical disk by using the Disk Administrator contained in the Administrative Tools program group). By having the paging files on multiple disks, the disk bottleneck that can often occur when a heavily loaded system is accessing the paging file will be reduced.

1. Choose Start|Settings|Control Panel. The Control Panel window appears.

2. Double click the System icon. The System Properties sheet appears.

3. Click the Performance tab to display the Performance page. Click Change, and the Virtual Memory dialog box is displayed.

4. Select the drive you want to create the paging file on. The Virtual Memory display will change to reflect the paging file size of the drive you have selected. This drive does not have a paging file on it, so the box will be blank.

5. Enter the initial and maximum sizes for the paging file into the relevant boxes. Click Set, as shown in Figure 1.7. Click OK.

6. You are returned to the System Properties window. Click Close. You'll need to reboot for the changes to take effect. Click Yes to reboot.

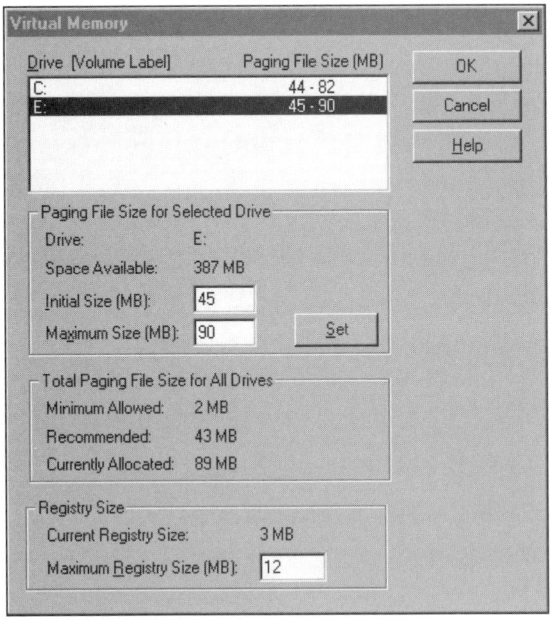

Adding a paging file.
Figure 1.7

Removing A Paging File

You have installed an additional disk controller with several more fast SCSI disks attached to it. On one of these disks, you have created quite a large paging file, which leaves you with a small paging file contained on an old, slow disk that you no longer require. Removing this unwanted paging file has puzzled you for a while. Deleting it while Windows NT is running is not possible, because the file is permanently held open by the operating system. Well, draw nearer to the fire, and as the smoke rises, all will become clear.

1. Choose Start|Settings|Control Panel. The Control Panel appears.

2. Double click the System icon. The System Properties window appears.

3. Click the Performance tab to display the Performance page.

4. Click the Change button, which is located in the Virtual Memory pane. The Virtual Memory dialog box appears.

5. Select the disk drive that contains the paging file you want to remove. Clear the values set in both the Initial Size and Maximum Size value boxes, as shown in Figure 1.8.

6. Choose Set. The paging file is removed from the paging file list.

7. Click OK, and then click Close. The computer must be restarted for the changes to take effect.

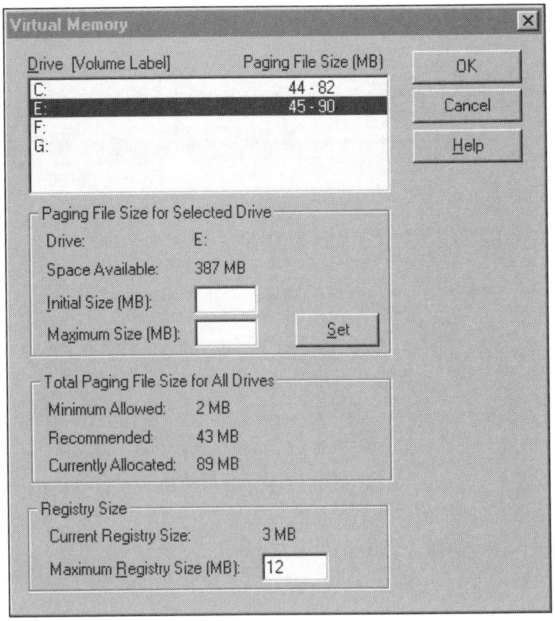

Virtual Memory

Drive [Volume Label]	Paging File Size (MB)
C:	44 - 82
E:	45 - 90
F:	
G:	

OK
Cancel
Help

Paging File Size for Selected Drive

Drive: E:

Space Available: 387 MB

Initial Size (MB): [   ]

Maximum Size (MB): [   ]   Set

Total Paging File Size for All Drives

Minimum Allowed: 2 MB

Recommended: 43 MB

Currently Allocated: 89 MB

Registry Size

Current Registry Size: 3 MB

Maximum Registry Size (MB):   [12   ]

Removing a paging file.
Figure 1.8

Starting A Process With A Higher Priority

You have a database-rebuild job that you want to run as fast as possible so you can get home at a reasonable time. You remember that you can use some Start switches to set the start priority of a process. (Isn't it amazing what can be accomplished with a little knowledge?)

1. Choose Start|Programs|Command Prompt.

2. Enter the process start line in the following format:

```
start program_name /high
```

An example of using the Start command line is shown in Figure 1.9.

 There are three other base priorities that can be set when a process is started: /low, /realtime, and /idle. Starting applications with the realtime priority is not advised, because these priorities will be running at the same priority as the operating system. This can cause the operating system to become unstable.

Start command line example.
Figure 1.9

Changing Foreground Performance Relative To Background

In the effort to squeeze every last bit of network performance out of your Windows NT Server, you have decided to set the foreground performance—in other words, assign the process using the mouse, screen, and keyboard a lower priority than the background. (I just have one question: What are you doing letting users log on to the server in the first place?)

1. Choose Start|Settings|Control Panel. The Control Panel is displayed.

2. Double click the System icon to access the System Properties sheet.

3. Click the Performance tab. The Performance page appears. The Application Performance pane contains a slider that can be used to select the performance boost for the foreground application. Set the required setting, and click OK.

Changing A Process's Base Priority

You have a process running that seems to be slowing down the server. It's not a very important process, so you decide to reduce its priority, at least for the time being. (If someone complains that their process has slowed down, you can always increase their priority.)

As a general rule, it is often advisable not to change the priorities of running processes; by default, Windows NT will be balancing the computer's resources against the demands being made on it by all of the running processes. However, business needs often overrule what is an advisable practice.

1. Right click the taskbar, and from the pop-up menu that appears, select Task Manager. The Windows NT Task Manager appears.

2. Click the Processes tab. The Processes page appears, showing all running processes on this computer.

3. Select the process you want to change the base priority of and right click. From the pop-up menu that appears, select Set Priority. The four base priorities appear, as shown in Figure 1.10.

4. From the list, select the priority you want to set. A Task Manager Warning dialog box appears, as shown in Figure 1.11. Click Yes, and the priority class is changed. You are then returned to the Task Manager.

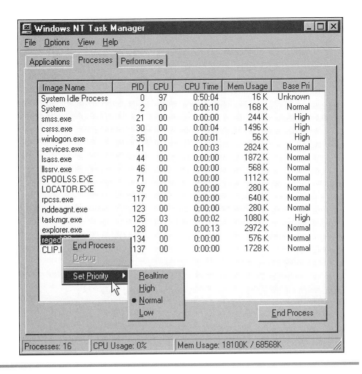

Setting a process's base priority.
Figure 1.10

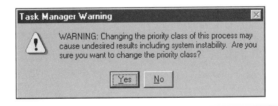

The Task Manager Warning.
Figure 1.11

Quick Reference Specifications

The following are the bare-bones facts and figures.

- *The hardware abstraction layer, or HAL, standardizes hardware platforms.*

- *The microkernel is responsible for scheduling all processes.*

- *Thirty-one priorities are used in the scheduling of processes.*

- *The 31 priorities are grouped into 4 priority classes: idle, low, realtime, and high.*

- *Windows NT automatically adjusts process priorities by ±2.*

- *Each process is provided with 4 GB of virtual memory address space.*

- *Windows NT is a fully 32-bit-based operating system.*

- *The initial paging file size should be at least the memory size plus 12 MB.*

Utilities To Use

The utilities used in this chapter and their functions are listed in this section. Consider this as a memory aid for the busy system administrator.

Command Prompt

- *Starting processes with different priorities.*

System Icon

- *Changing and creating paging files.*
- *Removing a paging file.*
- *Performance-boosting the foreground application.*

Task Manager

- *Changing a process's base priority class.*

Registry Editor

- *Searching the Registry for a particular key.*
- *Managing the Registry on a remote computer.*
- *Saving a Registry key.*

Chapter 2

System Security

Administrator's Notes...

Chapter 2

Components of the Windows NT security system are encountered in virtually all chapters of this book. This is because the Windows NT security system is a fundamental and underlying component of the operating system. The points covered in this chapter are pure security issues, along with the technology used to implement the security system. (For a more complete picture of Windows NT security, these points should be combined with the account information in Chapter 5 and the NTFS permissions discussion in Chapter 4.) In addition, Chapter 8 provides details on examining the security audit log.

A key point regarding Windows NT security is that the security system can only protect data when the operating system is in use. In other words, physical security needs to be considered. If the Windows NT system can be restarted using a different operating system, the data held on Windows NT volumes can be accessed. Like all other operating systems, Windows NT does not encrypt the data held on disk.

The Logon Process

The following steps describe the components used in the validation of an interactive logon for a user. Key components are then covered in more detail.

1. Pressing Ctrl+Alt+Del invokes the Windows NT Logon Information dialog box.

2. The user enters the user account details, i.e., username and password.

3. The logon process called the Local Security Authority (LSA) runs the logon authentication package.

4. The username and password are verified by the authentication package against the account information contained in the Security Accounts Manager (SAM).

5. If the logon information is found to be incorrect, the logon attempt is rejected, and the Logon Message dialog box appears, displaying a logon failure warning message.

6. If the logon information is valid, the authentication package creates a logon session and passes the necessary account information to the LSA for the Security Access Token (SAT) to be created.

7. The Win32 subsystem is called by the logon process to create a user process to which the Security Access Token is attached. The Win32 subsystem starts the Windows NT desktop.

Local Security Authority (LSA)

The Local Security Authority plays a key role in the Windows NT security system and provides the software interface between the user and kernel modes of Windows NT. Its main functions include:

- Calling the appropriate user authentication package

- Generating the Security Access Token

- Logging audit messages generated by the Security Reference Monitor

- Controlling the Audit policy

Security Access Token (SAT)

When a Windows NT logon occurs, the operating system generates a Security Access Token (SAT) containing the Security ID (SID) of the user who is logging on, the Security ID of any groups to which the user belongs, plus any user rights assigned to the user. The Security ID is discussed further in Chapter 5.

The SAT is only generated upon logon, so any changes made to either the user's rights or to the groups to which the user belongs will only take effect when the user next logs on. In other words, if a user is currently logged on and added to the Administrators group, this group membership will only take effect when the user logs off and back on again. By comparing the Security IDs contained in the SAT to the permissions assigned to the object, Windows NT can verify that the user has sufficient permissions to access an object. Each process that runs on behalf of a user receives a copy of the SAT, which the process will use to access objects.

Security Reference Monitor

The Security Reference Monitor verifies whether the requested access to an object is allowed and whether the requesting process has permission to perform the required operation on the object. The Security Reference Monitor is also responsible for generating audit messages.

Access Control List (ACL)

The access control list (ACL) contains access control entries (ACEs). The ACEs contain access masks, which are used to identify which users or groups have been granted or denied access to an object. When access to an object—for instance, a file, printer, or folder—is requested, the security system searches the ACL to see if the requested access is allowed. The ACEs are ordered in the ACL so that the no-access ACEs are listed first. If the access to the object has been blocked, this ACE will be reached before the grant-access ACEs. Therefore, if a user requests access to a file with an ACE that allows access, but the user is also a member of a group that is denied access, the user will be denied access.

The following steps show the method used to either allow or deny access to an object.

1. When access to an object is requested, a desired access mask is created that contains the process's access request.

2. The process's SAT is compared to the first ACE in the ACL. If a match is found between the Security IDs contained in the SAT and those contained in the ACE, further processing of the access request is done. If no match is found in this ACE, the next ACE is checked in the same way. If no match is found in any ACE contained in the object's ACL, access to the object is denied.

3. If access is denied, the desired access mask is checked to see whether the request is to change the object's permissions. If it is, and the process requesting the access is either the owner of the object or an administrator, the access will be allowed. If not, access to the object will be denied and no further ACEs will be checked.

4. If the access is allowed, the ACL entries are checked until an ACE is found with the exact match to the desired access mask. If the match is found, the access is allowed; if not, the access is denied.

Access Masks

The ACEs' access masks contain a list of possible access permissions based on the object type. These permissions are used to grant or deny access to the object. The different possible access permissions are defined as three separate groups, as shown in Table 2.1.

Security Accounts Manager (SAM)

The Security Accounts Manager (SAM) database is where all the user and group security information is held. In a workgroup, each workstation uses its own SAM, so all users and groups are local to that workstation. In the domain configuration, a single central SAM is used, which is administrated by the User Manager For Domains tool.

The SAM is also known as the directory service database. The actual security data is contained in the HKEY_LOCAL_MACHINE\SAM Registry key. By default, the Registry contents of this key cannot be viewed directly due to the permissions configured on it. The permissions can be changed on this key, but, as with all Registry keys, the preferred method of administrating this key is to use the relevant system administration tool—for instance, User Manager For Domains.

Administrative Accounts

The built-in Windows NT Administrator account has some special properties associated with it:

- Account cannot be deleted.

- Account will not be locked by bad logon attempts.

Any user account can be given Administrator rights, but only the built-in Administrator account has these special properties, as shown in Figure 2.1. The Administrator

Type	Description
Specific	Contains the access mask information specific to that particular object type. Each object can have up to 16 specific types defined.
Standard	Contains the access mask information that applies to all objects.
Generic	Contains mappings to both specific and standard types.

Table 2.1 Access mask types.

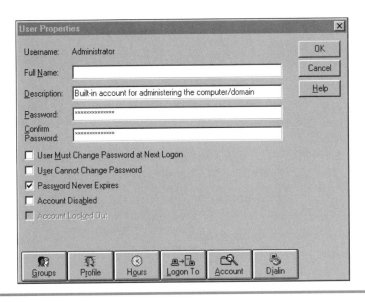

User Properties for the Administrator account.
Figure 2.1

account is a potential security risk; any number of passwords could be tried and the account would not be locked, regardless of the account policy in force. Renaming the Administrator account helps to reduce this risk, because any potential hacker would need to guess the account name in addition to the password.

As with any operating system, accounts with Administrator rights should only be used when performing administrative tasks. Normal user accounts should be used on a day-to-day basis to avoid accidental changes to the operating system.

By default, the Administrator account is a member of the Administrator, Domain Admins, and Domain Users groups on Windows NT Server. Further details on these groups is given in Chapter 5.

The Guest Account

General users who don't have an account on the relevant system can use the built-in Guest account to log on. The Guest account is, by default, disabled on Windows NT Server and enabled on Windows NT Workstation. The use of this account is often prohibited in the corporate environment because of the lack of accountability that occurs when multiple users are using the same account.

A common use for the Guest account is in small workgroups where the Guest account is enabled on all workstations with either no password or the same password set on all systems. When a user on one station wants to connect to a share offered by another, Windows NT attempts to make the share connection using the user's username and password. If the user doesn't have an account on the remote workstation, the Guest account is used to establish the connection instead.

By default, the Guest account is a member of the Domain Guest group for Windows NT Server. Further details on these groups are given in Chapter 5.

Locking The System

Standard security practice is to ensure that a Windows NT system is never left unattended with a user account logged on. This is especially important if an Administrator account is in use. Instead of logging off each time the system is unattended, the user can lock the system. Once locked, the user's logon password must be entered to unlock the system. This lock can be overridden by an administrator.

Windows NT screen savers can be used to automatically lock the system after a user-definable period of inactivity. The system will continue to function, accepting network connections and so on. Only the local display, keyboard, and mouse will be locked.

C2 Security

Windows NT has been evaluated as being C2-compliant by the National Computer Security Center (NCSC). The C2 security level is based on the requirements outlined in the U.S. Department of Defense Trusted Computers System evaluation criteria, also known as the "orange book." (The book is a member of the "rainbow range," with each book being a different color.)

The DOD security categories range from D, which provides minimal protection, to A, which is verified to be secure. A PC running DOS would be classed as D. Table 2.2 lists the current security levels.

Let's look at the C2 level more closely. C2 security features the following:

- Object protection on a user and group basis.

- Password is protected with a secure authorization database. Unique usernames are required.

Level	Provides
D	Minimal protection.
C	Discretionary protection division.
C1	Discretionary security protection.
C2	Controlled access protection.
B	Mandatory protection division.
B1	Labeled security protection.
B2	Structured protection.
B3	Security domains.
A	Verified protection division.
A1	Verified protection.
A2	Not yet defined.

Table 2.2   Security levels.

- Auditing of security-related events.

- Authorization for access may only be assigned by authorized users.

- Objects must be protected from reuse. For instance, memory freed by one process shouldn't be able to be read by another.

Provided with the Windows NT Resource Kit is the C2 Configuration Manager, which can be used to configure Windows NT to meet the C2 security level.

Practical

Guide To

System

Security

The following section provides real-life examples and step-by-step instructions on how to administrate Windows NT security. As previously stated, the Windows NT security system cannot be separated from the total operating system, so examples on using and configuring security can be found in most chapters. Some of these examples use the Registry Editor REGEDT32 to directly change the Registry. Be careful when using REGEDT32; incorrect changes to the Registry can prevent Windows NT from functioning.

Removing The Last Logged On Username

You have a lot of general-user Windows NT workstations—in other words, systems not allocated to any particular user but available for anyone to use. You often find that users are trying to log on using the wrong username, and at the moment, the last logged on username is displayed. This isn't a particular security issue for you, but it does mean that user accounts are getting locked by mistake. You decide to remove the last logged on username from the logon screen.

The last username is removed by changing the Registry. This can be done in one of three ways:

a. Using the System Policy Editor in a domain to create a domain policy.

b. Using the System Policy Editor to change the local Registry.

c. Using the Registry Editor REGEDT32 to change the Registry.

Method A—Creating A Domain Policy

1. Choose Start|Programs|Administrative Tools|System Policy Editor. The System Policy Editor window appears.

2. Choose File|New Policy. The Policy window shows the Default Computer and Default User icons. Double click the Default Computer icon to display the Default Computer Properties window.

3. Double click the Windows NT System icon, then the Logon Book icon.

4. Select the Do not display last logged on user name option, as shown in Figure 2.2. Click OK. You are returned to the System Policy Editor window.

5. Choose File|Save As, and save the policy file to the NetLogon folder of the Primary Domain Controller with a file name of NTCONFIG.POL.

Method B—Changing The Local Registry

1. Choose Start|Programs|Administrative Tools|System Policy Editor. The System Policy Editor window appears.

2. Choose File|Open Registry. The local Registry is opened.

3. Double click the Local Computer icon. The Local Computer Properties window appears.

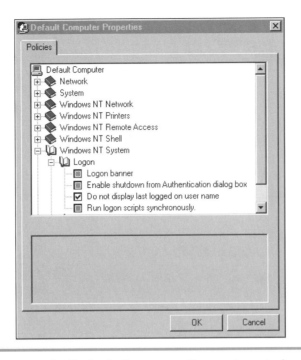

Logon policy settings in the Default Computer Properties window.
Figure 2.2

4. Double click the Windows NT System icon, then double click the Logon Book. Check the Do not display last logged in user name option. Click OK. You are returned to the System Policy Editor window. Click File|Save to save the changes to the local Registry.

Method C—Changing The Registry Directly

1. Choose Start|Run. The Run dialog box appears.

2. Use the Browse button to select the Registry Editor REGEDT32, which is located in the SYSTEM32 subfolder, as shown in Figure 2.3. Click OK. The Registry Editor window appears.

3. Select the HKEY_LOCAL_MACHINE hive. Select the SOFTWARE\Microsoft\Windows NT\CurrentVersion\Winlogon subkey.

4. If the DontDisplayLastUserName value entry doesn't exist, you need to create it. Choose Edit|Add Value. The Add Value dialog box appears. Enter "DontDisplayLastUserName" into the Value Name field, and select REG_SZ in the Data Type field. Click OK. The

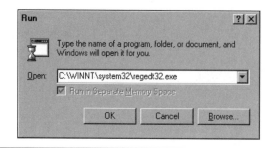

The Run dialog box.
Figure 2.3

String Editor dialog box appears. Enter "1" into the dialog box, and click OK. The Registry value entry will be created.

5. If the DontDisplayLastUserName value entry does exist, double click the entry. The String Editor dialog box appears. Enter "1" into the dialog box, and click OK. The Registry value entry is updated.

When the users now log on, the Username field in the Windows NT logon screen will be blank.

To change back to having the last username displayed, either change the DontDisplayLastUserName entry to 0 or delete the value completely.

Displaying A Logon Message

As a gentle reminder to all users, it has been decided that a logon message should be displayed informing users that they must not disclose their passwords to anyone and should only use their own accounts. The message can be set in two ways: the first uses the System Policy Editor and the second uses the Registry Editor.

Method A—Using The System Policy Editor

1. Choose Start|Programs|Administrative Tools|System Policy Editor. The System Policy Editor window appears.

2. Choose File|Open Registry. The Local Registry window appears.

3. Double click the Local Computer icon to access the Local Computer Properties window. Double click the Windows NT System icon, and then double click the Logon Book icon. Select the Logon banner option box.

4. The logon banner may now be set in the lower pane, as shown in Figure 2.4. Enter the title for the message into the Caption box and the actual message into the Text box. Click OK. You are returned to the System Policy Editor window.

5. Choose File|Save to save the changes to the Registry.

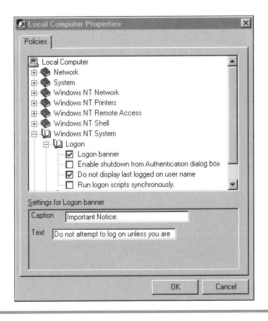

Setting the logon banner.

Figure 2.4

Method B—Using The Registry Editor

1. Choose Start|Run. The Run dialog box appears.

2. Use the Browse button to select the Registry Editor REGEDT32, which is located in the SYSTEM32 subfolder. The Registry Editor window appears.

3. Select the HKEY_LOCAL_MACHINE hive. Select the SOFTWARE\Microsoft\Windows NT\CurrentVersion\WinLogon subkey.

4. If the LegalNoticeCaption value entry doesn't exist, choose Edit|Add Value to access the Add Value dialog box. Enter "LegalNoticeCaption" into the Value Name field, and select REG_SZ in the Data Type field. Click OK. The String Editor dialog box appears. Enter the title message for the logon message. Click OK.

5. If the LegalNoticeCaption value entry does exist, double click the entry. The String Editor dialog box appears. Enter the title message for the logon message. Click OK.

6. If the LegalNoticeText value entry doesn't exist, choose Edit|Add Value. The Add Value dialog box appears. Enter "LegalNoticeText" into the Value Name field, and select REG_SZ in the Data Type field. Click OK. The String Editor dialog box appears. Enter the text you want displayed. Click OK.

7. If the LegalNoticeText value entry does exist, double click the entry. The String Editor dialog box appears. Enter the text you want to be displayed. Click OK.

The logon message will now be displayed to all users upon logon. The message must be acknowledged for the logon process to continue.

Allowing Automatic Logons

A workstation has been installed in the company reception area for use by visitors. This system is mainly used for checking the online phone directory and accessing the corporate intranet. To make it easier to use, it has been decided that the system should automatically log on when rebooted.

1. Choose Start|Run. The Run dialog box appears.

2. Use the Browse button to select the Registry Editor REDEDT32, which is located in the SYSTEM32 subfolder. Click OK. The Registry Editor window appears.

3. Select the HKEY_LOCAL_MACHINE hive. Select the SOFTWARE\Microsoft\Windows NT\CurrentVersion\Winlogon subkey.

4. Choose Edit|Add Value from the Registry Editor menu. The Add Value dialog box appears. Enter "AutoAdminLogon" into the Value Name field. In the Data Type field, select REG_SZ, as shown in Figure 2.5. Click OK. The String Editor dialog box appears. Enter "1" into the box, and click OK.

5. Double click the DefaultUsername entry. The String Editor dialog box appears. Enter the username of the account you want to automatically log on. Click OK.

6. Choose Edit|Add Value from the Registry Editor menu. The Add Value dialog box appears. Enter "DefaultPassword" into the Value Name field. In the Data Type box, select REG_SZ. Click OK. The String Editor dialog box appears.

7. Enter the password for the default user account. (Remember, Windows NT passwords are case sensitive.) Click OK. Exit the Registry Editor.

The Add Value dialog box.
Figure 2.5

When the system is restarted, the default user will automatically be logged on. When the user logs off, the default account will automatically be logged on again. To inhibit this automatic logon, the user must press and hold down the Shift key while the logon is in progress.

When the default user information is stored in the Registry, the user password is stored in plain text. By default, any user can view the WinLogon Registry key, which can present a security issue, especially if the automatic logon account is an administration account. To overcome this, the permissions on the Registry key can be changed. The next example shows how to do this.

Setting Permissions On Registry Keys

Now that a password has been set to allow an automatic logon on startup, steps need to be taken to ensure that users don't find out the password used for the automatic logon account. This can be done by changing the permissions on the relevant Registry key.

1. Choose Start|Run. The Run dialog box appears.

2. Use the Browse button to select the Registry Editor REGEDT32, which is located in the SYSTEM32 subfolder. Click OK. The Registry Editor window appears.

3. Select the HKEY_LOCAL_MACHINE hive. Select the SOFTWARE\Microsoft\Windows NT\CurrentVersion\Winlogon subkey.

4. Choose Security|Permissions to access the Registry Key Permissions window for the Winlogon key, as shown in Figure 2.6. By default, the group Everyone has the Read permission on this key. Therefore, any user would be able to view the automatic logon account password. To inhibit this, the group Everyone permission to this key can be removed.

5. Select Everyone from the Name list. Click Remove, and the group is removed from the Name list. Click OK. The Registry permissions are updated.

This Registry key will now appear grayed-out to non-privileged users, and no key entries will be displayed.

 Changing permissions on Registry keys must be done with great care. Windows NT can be locked out from Registry keys just as users can. The next section shows how Registry events can be audited in case such a problem occurs.

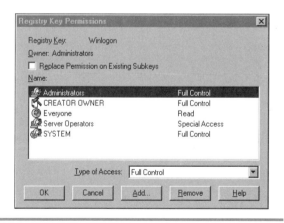

The Registry Key Permissions window.
Figure 2.6

Setting Auditing On Registry Keys

It's a good idea to set auditing for failure on a Registry key that you are changing the permissions on. This way, if a change you have made causes problems, it will at least be logged in the event log. (So don't forget to destroy the evidence before the questioning starts.)

1. Choose Start|Run. The Run dialog box appears.

2. Use the Browse button to select the Registry Editor REGEDT32, which is located in the SYSTEM32 subfolder. Click OK.

3. Select the key on which you want to audit the events. Choose Security|Auditing. The Registry Key Auditing window appears.

4. Click the Add button, and select the user or group you want to audit from the Names list. Click the Add button again. The selected name appears in the Add Names pane. Repeat for each user or group you want to add. Click OK. You are returned to the Registry Key Auditing window.

5. Select the events you want to audit by selecting the option boxes in the Events to Audit pane, as shown in Figure 2.7. Click OK, and the auditing configuration is implemented.

If it is not already configured, the Audit policy needs to be set to log the Registry audit events. The procedure is as follows:

1. Choose Start|Programs|Administrative Tools|User Manager For Domains.

2. In the Policies menu, choose Audit. The Audit Policy window appears.

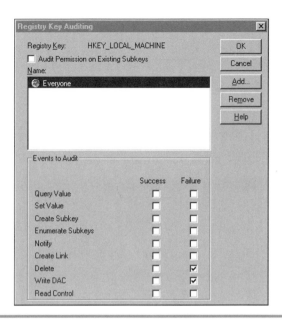

Registry Key Auditing window.
Figure 2.7

3. If it isn't already selected, choose Audit These Events. Select the File And Object Access option. Set either the Success or Failure box, depending on what type of event you are auditing. Click OK. Exit User Manager For Domains.

Any Registry audit events will now be logged in the security event log. Details on how to view and administrate the event logs can be found in Chapter 8.

Changing The Logon Screen

It has been decided by people far more important than you that the company logo should appear on the logon screen. The graphics department has provided you with a bitmap file of the logo. True, the logo is a bit boring, but after some company joker devised a screen saver featuring photos of you at the last office party, you decide the logo isn't that bad.

1. Choose Start|Run. The Run dialog box appears.

2. Use the Browse button to select the Registry Editor REGEDT32, which is located in the SYSTEM32 subfolder. Click OK. The Registry Editor window appears.

3. Select the HKEY_USERS hive. Select the DEFAULT\Control Panel\Desktop subkey.

4. Double click the Wallpaper key. The Registry Editor appears, as shown in Figure 2.8. In the dialog box, enter the name of the bitmap file you want to use as the logon screen. Click OK. Exit the Registry Editor.

When you log off and log back on, you will see the new logon screen in operation.

 The bitmap files you want to use as logon screens must be located in the Windows NT system root folder.

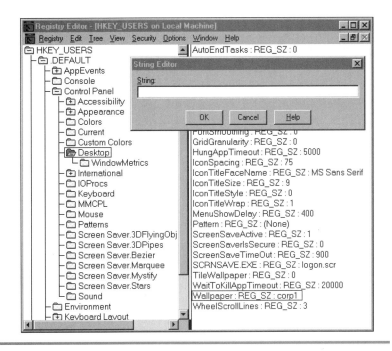

The Registry Editor.

Figure 2.8

Locking And Unlocking Windows NT

A new user approaches you with a worried look on his face and confesses that he can't find the key for his workstation anywhere. This puzzles you, until on questioning the user further, you find he has been told by his new boss to lock his workstation before going to lunch. (Well, what do you think? Should we play with this user for a bit or set him straight? Okay, we'll tell him.) To lock and unlock a workstation:

1. Press Ctrl+Alt+Del. The Windows NT Security window appears.

2. Click the Lock Workstation button. The system locks and the Workstation Locked dialog box appears.

3. To unlock the system, press Ctrl+Alt+Del. The Unlock Workstation window appears. Enter the user password to unlock the system or override the lock by entering an Administrator username and password, which, although unlocking the workstation, will cause the user to be logged off.

In this and the following discussion, the term workstation refers to both Windows NT Workstation and Server.

Configuring A Screen Saver To Automatically Lock

The advancing years are beginning to take a toll on your memory: you keep walking away from your desk without locking your workstation. This is, of course, in direct opposition to the corporate security policy. You decide to set the screen saver to automatically lock the screen after 15 minutes of inactivity. Now, the next time you fall asleep at your desk, at least your workstation will be secure.

1. Choose Start|Settings|Control Panel. The Control Panel window appears.

2. Double click the Display icon. The Display Properties sheet appears.

3. Click the Screen Saver tab. The Screen Saver page appears. Select a screen saver from the Screen Saver pane, and select the Password Protected option box. The selected screen saver is displayed, as shown in Figure 2.9.

4. Set the timer for the length of inactivity before the system is locked, and click OK.

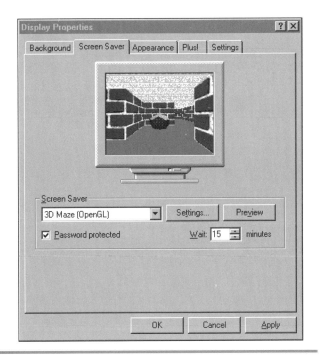

Screen Saver page in Display Properties.
Figure 2.9

Quick Reference Specifications

The following are the bare-bones facts and figures.

— *Local Security Authority (LSA) is the heart of the security system and the interface between the user and the security system.*

— *Security Reference Monitor (SRM) checks user-requested access against permissions defined on the object.*

— *Security Access Token (SAT) is only updated at logon and contains the user Security ID (SID) and the groups to which the user belongs.*

— *Access control list (ACL) contains the access control entries.*

— *Access control entries (ACEs) contain access masks, which list the permissions assigned to any object.*

— *The built-in Administrator account can be renamed but not deleted; it will not be locked by bad logon attempts.*

— *The Guest account can be used for general user access.*

— *Windows NT has been evaluated as C2 compliant.*

Utilities To Use

The utilities used in this chapter and their functions are listed in this section. Consider this as a memory aid for the busy system administrator.

Display Icon

- Configure password-protected screen saver.

System Policy Editor

- Remove last logged-on username.
- Display security logon message.

Registry Editor

- Remove last logged-on username.
- Display security logon message.
- Configure automatic logons.
- Set Registry key permissions.
- Set auditing on Registry keys.

User Manager For Domains

- Configure the Audit policy.

Chapter 3

System Startup And Shutdown

Administrator's Notes...

Chapter 3

The system startup of Windows NT is a potential problem area for the Windows NT administrator. This chapter concentrates on the actual startup procedure, the files involved, and recovery techniques. When combined with the information in Chapter 9, which is the troubleshooting chapter, these techniques will help you diagnose and resolve startup problems. It should be noted that the specific startup process depends on the processor architecture on which the computer is based.

System Startup

When an Intel x86-based system is started, the Windows NT startup sequence is as follows:

1. Power-on self tests are run.

2. The boot device is located, and the master boot record is executed.

3. The master boot record locates the system partition and loads the boot sector from it.

4. The Windows NT boot loader, NTLDR, is loaded into memory and executed.

5. The processor is switched into 32-bit mode. The relevant minifile system is now started, supporting either FAT or NTFS volumes.

6.   The BOOT.INI file is read, and the available operating system selections are displayed. The selections will appear for the length of time specified in the display list configuration line in BOOT.INI.

7.   NTLDR runs NTDETECT.COM, which will detect the currently installed hardware and prepare a list. The list is passed back to NTLDR.

8.   NTLDR then inquires if you want to invoke the Hardware Profile/Last Known Good. Pressing the spacebar while this message is displayed will invoke the relevant menu.

9.   NTLDR then loads the Windows NT kernel, NTOSKRNL.EXE, and passes to it the hardware information gathered by NTDETECT.COM. At this point, the relevant device drivers are loaded but not initialized.

10.   The kernel initializes and turns the screen blue when it has successfully taken control.

11.   The device drivers that were loaded during the kernel load are now initialized. In addition, a second group of drivers is loaded and initialized by the kernel.

12.   The high-level operating subsystems and services are now initiated by the session manager, SMSS.EXE.

13.   An automatic boot time, CHKDSK, is run on each partition to verify partition integrity.

14.   The paging file (or swap file) is set up.

15.   The required subsystem is started—for example, the Windows subsystem, WIN32, which controls all I/O from the video screen.

16.   WIN32 starts WINLOGON.EXE, which, in turn, starts the local security administrator, LASS.EXE. At this point, the Logon dialog box appears, inviting you to log on.

17.   Although you can now log on, the startup process will continue and the necessary system services will be started in the background. Once a user has successfully logged on, the startup is considered good. The HKEY_LOCAL_MACHINES\System\LastKnownGood registry subkey is updated to point to the registry key that contains the configuration used to start the operating system successfully.

The RISC startup is more dependent on the processor hardware. Table 3.1 points out which files are used for both x86- and RISC-based architectures, along with their location, attributes, and function.

File	Location	Attributes	Function
NTLDR	Root folder of boot drive	Hidden, read-only system file	Windows NT system loader; also allows the loading of other operating systems; x86-based systems only.
BOOT.INI	Root folder of boot drive	Read-only system file	Provides the operating system selection list; x86-based systems only.
BOOTSECT.DOS	Root folder of boot drive	Hidden system file	Used to boot a different operating system from within NTLDR, e.g., MS-DOS.
NTDETECT.COM	Root folder of boot drive	Hidden, read-only system file	Builds installed hardware list and passes back information to NTLDR; x86-based systems only.
OSLOADER.EXE	\Os\Winnt40		The operating system loader for RISC systems. This provides, along with the RISC hardware, the same functions as NTLDR.
NTOSKRNL.EXE	%systemroot% \System32		The Windows NT kernel.

Table 3.1 The Windows NT startup files.

As you will see in Chapter 9, there are various problems that can occur during startup that can be corrected by a competent system administrator. The system startup configuration can be modified by using the System icon contained in the Control Panel. The Startup/Shutdown tab is shown in Figure 3.1.

BOOT.INI

The BOOT.INI file supports the starting of not only Windows NT, but a selection of other operating systems, including non-Microsoft products. Figure 3.2 shows the BOOT.INI file configured for a dual-boot system. The operating systems in this case are Windows NT and MS-DOS.

There are two lines of code used to start Windows NT. One line is the normal Windows NT startup line. The second is the VGA start line and is used to boot a standard VGA

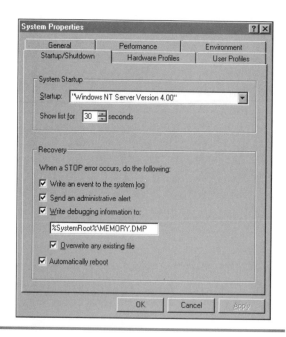

The Startup/Shutdown management utility.

Figure 3.1

configuration. This uses the /BASEVIDEO switch to overcome display problems caused by selecting the wrong video driver—which may mean that you can't read the display upon firing up Windows NT (which makes managing a Windows-based system slightly difficult, to say the least).

The VGA start line shown in Figure 3.2 also uses the /SOS boot switch. This switch displays the name of each device driver as it is loaded. The /SOS switch is useful if the system won't boot because a particular driver is missing. Table 3.2 shows a list of the most useful switches for system administrators.

The BOOT.INI file uses the Advanced RISC Computer (ARC) naming convention to identify the path and file names of Windows NT. In addition, there are two types of boot format: multi() and SCSI(). Multi() indicates that the system BIOS should be used to start the operating system. SCSI() indicates that the SCSI device should be used.

SCSI drives are not always accessed via the SCSI() parameter, but could be accessed via multi(). In other words, the system BIOS will be used to start Windows NT.

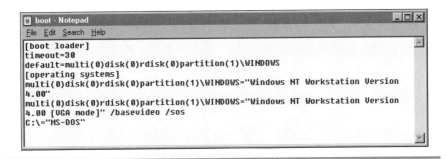

The BOOT.INI file.
Figure 3.2

The full command-line parameters used in BOOT.INI for both multi() and SCSI() are:

```
SCSI/multi(w) disk(x) rdisk(y) partition(z)
```

The possible values for both of these boot formats are shown in Table 3.3.

Hardware Profile/Last Known Good

When the startup has collected the hardware information using NTDECTECT.COM, a selection line is displayed, allowing you to press the spacebar to invoke the Hardware Profile/Configuration Recovery menu. This menu lets you select different hardware profiles or invoke the configuration used the last time the system was successfully started, called Last Known Good. (A successful startup is when the system has completed all of its startup tasks and has had successful user logon.)

Switch	Description	Function
/BASEVIDEO	Causes Windows NT to start with standard VGA.	Fixes display driver problems.
/MAXMEM	Limits the amount of memory used by Windows NT.	Can be used to diagnose memory problems.
/NOSERIALMICE	Inhibits the auto-detection of serial mice.	Can be used to stop modems, etc. from wrongly being detected as mice.
/SOS	Displays device drivers as they are loaded.	Useful if Windows NT won't start and the problem is driver- or hardware-related.

Table 3.2 The BOOT.INI configuration switches.

Parameter	Multi() Definition	SCSI() Definition
w	Controller number always 0.	Set to relevant controller number.
x	Unused, always set to 0.	SCSI ID of the target drive.
y	0 or 1 for drives connected to primary controller.	SCSI logical unit number of the target drive; usually set to 0.
z	Partition number—partition numbering starts at 1; all other parameters at 0.	

Table 3.3   ARC naming conventions.

The Hardware Profiles tab found under System Properties can be used to create hardware profiles that can start Windows NT with different hardware configurations. This is particularly useful for portables that can be used with docking stations, because it allows one profile to be created for use with the docking station and another profile for use without the station. The Hardware Profiles management window is shown in Figure 3.3. The required services can also be enabled and disabled on a per-profile basis.

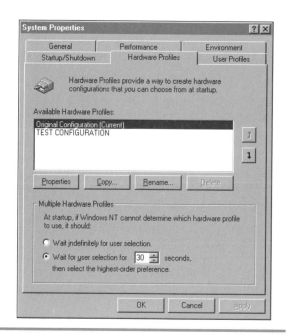

The Hardware Profiles management tab.
Figure 3.3

System Services

At the point when you can actually log on to Windows NT, there might well be some system services still starting up. These services provide the background functionality for Windows NT. The system services can be set to automatically start when Windows NT is started, or they can be started manually by using the Services start option in the Control Panel. The actual services on the system will depend on the products installed and the configuration used. Many of the system services will not be seen as separate processes when the system is viewed using the Task Manager Processor tab to display current processes. This is because these services are being run by the services process, which is a shared process used to conserve system resources. Table 3.4 shows the most important default services and their functions.

The Services management window is shown in Figure 3.4, and the Service startup window is shown in Figure 3.5.

Service	Function
Alerter	Notifies of any system alerts that have occurred on the system.
Computer Browser	Maintains list of available computers.
Directory Replicator	Replicates folders and the contents of the folder to remote systems.
Event Log	Records the system, security, and application events.
Messenger	Sends and receives alert messages.
Net Logon	Used in the verification of logons and the synchronization of domain databases on Windows NT servers.
Schedule	Used by the AT command to schedule events to run at specified times.
Server	Provides file and print services, as well as other network facilities.
Spooler	Print spooler service.
UPS	Manages the uninterruptible power supply (UPS) connected to the system.
Workstation	Provides the basic network functions.

Table 3.4   System services and functions.

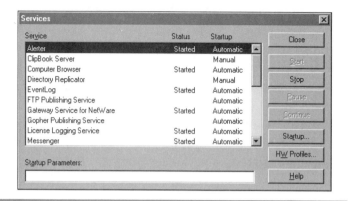

The Services management window.
Figure 3.4

The Service startup window.
Figure 3.5

System Shutdown

Like all multiuser operating systems, Windows NT needs to be shut down gracefully to avoid losing data. The shutdown process ensures that all data is flushed to disk before the system displays a message that it is safe to switch off the system.

To shut down Windows NT, the Shut Down The System user right is required by default. With Windows NT Workstation, this right is assigned to the groups Users and Everyone, so each user can shut down their particular workstation. You can remove this right from these groups if you do not want users to shut down their workstations. If you do, the right will still be assigned to the Administrator, Operator, and Power user groups. When using Windows NT Server however, this point is academic, as the default policy is to not allow users to log on locally to the server.

When you are logged on to Windows NT, the operating system can be shut down or restarted in several ways, including using the Shutdown option on the Start menu. Also, a Shutdown button can be displayed on the Logon box to shut down the system; this button is available as a default on Windows NT Workstation but is disabled on Windows NT Server. This configuration can be changed to suit your working practices by using the System Policy Editor (see Figure 3.6) or the Registry editor Regedt32.exe. The Shutdown button is controlled by the Shutdown without the logon registry entry contained within the \Microsoft\Windows NT\Current version\winlogon key of the HKEY_LOCAL_MACHINE\Software. The practical guide in the next section of this chapter contains an example for changing this configuration.

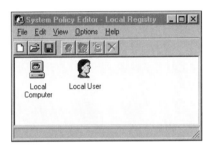

The System Policy Editor.
Figure 3.6

Practical

Guide To

Startup And

Shutdown

The following is a real-world guide to managing the system startup and shutdown configurations.

Changing The System Selection List Display Time

You have multiple operating systems on your workstation. (Yes, I know, it's a pain, but do you really want to have to rewrite that DOS application that's used twice a year to file some accounts?) Anyway, each time you restart your system to start MS-DOS, the phone rings or you go to grab a cup of coffee and the system automatically goes into Windows NT, which means you have to restart again. This happens to me all the time and drives me nuts. To fix this, we'll need to adjust the length of time that the selection list is displayed.

1. Choose Start|Settings|Control Panel.

2. Double-click the System icon. The System Properties window will be displayed.

3. Choose the Startup/Shutdown tab. In the System Startup pane, change the display time in the Show List For dialog box; the default is 30 seconds. Once set, click OK, and the BOOT.INI file will be modified.

You can also decrease the display time to speed up the start time of a system; this is frequently done on servers. (If you do decrease the display time, remember not to make it too fast, or you won't have time to select the VGA Boot option should you ever need to.) You can press the Enter key when the timer is counting down. Whichever operating system option is highlighted will be the one used to start the system immediately.

Setting The Default Operating System

You have a Windows NT workstation that most of the time runs MS-DOS to communicate with some old laboratory equipment. This equipment collects data 24 hours a day, but some of the data was recently lost due to a power outage. When the computer restarted, it automatically started Windows NT, and that's how it stayed until you showed up in the morning.

The chief egghead tells you that the UPS will be budgeted for next year (honest!), but in the meantime, you need to make sure it doesn't happen again. You'd better change MS-DOS to be the default operating system on startup.

1. Choose Start|Settings|Control Panel.

2. Double-click the System icon; the System Properties window will be displayed.

3. Choose the Startup/Shutdown tab. In the System Startup pane, the current default startup operating system will be displayed. Select the required operating system from the drop-down list.

4. Click OK to save your selection and to exit the System Properties window.

Now when you start the system, the specified operating system will be highlighted as the default.

Hangs During System Startup

You just couldn't leave things alone, could you? You just had to mess with a perfectly adequate configuration and now the system hangs on startup. You have three courses of action:

- Restore the operating system from backup.

- Start the operating system with an SOS switch and see if a particular driver is causing the problem. Perhaps you deleted it, or it is corrupted.

- Start the system using the Last Known Good configuration—or, the configuration before you screwed it up.

As usual, the system hasn't been backed up for a while, so it's down to SOS or Last Known Good. Let's start with SOS.

Because the system is hanging, no changes can be made to the BOOT.INI file if it is on an NTFS volume. However, if the volume is FAT, you could start MS-DOS and edit the default start line in BOOT.INI to include the SOS switch. Either way, this is really unnecessary, because the VGA-mode start command in BOOT.INI will already include the SOS switch. This line is created by default when Windows NT is installed, so it's a very good idea to leave this line in.

1. When the operating system start list is displayed, use the up or down arrow to select the VGA-mode startup. Press Enter to continue.

2. As the drivers are loaded, the file name and path name of each driver will be displayed.

3. If there is more than one profile available, a selection list is presented, allowing you to choose the relevant profile.

4. The file system volumes are then checked with the boot time version of CHKDSK, and the file systems being checked are displayed.

The SOS start option won't cure any start problems you might have, but it might show you where a particular problem lies—particularly if the problem is being caused by a missing or corrupted device driver.

The Last Known Good startup facility will start the operating system using the configuration that was used the last time the system was successfully started and a user successfully logged on. This makes it the quickest way of correcting most configuration problems. Keep in mind, however, that if you deleted a driver or software component, the Last Known Good facility won't put it back.

1. To invoke the Last Known Good facility, start the system, and select the operating system you want to start.

2. NTDETECT will run, and then a message will be displayed for a short time informing you that if the spacebar is pressed, the Last Known Good configuration can be invoked. Press the spacebar at this point.

3. If more than one profile is available, you will also be offered a selection list.

The Last Known Good configuration will be used to start the system and should correct any configuration errors. If the startup is failing because of problems not related to configuration, refer to Chapter 9, the troubleshooting chapter, on how to correct these.

Creating And Using A Hardware Profile

You have been "transferred" out into the field (apparently, you made quite a spectacle of yourself at this year's office party), so your trusted desktop system has been replaced with a portable and docking station. That's okay, but it does mean that you have two completely different hardware configurations, depending on whether or not you're using the docking station.

Windows NT has a built-in feature just for you that enables different hardware configuration profiles to be built and selected on system startup.

1. Choose Start|Settings|Control Panel.

2. Double-click the System icon. Choose the Hardware Profile tab on the System Properties window. The original configuration will be displayed, which we will assume is the full configuration profile used when the portable is docked. You need to copy this to use as a template for your additional hardware profile.

3. Choose the Copy button. The Copy Profile dialog box will be displayed. Type in an appropriate profile name—for instance, "Mobile", and click OK.

4. The Mobile profile will now be added to the list of available hardware profiles.

5. With the Mobile profile selected, choose the Properties button. The Mobile Properties window will be displayed, as shown in Figure 3.7. Select the Portable Computer checkbox and the appropriate docking state.

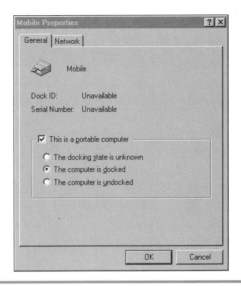

The Mobile Properties window.
Figure 3.7

6. Choose the Network tab, and ensure that the network components are disabled. Click OK. You will be returned to the System Properties window. Click OK again to confirm the profile changes.

7. To use the profile you have just created, restart the system. When the profile/Last Known Good option is displayed, press the spacebar, and select the required profile from the profile list.

Setting System Service For Hardware Profiles

If you're going to use a different profile to start your Windows NT system and the profile doesn't have any network capability, starting the network services is a waste of time. They will just fail and be logged into the event logs, so disabling them would be a good idea.

1. Choose Start|Settings|Control Panel.

2. Double-click the Services icon. The Service Management window will be displayed.

3. Choose the service you want to disable. Choose the HW Profiles button; a list of the defined profiles will be displayed, as shown in Figure 3.8. Choose the relevant profile, and select the Disable or Enable button. Click OK to activate the change.

4. You will be returned to the Service window. Repeat the process for each additional service you want to change when using a particular profile. When you're finished, click the Close button.

Remember, you don't need to be using a particular hardware profile to make changes to it; however, you won't see the effect to the profile until you start Windows NT using that profile.

The Service profile window.
Figure 3.8

Starting And Stopping System Services

There is a service that runs on your system that you no longer need. (At least, you hope you no longer need it. If you do, get ready to restart it quickly and blame sunspots for the loss of service.)

1. Choose Start|Settings|Control Panel.

2. Double-click the Services icon. Choose the service you want to either start or stop, and choose the relevant state button.

3. If you are stopping a service, a confirmation box will appear for you to confirm that you want to stop the service, and a clock will be displayed while the service is stopped. If you are starting a service, no confirmation is required. When you're finished, click the Close button.

Setting System Services To Start Automatically

You want a service to run automatically when Windows NT is started. At the moment, however, each time Windows NT is started, you have to go and manually start the service. This should be an easy one to change.

1. Choose Start|Settings|Control Panel.

2. Double-click the Services icon. Choose the required service, then click the Startup button.

3. A Service Startup configuration window will be displayed. You can use this window to define the service startup configuration, either manual or automatic, when Windows NT is started.

4. In the Startup Type pane, choose the startup option required. Click OK. You will be returned to the Service window. When finished, click Close.

Adding The Shutdown Button

In Windows NT Workstation, a Shutdown button is provided on the Logon display as a default. This button allows users to shut down the system without first having to log on to it. However, the option is disabled on the Server product, and the button is grayed out. You might want to change this on your servers. Quite often, servers are located at remote locations with no IT professionals. By making the Shutdown button a default, you'll allow local users to shut down the server without logging on to it.

To change these configurations, either the System Policy Editor or the Registry Editor can be used.

Using The System Policy Editor

1. Choose Start|Programs|Administrative Tools|System Policy Editor. The System Policy Editor window will be displayed.

2. Choose the File Menu option, and in the drop-down list, choose Open Registry.

3. Double-click the Local Computer icon. The Local Computer Properties window will be displayed, as shown in Figure 3.9.

The Local Computer Properties Policies window.

Figure 3.9

4. Double-click the Windows NT System book, then double-click the Logon sub-book. The Enable Shutdown From Authentication checkbox will appear. Select this option to enable the Shutdown button. Click OK.

5. You will be returned to the System Policy Editor window. Close this window. You will be prompted to save the registry changes you have just made. Choose the Yes button. Your changes will be saved, and you will exit Policy Editor.

If you now log off from Windows NT, you will see the relevant Shutdown button in the Logon dialog box.

Using The Registry Editor

1. Choose Start|Run. The Run window will be displayed.

2. Use the Browse button to select the Regedt32.cxc program located in the system32 folder. Click OK, and the Registry Editor will be displayed.

3. Select the HKEY_LOCAL_MACHINE window. Double-click the Software key to expand it. Then expand Microsoft|Windows NT|Current version. Click Winlogon.

4. Double-click the ShutdownWithoutLogon, as shown in Figure 3.10. The String Editor window will appear. Set the value of this parameter to 1. Choose the OK button, and the registry entry will be updated. Exit from Regedt32.

If you now log off from Windows NT, you will see the relevant Shutdown button in the Logon dialog box.

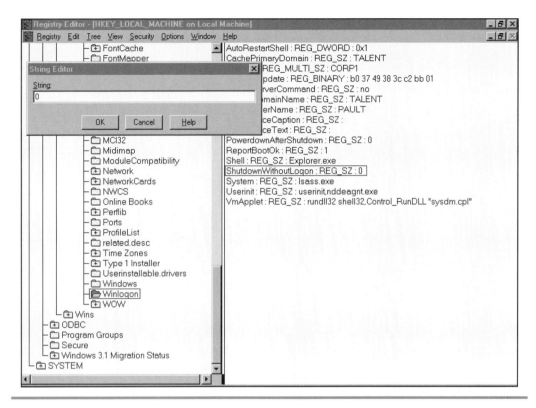

Registry Editor Shutdown button changes.

Figure 3.10

Removing The Shutdown User Right

You have several Windows NT Workstations in a workgroup configuration. One of these workstations is located in the print room and is used to provide network shares for the larger printing devices.

This workstation happens to be a dual boot system with the facility to be started using MS-DOS. As the print room is located in the basement, out of sight of the boss, the guys who work down there are forever shutting down Windows NT and starting MS-DOS so they can play games! Which means that you end up getting calls from the users saying that something has gone wrong with the printing.

Removing the shutdown right from these guys should make them think twice about playing games. As this is a workgroup configuration, you will have to make the user rights changes at the actual workstation.

1.   Choose Start|Programs|Administrative Tools|User Manager.

2.   Click Policies|User Rights. The User Rights Policy window will be displayed. In the Right selection box, choose Shut down the system, as shown in Figure 3.11.

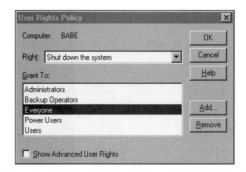

The User Rights Policy window.
Figure 3.11

3. Select the Everyone group in the Grant To box, and click the Remove button. Then, do the same for the Users group. Click OK to close the User Rights Policy window, and the user rights will be updated.

Now when these guys try to shut down this workstation, the request will be refused, as shown in Figure 3.12.

 Remember to remove the Shutdown buttons from the logon window as well, or they will still be able to shut down the workstation without being logged on.

Shutdown refused.
Figure 3.12

Shutting Down Windows NT

I know...a Windows NT administrator who can't shut the operating system down doesn't inspire too much confidence, but, hey, we all suffer from mental blocks from time to time. This section will serve as a refresher on the four methods used to safely shut down NT. Just make sure to hold this book under the desk so no one can see you're referring to it. The four methods are:

- If the button is available, choose Shutdown on the Logon window.

- Choose Start|Shut Down. In the Shut Down Windows dialog box, select the required shutdown option. Click the Yes button to proceed.

- Press Ctrl+Alt+Del. Click the Shutdown button, and select the required shutdown option from the Shutdown window. Click the Yes button to proceed.

- Press Alt+F4, and select the required shutdown option. Click the Yes button to proceed.

There is an old saying that goes along the lines of "if it ain't broke, don't fix it." This also applies to shutting down computers—if you don't need to shut it down, don't.

Quick Reference Specifications

The following are the bare-bones facts and figures.

- *BOOT.INI contains the operating system boot selection list.*

- *Startups are only considered good once a local logon has occurred.*

- *The VGA start line can be used to overcome video driver problems.*

- *Hardware Profiles can be used to set up different hardware configurations.*

- *You need to be assigned the Shut Down The System right to shut down Windows NT when logged on.*

- *The default is for the Shutdown button to be enabled on the Logon window for Windows NT Workstation and disabled on Windows NT Server.*

Utilities To Use

The utilities used in this chapter and their functions, are listed in this section. Consider this section to be a memory aid for the busy system administrator.

System

- *Change default startup operating system.*
- *Change show list timer.*
- *Create hardware profiles.*

Services

- *Start and stop system services.*
- *Change service startup types.*

System Policy Editor

- *Adding and removing the Shutdown button.*

Registry Editor

- *Adding and removing the Shutdown button.*

User Manager

- *Removing the Shutdown user right.*

Chapter 4

The Disk And File Systems

Administrator's Notes...

Chapter 4

The disk subsystem can be defined as encompassing the necessary hardware and software components to implement a robust file system. In this chapter, the hardware components are discussed in generic terms as adhering to the design goals of Windows NT, and our discussion will remain hardware-independent. In addition, the fault-tolerance issues discussed are based on the standard software functions of Windows NT and are not reliant on hardware-based, fault-tolerant solutions.

The Disk Subsystem

The disk subsystem is controlled by the I/O Manager, which controls all input and output requests for Windows NT. The I/O Manager is a component of the NT Executive, which acts as the interface between the high and low-level components of the operating system—in other words, between the kernel (low) and the Win32 subsystem (high).

The I/O Manager consists of a series of layered drivers that communicate with each other via the Executive I/O Manager, as shown in Figure 4.1. For example, for the file system driver to communicate with a disk drive, an I/O request would have to be routed via the I/O Manager. The I/O Manager, in turn, communicates with the disk driver and the disk controller. Because the I/O Manager is used to pass I/O requests

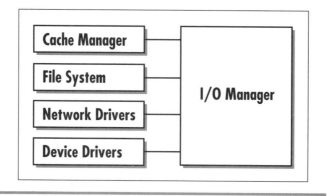

The I/O Manager and layered drivers.
Figure 4.1

between the drivers, each driver is kept as a self-contained module, making it easy to replace, remove, or add a driver without affecting the entire operating system.

A good analogy for the way the I/O Manager and drivers interact is an elevator in an office block. To move from one floor to the next, employees have to use the elevator. If a particular floor is closed, the elevator still delivers the other employees to their required locations, and the organization as a whole continues to function. If you substitute I/O requests for employees, drivers for floors, and the I/O Manager for the elevator, you end up with a pretty good idea of how the disk subsystem works.

The Disk Administrator

The disk subsystem is managed with the Disk Administrator, which is a graphical system management tool accessed via the Administrative Tools menu. The Disk Administrator can be used to perform the following tasks:

- Create and delete partitions

- Create, delete, format, label, and extend volumes and volume sets

- Create and delete stripe sets

- Assign drive IDs

- Save and restore the drive configuration

In addition, with Windows NT Server, the Disk Administrator can do the following:

- Establish and break disk mirroring or duplexing

- Create, delete, and regenerate stripe sets with parity

To use the Disk Administrator, you need to be a member of the Administrator group. When you invoke the Disk Administrator for the first time, a signature is written to disk 0. This signature does not overwrite any data and is used internally by Windows NT.

Disk Administrator provides two views of the disk configuration: *partition view*, shown in Figure 4.2, and *volume view*, shown in Figure 4.3.

To use the Disk Administrator effectively, you need to have an understanding of both the terminology and underlying technology, which is explained in the following section.

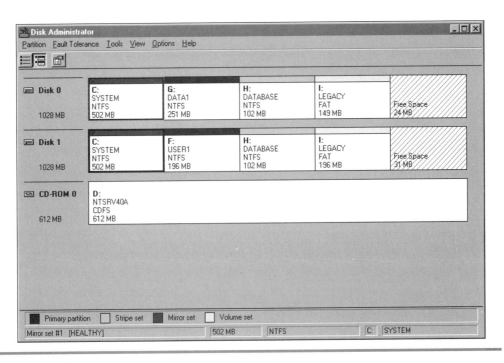

The Disk Administrator partition view.
Figure 4.2

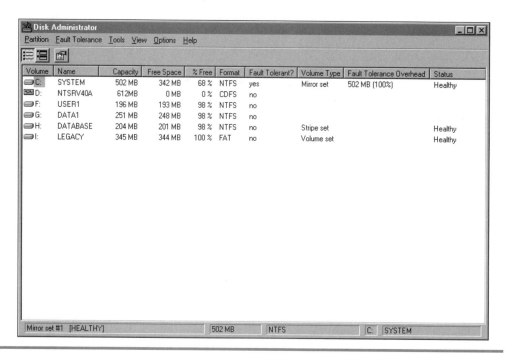

The Disk Administrator volume view.
Figure 4.3

Windows NT Workstation And Server

The following terms apply to technology and features common to both the Server and Workstation versions of Windows NT:

- *System and boot partitions*—Under Windows NT, the *system partition* is the volume that contains the files required to load Windows NT. This must be on the disk that is accessed by the computer system on startup. On x86-based systems, this partition must be marked as active. The *boot partition* contains the Windows NT operating system files. This partition can be the same partition as the system partition, but it doesn't have to be. RISC-based systems do not use an active partition to boot, but instead have a hardware-based boot configuration.

- *Primary partition*—A partition that can be marked as active and could be used to load an operating system. There can be a maximum of four primary partitions per physical disk.

- *Extended partition*—This is used to subdivide free disk space into smaller logical areas. There can be only one extended partition per disk.

- *Volume*—An area of disk that is partitioned and formatted for any of the Windows NT-supported file systems.

- *Volume sets*—Disk partitions joined together into a single logical area. The partitions can be on the same or different physical disks and can include disks of different types. There can be up to 32 separate areas of disk joined together to form a single volume set. The data is written to volume sets in a sequential fashion, i.e., one area of the volume set is filled up before moving on to the next. The system and boot partitions cannot be part of a volume set.

 Both volumes and volume sets can be extended in size without reformatting the volume, as long as the volume is formatted for use by NTFS. If the volume you wish to extend is formatted for FAT use, you must first convert it to NTFS and then extend it. The conversion from FAT to NTFS is a one-way process.

- *Stripe sets*—In a stripe set, data is written across different physical disks in 64 K stripes on partitions of equal size, as shown in Figure 4.4. This technique is often used to increase the disk I/O performance; because the I/O load is spread over a number of disk spindles, I/O throughput is increased. Stripe sets can be configured over 2 through 32 physical disks. Disk striping provides no fault tolerance. If any of the disk drives containing a stripe fails, all data in that stripe set will be lost.

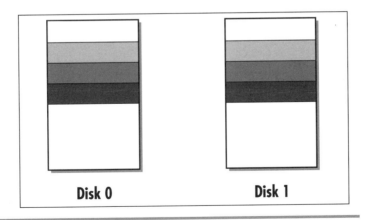

Disk 0   **Disk 1**

Stripe sets.
Figure 4.4

Windows NT Server

The following terms and technology apply to features only available with Windows NT Server:

- *Stripe sets with parity*—In a stripe set with parity configuration, the data is still striped across the disk drives; however, one of the stripes on the drives is used to provide a parity check (see Figure 4.5). If any one of the disks fails, the data can be reconstructed using the parity data. Windows NT will continue to function using the parity data until a convenient time arises when the system can be shut down and the faulty drive replaced. Once the drive has been replaced, the data can be reconstructed on the new disk using the Regenerate function of Disk Administrator.

- *Disk mirroring*—Keeps exact copies of two partitions on two separate disks (see Figure 4.6). Both disks are said to be members of a *mirror set*. All disk writes are automatically performed on both mirror set members. In the event that one of the mirror set members fails, the other will continue to be used as a single-member mirror set until the failed drive can be replaced and the mirroring relationship can be reestablished. The actual mirroring is done on a partition-by-partition basis.

- *Disk duplexing*—This functions the same way as disk mirroring, except that each drive is connected to a separate disk controller, as shown in Figure 4.7.

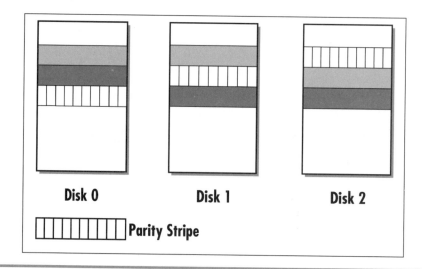

Stripe sets with parity.
Figure 4.5

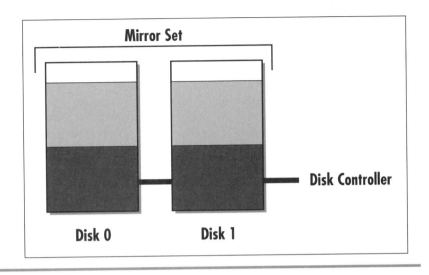

Disk mirroring.
Figure 4.6

This means that even though a single disk or controller may fail, the data will still be available from the remaining duplexed drive. Windows NT boot partitions can be mirrored or duplexed to obtain a fault-tolerant solution, but they cannot be members of a stripe set.

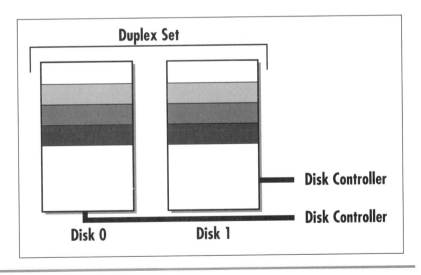

Disk duplexing.
Figure 4.7

Redundant Array Of Inexpensive Disks

Most of the disk configurations discussed in the previous section are actually based on the redundant array of inexpensive disks technology, commonly known as *RAID*. The complete list of the RAID levels and their key features include:

- *RAID 0*—This is a disk striping technique in which data is striped across the stripe members in 64 K blocks. No fault tolerance is provided with RAID 0. This level is currently implemented in both Windows NT Workstation and Server.

- *RAID 1*—This level is used to implement disk mirroring, or duplexing, and is the most common form of RAID technology in use today. Although RAID 1 does provide fault tolerance, it imposes a 100 percent reduction in available disk space to achieve this. It is currently implemented in Windows NT Server.

- *RAID 2*—This is also a disk striping technique, but the data is striped at a bit level, instead of a block level. One disk in the stripe set is reserved for data recovery. This level is not currently implemented in Windows NT.

- *RAID 3*—This level provides disk striping at the bit level, with one disk reserved for the parity data to dynamically reconstruct data that is lost when a stripe member fails. This level is not currently implemented in Windows NT.

- *RAID 4*—RAID 4 provides disk striping at block level, with one disk reserved for the parity data. It is not currently implemented in Windows NT.

- *RAID 5*—This provides disk striping at block level. The parity data is evenly spread across all disk stripe members, instead of being confined to a single drive—as is the case in a RAID 4 configuration. Spreading the data across all disk stripe members avoids the I/O bottleneck often found with a single parity drive. RAID 5 is currently implemented in Windows NT Server.

The File Systems

Windows NT was designed for use with multiple file systems to enable the support of existing data and applications. Windows NT currently supports the following file systems:

- *FAT*—File allocation table

- *CDFS*—Compact disk file system

- *NTFS*—New technology file system

In addition, networks are considered to be a special kind of file system. Because FAT and NTFS are the file systems of most interest to Windows NT administrators, we'll take a closer look at them in the following sections.

FAT

The FAT file system is currently the most widely used file system in the world. Originally designed to be used with floppy disks, this system has had to undergo many modifications to support today's high-capacity disk drives. Windows NT formats all floppy disks in the FAT format.

The key features of the FAT file system are as follows:

- Can be accessed under MS-DOS, OS/2, and Windows NT

- Standard FAT file names are 8.3 format

- No local security

- When used with Windows NT, allows long file names of up to 255 characters

- No automatic file recovery

- File size is limited to 4 GB

NTFS

NTFS is the new technology file system that was developed specifically for use with Windows NT and operates in the same way as a relational database. If the system should fail for any reason, the operating system can use the transaction logs to undo or redo any incomplete transactions. By doing this, the file system is left in a known state.

The key features of NTFS are as follows:

- Local security can be set up at the volume, folder, and file level

- Allows long file names of up to 255 characters

- Automatic generation of 8.3 file names for DOS application compatibility

- Designed for files and disk drives of up to 16 EB, or 16 billion-billion bytes, in size

- Case-sensitive file names for compatibility with POSIX standards

- Recoverable file system based on a relational database design

- Requires a 2 MB disk overhead; not recommended for very small drives

- Available for use only under Windows NT

Bad Cluster Recovery

NTFS uses a recovery technique known as *cluster remapping* to recover from disk errors caused by bad sectors. If a disk error occurs on a disk write operation, NTFS will automatically assign a new cluster to which the data will be written. The cluster that contains the sector that caused the error will be added to the bad cluster file to ensure that the bad sector is not used in any future operations. No data is lost during this operation.

If the error occurs on a read operation, the cluster is added to the bad cluster file in the same way as a write error, and an error is returned to the application that called the read operation. The data contained in the failing cluster will be lost, although all other clusters containing data for this file will still be accessible.

When a partition is initialized and formatted for use by the disk administrator, a default cluster size will be chosen that is appropriate for the size of the partition to be used.

Disk sectors are the smallest area of addressable disk space and are usually 512 bytes in size. Disk clusters are a collection of disk sectors. The number of sectors per cluster is determined by the cluster size used on that particular volume, which is defined when the volume is formatted.

The minimum cluster size is 512 bytes, and this will contain one sector. This cluster size is used for partitions of less than 512 MB in size. The cluster then doubles in proportion with the partition size—for example, a 4 GB partition will have a 4 K cluster, and an 8 GB partition will have an 8 K cluster that will contain 16 sectors per cluster. The maximum cluster size is 64 K and is used for partitions that are larger than 32 GB in size.

Short Names

NTFS will by default automatically generate short names in the 8.3 DOS format. These names are required to allow DOS-based applications to access files with long file names.

The short file names are generated by taking the first six characters of the long file name and appending a tilde to it along with a number. For example, a file with the long file name of THISISAVERYLONGFILENAME.TXT would have a short name of THISIS~1.TXT. If the six characters of a long file name do not give a unique file name, the number appended to the short name is incremented, thus making it unique. So, you may have two similar long file names, having the short names of THISIS~1.TXT and THISIS~2.TXT.

The number appended to the short file names is only incremented up to four. So if you have five similar long file names, a different technique is then used to generate the short names on the fifth and subsequent files. This involves just using the first two characters of the long file name and performing a mathematical operation on the remainder of the long file name to generate the next four characters for the short name. A number is then appended along with the tilde, but in this case, the number will always be 1, as the mathematical calculation is actually providing the unique part of the name.

The automatic generation of short names can be disabled if you have no requirement for them, and this may improve performance on volumes with large numbers of similarly named files.

NTFS Security

One of the strongest areas of NTFS, and an important reason for its popularity among corporate users, is the security facilities available within the standard Windows NT product. NTFS security access, or permissions, are assigned and viewed by using the Windows NT Explorer System Administrator tool. The permissions can be assigned for access on both a user and group basis. The permissions assigned are cumulative—members of groups receive both the permissions of the groups and their own individual user permissions.

File permissions take priority over any folder permissions that might be assigned (see Figure 4.8). The No Access permission is an exception to this rule, however. No Access on a folder will block access to any files in that folder, regardless of the permissions assigned to the files.

When an NTFS volume is first created, the permissions are set to Everyone With Full Control, or no effective security at all. At this point, you must implement your required security.

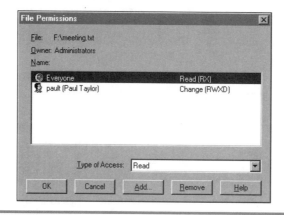

NTFS File Permissions window.
Figure 4.8

Ownership

The owner of an object (such as a file or folder) is allowed special access to that object regardless of the actual permissions assigned to it. This access allows the owner to change the permissions on the object even if the permissions have been configured for No Access to the owner. In addition to the owner, the Administrator group may also take ownership of any object. As the owner of the object, the group may then change the permissions assigned to it.

Copying And Moving Files

When you copy files between NTFS folders, the files inherit the permissions of the destination parent folder. These inherited permissions replace the existing permissions of the files. When you move files between NTFS folders on the same volume, the files retain their existing permissions. However, when you move files between folders on different volumes, the files inherit the permissions of the destination parent folder. In effect, moving a file between volumes is treated as a copy operation, with the source file being deleted after the move.

Here's an example. The Sales_info folder has the following permissions assigned: Administrators (All), Manager (RWXD), and Sales (RX). The folder contains the file text of a sales meeting, the permissions for which are shown in Figure 4.9.

The file named Text of Sales Meeting is needed in the Test folder, which has the following permissions assigned: Administrators (All) and Everyone (RX). The file is

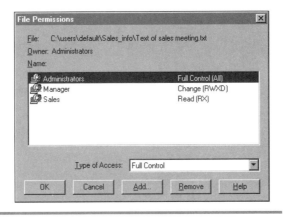

Source file permissions for the Sales_info folder.
Figure 4.9

copied from the Sales_info folder to the Test folder, and the resulting permissions can be seen in Figure 4.10. When the same file is *moved* between the same two folders, the resultant file permissions appear as shown in Figure 4.11.

Cumulative Permissions

As previously stated, NTFS user and group permissions are cumulative. Say, for example, that User A is a member of both the Sales and Manager groups. The group access assigned to the Sales_info folder is shown in Figure 4.12. The effective permissions

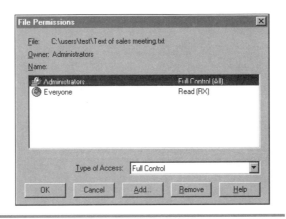

File permissions when a file is copied to another folder.
Figure 4.10

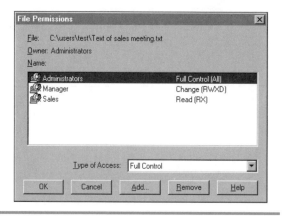

File permissions when a file is moved to another folder.
Figure 4.11

on this folder for User A would be Read, Write, Execute, and Delete. If User A was removed from the Manager group, the effective permissions would be reduced to Read and Execute only.

If User A was then added to the Leavers group, all access to this folder would be blocked, since the Leavers group has been assigned No Access. Even though User A is still a member of the Sales group, this authorization has been overridden. All other members of the Sales and Manager groups would be unaffected.

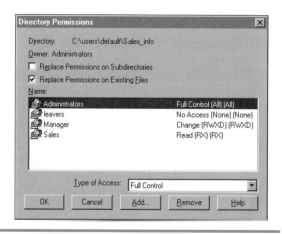

Cumulative permissions.
Figure 4.12

One point to remember is that if User A was added to the Leavers group while he was still logged on, the No Access block would not take effect until User A logs out and back on again. This is because the changes made to the User A account are not dynamically made to the Security Access Token of User A. This token is at the heart of Windows NT security and is generated upon logging on to the system. Once generated, no changes are made to it.

The complete list of permissions that can be assigned to files is shown in Table 4.1, and permissions for folders are given in Table 4.2. Because of the different uses of folders and files, there are two sets of standard permissions, as well as special sets of permissions to define more selective access. The folder permissions contain and display two sets of permissions; the first set refers to the folder access, and the second set refers to the file or subfolder permissions on objects contained within the folder.

Permission	Description
Standard File Access Permissions	
No Access (None)	All access to the file is blocked, overriding all other permissions.
Read (RX)	Allows data to be viewed and executed if it is a program.
Change (RWXD)	Same access as Read, plus data may be modified or the file deleted.
Full Control (All)	Same access as Change, plus file permissions may be changed and ownership of the file taken.
Special File Access Permissions	
Read (R)	File may be opened and data viewed.
Write (W)	File data may be modified.
Execute (X)	Allows execution of program file.
Delete (D)	File may be deleted.
Change Permissions (P)	File access permissions may be changed.
Take Ownership (O)	Allows ownership of the file to be taken.

Table 4.1   File permissions.

Permission	Description
Standard Folder Access Permissions	
No Access (None)(None)	Blocks all access to the folder, overriding all other permissions.
List (RX)(not specified)	Allows listing of file names and moving to subfolders.
Read (RX)(RX)	The same as List, plus files may be viewed and executed.
Add (WX)(not specified)	Allows files to be added to the folder and subfolders created.
Add & Read (RWX)(RX)	The same as List, plus Add at folder level. Files may be viewed and executed.
Change (RWXD)(RWXD)	The same as Add & Read at folder level, plus folder may be deleted. Files may be viewed and executed. Files and subfolders may be modified and deleted.
Full Control (All)(All)	The same as Change, plus file and folder permissions may be changed, and ownership of folder and files may be taken.
Special Folder Access Permissions	
Read (R)	File and subfolder names may be listed.
Write (W)	Files and subfolders may be added to the folder.
Execute (X)	Moving to subfolder permitted.
Delete (D)	Folder may be deleted.
Change Permission (P)	Folder permissions may be changed.
Take Ownership (O)	Ownership of folder may be taken.

Table 4.2   Folder permissions.

If a group or user has been granted Full Control permissions on a folder, any file contained in that folder may be deleted, regardless of the permissions assigned to the file.

Auditing

It is possible to enable auditing on NTFS volumes to allow selected events to be recorded in the security event log. The auditing can be used to either log possible security breaches or to provide an audit trail on which operations have been performed on the file system. Auditing can be enabled for failed operations, successful operations, or both at the file or folder level. Remember, file and folder auditing may only be implemented on NTFS volumes. Figure 4.13 shows the File Auditing screen.

Data Compression

Files and folders on NTFS volumes can be compressed by using the Windows NT Explorer. In fact, when NTFS volumes are formatted, the compression can be enabled at this point. Once a folder has been compressed, all files or subfolders copied to that folder are automatically compressed as well. However, when a file or folder is moved into a compressed folder on the same NTFS volume, the file or folder retains its compression state and isn't automatically compressed. The actual compression is transparent to applications, both when the files or folders are being compressed and once the compression is completed.

Compression can only be used with volumes that have a cluster size of 4 K or less. All compression options will be grayed out on volumes with larger cluster sizes due to performance issues when compressing data on these volumes.

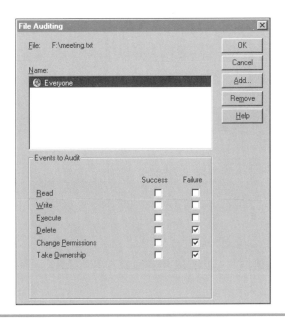

The File Auditing screen.
Figure 4.13

The Windows NT Explorer

The Windows NT file system folders and files are viewed by using either the My Computer icon or the Windows NT Explorer. (As a Windows NT administrator, you will probably use the Windows NT Explorer to accomplish your system administrator tasks; it is the more direct method.) The Windows NT Explorer presents a vertically split window (shown in Figure 4.14). The left window is used to display disk drive icons, as well as folders and files. The right side displays the contents of the item that you clicked on the left.

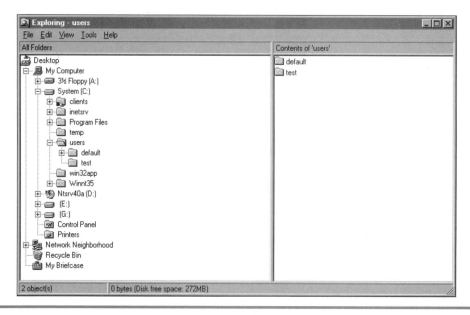

The Windows NT Explorer.
Figure 4.14

Practical

Guide To

Disk And File

Administration

The following section provides real-life examples and step-by-step instructions on how to successfully administrate your file and disk subsystem. These examples make use of the graphical system-management tools; however, most functions do have a corresponding command-line tool that you can use instead. Accessing Help at the command prompt will provide you with more information on these command-line tools and their usage.

After each change to the disk configuration, you will need to commit the changes and will be reminded to update your emergency repair disk to reflect your new configuration. The use of this disk configuration data is covered in more detail in Chapter 9.

Modifying The Disk Administrator Display

It's your first day at a new job. You have been given a phone, a desk, and the administrator's password. No one seems to know what you should be doing; the boss is away, and your new coworkers never understood exactly what your predecessor did.

Oh well, might as well spend some time getting to know your new systems before everyone starts dumping work on you. Where to start though? How about if you start with the disk configuration:

1. Click the Start button on the taskbar. Choose Programs, then Administrative Tools, then Disk Administrator.

Wow, man, what a color scheme! Your predecessor must have been on some heavy medication. Quick, check the desk drawers to see if any is left. Nope, out of luck. Well, since you can't reach that higher plane your predecessor was working on, you'd better tone that display down before it blows your mind.

2. Open the Options menu at the top of the Disk Administrator display. The following options are available for display configuration: Colors & Patterns, Disk Display, Region & Display, and Customize Toolbar.

First things first. Let's change the color and patterns being used for the boot disk mirror set.

3. Choose Colors & Patterns from the Options menu. A Colors & Patterns option window will display the colors and patterns available. Click the arrow on the Color & Pattern

For selection window, and click Mirror Set. The currently selected color and pattern are shown with an emphasized border. Now, click the color and pattern that appeals to you and then click OK. You will be returned to the Disk Administrator main screen with the new color and pattern applied. Enjoy.

If you don't see a graphical representation of the disk drives when you access the Disk Administrator, you probably have the volume display selected. In the View menu, choose Drive Configuration, or use Ctrl+D to change displays.

Now that the color is a bit easier on the eyes, how about setting the rest of the display to suit? The Disk Display option is used to select whether disks are displayed as all the same size or based on their actual capacity. Region Display is used to set the way disk regions are displayed on a per-disk basis. The size of regions may be based on actual capacity, or they all may be the same size. You can also let Disk Administrator set the size of the regions. (If computers ever start making real decisions, I'm going to look for another job!)

The icons available on the toolbar can be modified by using the Customize Toolbar option:

1. In the Options menu, choose Customize Toolbar. Select the button you want to add from the available buttons list, and click the Add button.

2. To remove a button, select the toolbar button you want to remove, and then click the Remove button. Click Close to exit.

Creating And Preparing A Partition/Volume

Your friendly local hardware engineer has just installed a new disk drive for you. (Is it me or are these guys getting younger?) Anyway, the kid...sorry...the *engineer* wants you to sign his paperwork so he can hit the road. Well, better check out this new drive before signing anything, so here goes:

1. Click Start|Programs|Administrative Tools|Disk Administrator.

2. Okay, you can see the drive in Disk Administrator. So far, so good. Click anywhere on the drive—the border will be emphasized. In the Partition menu at the top of the display, choose Create. A Create Logical Drive dialog box appears, which allows you to see the size of the logical drive (the partition size). The default size is the maximum amount of free space on the drive. Select the required size, and click OK.

3. Now, select Partition|Commit Changes Now. Confirm the saving of the changes, and acknowledge the informational message regarding the emergency repair disk.

4. Click the newly created partition. In the Tools menu, choose Format. A Format window will appear, which allows you to select the file system for the format and volume label operations. You can choose whether you want to perform a quick format and whether you want compression to be enabled on the volume. You can also change the default allocation unit size if you choose.

5. It's getting close to lunch, so how about creating an NTFS volume using Quick Format with compression enabled and a volume label of Backup1? Click the arrow on the File System option, and choose NTFS. Click the Volume Label box, and type "Backup1". Select the Quick Format and Enable Compression checkboxes. Click the Start button, and confirm the format operation.

6. The status bar at the bottom of the Format window displays the progress of the format operation, although with Quick Format, you might not have time to see this. When the format is complete, click the confirmation box. You should be returned back to the Format window. Click Close. There it is, the brand-new, all-singing, all-dancing disk just waiting to start work. Let's get some lunch.

Assigning Drive Letters

You're planning a lazy afternoon just goofing off until it's time to go. You casually reach across and click on the online documentation. After a loud beep, you get an information message telling you that the online documentation can no longer be found in drive D. Okay...nobody move...who's taken the NT CD-ROM out of the drive? Silence. You remember that you have your own office these days, so there's no one to answer you. Curious-er and curious-er. Well, let's see if we can find out what's going on:

1. Choose Start|Choose Programs|Administrative Tools|Disk Administrator.

Hang on a minute, who set the CD-ROM up as drive E and where did that drive D come from? You remember that is the new drive that has just been installed. You have just been hit by the helpful-operating-system syndrome. Windows NT will automatically assign drive IDs for you; however, as we have just found out, this is not always what you want. Don't worry, you can reassign them, and manually assigned drive IDs are static, so they won't get messed up in the future.

2. Click the drive that has assumed the ID you want to use—in our case, the new drive D. Then choose Tools|Assign Drive Letter. The Assign Drive Letter window appears. Click the arrow on the list to select an appropriate drive letter. Click OK, and confirm you want the drive ID updated immediately. You have now moved the offending drive to a new ID and freed up the CD-ROM ID for reassignment.

3. Click the CD-ROM drive region display you want to reassign, then choose Tools|Assign Drive Letters. From the available drive letters, click on drive D, and confirm the selection. The Assign Drive Letter window is shown in Figure 4.15.

Now when you click the online documentation, everything is okay. You can get back to your lazy afternoon—that is, until the phone rings.

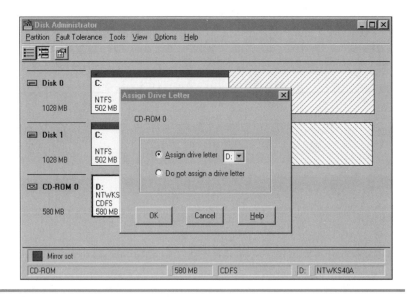

The CD-ROM drive letter assignment window.
Figure 4.15

Creating A Volume Set

It's a sunny Monday morning. You've had a great weekend, and everything in life is looking good. Just then, your boss walks into your office and says he has a five-minute job for you to do. Great, there goes the rest of the day.

Basically, the head of the accounts department has bought a new application and wants it installed right away. Your boss checked the software requirements on the box and turned pale when he realized it needs 600 MB of disk space. He knows full well that the maximum amount of space you have available on any one disk is 500 MB. The hardware budget has been spent for this year, so it's up to you to sort it out. Apparently, it's what you're getting paid for...isn't it? (I always wondered myself.) Because life is so great at the moment, you decide to help out. You vaguely remember that you can join together free areas of disk space into one logical volume. Where to start? The Disk Administrator, maybe? Cool, let's look there:

1. Click Start|Programs|Administrative Tools|Disk Administrator.

2. Okay, you have three free areas of disk space: one 500 MB, one 400 MB, and one 300 MB. Well, let's use the 400 MB and 300 MB areas. These areas don't have to reside on the same physical disk, but they do need to be free—in other words, not partitioned or formatted. Click the 400 MB area. While holding down the Ctrl key, click the 300 MB area. Release the Ctrl key. In the Partition menu, choose Create Volume Set. The Create Volume Set window appears. Select the size required (600 MB), then click OK.

3. The Volume Set window closes, and the volume set is displayed on the selected areas. In the Partition menu, choose Commit Changes Now. Confirm that you want to save the changes, and acknowledge the message about the emergency repair disk.

4. Click an area of the volume set; all areas will have emphasized borders. In the Tools menu, choose Format. You can now select the required format options and perform the format operation. When the format operation is over, the volume set will appear to users and applications as a single 600 MB logical drive.

Once again, you've saved the day. Life just gets better and better.

Extending A Volume Or Volume Set

Good news, the company is expanding, and you might even get that long-promised bonus (yeah, right). All these new employees are now starting to fill up your free disk space, the word-processing volume set is about to bust, and everyone assures you that they can't delete anything. So, it's time for Captain Volume to once again don the Administrator mask and save the day.

Two things to remember: Only NTFS volumes can be extended without reformatting, and a reboot will be required to create the extension. This reboot will be performed when you have extended the volume set, so be warned. If the volume or volume set you want to extend is formatted for FAT, you could first convert it to an NTFS partition and then extend it. Don't forget, though, that the conversion is a one-way process:

1. Click Start|Programs|Administrative Tools|Disk Administrator.

2. Click the volume set to be extended, hold down the Ctrl key, and click the free area you wish to use. In the Partition menu, choose Extend Volume Set. The Extend Volume Set window will appear, as shown in Figure 4.16.

3. Select the total volume size required, and click OK. In the Partition menu again, choose Commit Changes Now. Click Confirm to save changes, and acknowledge the informational message regarding the emergency repair disk. A Shutdown confirmation message now appears. Once confirmed, the system will restart.

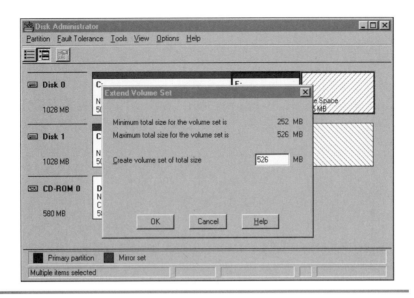

Extending a volume.
Figure 4.16

When the system reboots, the additional area of disk space will automatically be formatted for use with NTFS. The existing data will be unaffected by this operation.

Creating A Mirror Set

You have just finished talking—or should I say listening—to an old friend describe the trouble she has had at work since the system disk on her Windows NT Server failed. This reminds you that you haven't given any recent thought to your system disks, and it has been at least six months since you told your boss you were going to sort it out. So, let's get to it:

1. Click Start|Programs|Administrative Tools|Disk Administrator.

2. Click the volume that you want to mirror, then hold down the Ctrl key and click an area of free space as large as the volume you want to mirror. Keep in mind that this must be on a different physical disk.

3. Open the Fault Tolerance menu, and choose Establish Mirror.

4. In the Partition menu, choose Commit Changes Now. Confirm the changes. The mirror set is now established.

When the boot disk is made into a mirror set member, a mirror set boot floppy disk is required if the disk from which your system boots fails. The creation and use of this disk is discussed in the troubleshooting section later in the book.

A duplex set is created in the same way as a mirror set, but the disks must be connected to separate disk controllers. Remember, mirror sets are only available with Windows NT Server.

Breaking A Mirror Set

In a sudden fit of paranoia, you got so worried about losing a disk, you made all volumes into mirror sets and reduced your effective disk capacity in half. Nice going—disk manufacturers will love you. Perhaps the games volume shouldn't really be mirrored after all.

Breaking a mirror set is quick and painless; however, if the system volume is the mirror you are breaking, a reboot will be required:

1. Click Start|Programs|Administrative Tools|Disk Administrator.

2. Click the mirror set you want to break.

3. Open the Fault Tolerance menu, select Break Mirror, and confirm the break operation. Each member of the mirror set is assigned a unique drive ID. In the Partition menu, select Commit Changes Now. The mirror set will now be broken.

If files are open on the mirror set, a reboot is required to break the mirror relationship. Once broken, both members are assigned separate drive IDs. The Break Mirror window is shown in Figure 4.17.

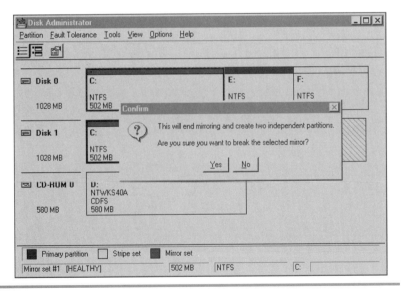

Breaking a mirror set.
Figure 4.17

Creating A Stripe Set

You have been fielding a few complaints from users that Windows NT Server seems to be running slow. Doing your best detective work, you decide that it's a certain application that is causing the problem because of the I/O load it's placing on the main application disk. Unfortunately, the application causing the problem is quite important, so removing it from the system isn't an option. But perhaps if the I/O load was spread across several disks, the problem might be eased. So, let's create a stripe set and spread the load. Remember that stripe sets can be created on a minimum of 2 and a maximum of 32 separate disks:

1. Click Start|Programs|Administrative Tools|Disk Administrator.

2. Click the first area of free space. Holding the Ctrl key down, click the second area and all additional areas that are required. Note that each one has to be located on separate physical disks.

3. Select Partition Menu|Create Stripe Set. Set the total size of the stripe set in the Create Stripe Set window. Click OK. Now choose Partition|Commit Changes Now. Click to confirm the changes, and acknowledge the message regarding the emergency repair disk.

4. Click on any area of the stripe set, then select Tools|Format. You can now select the required format options and format the stripe set.

The stripe set is now available for use. Disk striping is available with both Windows NT Workstation and Windows NT Server.

Creating A Stripe Set With Parity

One of the users who complained about the speed of the system has now heard through the grapevine that you are scattering his data across disks and is worried that this might erase some of his data if a disk fails. Valid point, since the mean time between failures is reduced in proportion to the number of disks the data is spread across. But don't you wish the users would just get on with their jobs and let you do yours? Anyway, to assuage the user's fear, you can create a stripe set with parity and copy the data to it.

Stripe sets with parity are only available with Windows NT Server. They can be created on a minimum of 3 and a maximum of 32 drives:

1. Click Start|Programs|Administrative Tools|Disk Administrator.

2. Click the first area of free space, then holding the Ctrl key down, click the second and third area, as well as any additional areas that are required. Remember that each area has to be located on a separate physical disk.

3. Select Fault Tolerance|Create Stripe Set With Parity. Select the size required from the Create window, and click OK.

4. In the Partition menu, choose Commit Changes Now. Click on any area of the stripe set. Select Tools|Format. You can now select the required format options to format the stripe set with parity.

Now you can tell the user that he can sleep soundly tonight. Any single drive in the stripe set can now be lost and the data can still be accessed, because parity data is also striped across the disk.

Setting And Viewing File And Folder Permissions

A group of users complain that they are unable to access a certain folder that contains data they need. To resolve this problem, there really is only one place to start: Windows NT Explorer. (Well, if you wanted, you could use the My Computer icon, but, again, as your experience grows with Windows NT, you'll find the Windows NT Explorer is considerably quicker to use.) Let's do it the easy way:

1. Click Start|Programs|Windows NT Explorer.

2. The Windows NT Explorer display is vertically divided, with the left side showing drives, folders, and files and the right side showing the contents of the left-side items. Locate the folder you require by clicking the correct folder path in the right display. Double-clicking the folders will expand the items in the folder.

3. Right-click the required folder. A pop-up menu will appear. Select the last item on this menu, Properties. The Folder Properties window appears with three selection tabs: General, Sharing, and Security. (If only the General and Sharing tabs are available, you are not using the NTFS file system on this volume. Only NTFS provides local security.)

4. Click on the Security tab. Three options are available in the Security dialog box: Permissions, Auditing, and Ownership. Click the Permissions button. The current permissions applied to the folder are displayed.

5. If the user group is not displayed in the list of current permissions, click the Add button. Locate the required group or even individual users required. Click the required group, and then click the Add button. The group is added to the Add Group window. Click the Type of Access Required arrow, and select the required access. Click OK.

6. You are returned to the Folder Permissions window. Two checkboxes are available regarding how the new permissions will affect existing files and subfolders. Select the appropriate box. Click OK. The new permissions will be applied.

The user group in question should now find that everything is working fine.

 Contained within Administrative Tools is an Administrator Wizard to help set file and folder permissions. This tool is great for users new to Windows NT, but for an administrator, it doesn't provide the full range of functions that you will require. It also is painfully slow, as it leads you screen-by-screen through the configuration process.

Copying And Moving Folders Or Files

As with most companies, once you get everything working smoothly, a company reorganization is announced. Usually aimed at refocusing personnel to more customer-oriented roles—sound familiar?—it is generally an annual event. (If I get any more customer interaction, I'll be sleeping with them—say no more.)

As the administrator, you're going to face the brunt of the reorganization, since you now have to move the users from their relevant groups, group folders, and so on to their new locations. So hold your mouse hand in the air, extend your clicking finger, and—up...down...up...down.... There, that's enough exercise for one day. (I can't say there's any medical benefit in doing this, but it does help to keep the users at arm's length. Barking at passing cars is another neat trick, but I think we should keep that in reserve for now.) Let's get cracking:

1. Click Start|Programs|Windows NT Explorer.

2. Locate the required item in Windows NT Explorer. Right-click on the item, and keeping the button depressed, drag the item to its new location and release the button. A pop-up menu is displayed that allows you to select whether the item is to be moved, copied, or shortcut-created. A *shortcut* is a logical link to the original item; the original is not relocated, so deleting a shortcut will not affect the original item.

3. As you are relocating users, you will probably want to move folders and files. Why use the Move function? Because moved items on the same volumes will retain their permissions. Select Move. The items will move to their new locations.

Remember, Move only retains permissions when objects are moved between folders on the same volume. If the folders are on different volumes, Move functions the same way as a copy operation—in other words, the items inherit their permissions from the destination parent folder.

Creating A New Folder

While spring-cleaning, you decide to collect various data files and store them in one location. You want to create a new folder to hold them. To do this:

1. Click Start|Programs|Windows NT Explorer.

2. Locate where you want to add the folder, using the left side of the Explorer window. Click the location where you want the new folder. Select File|New|Folder. The new folder is created and displayed in the right-hand side of the Windows NT Explorer window. Type the new folder name directly into the folder name box next to the icon.

That's it. You can now move the data to the new folder.

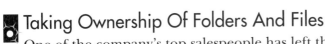 Taking Ownership Of Folders And Files

One of the company's top salespeople has left the company, and the sales manager wants you to check the data contained in the salesperson's account. (What's this? Don't trust your sales force?) However, when you try to access the relevant folders, you find access has been blocked. Hey, this salesperson was brighter than he looked. Of course, as the administrator, you can always take ownership of any object and then change the permissions on it:

1. Click Start|Programs|Windows NT Explorer.

2. Locate the relevant folder, and right-click on it. On the pop-up menu, select Properties. From the Properties window, click the Security tab, then the Ownership button, as shown in Figure 4.18. Confirm that you want to take ownership of the folder, and then confirm that you want to take ownership of the files and subfolders. The ownership will then be assigned to you.

3. You are returned to the Properties window. Click the Permissions button, and change the assigned permissions to allow you access to the folder.

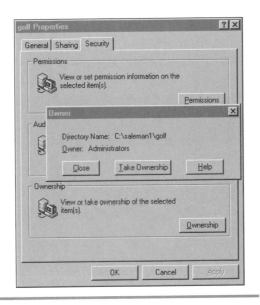

Taking object ownership.
Figure 4.18

After checking the files and folders, all you learned was the salesperson's golf handicap. The sales manager can sleep soundly knowing no company secrets have been compromised.

After lunch, the sales manager rushes into your office all smiles and tells you that the salesperson is coming back to the company. The sales manager wants the files and folders returned to the salesperson. You can take great pleasure in telling him that it is not possible to give the ownership back to the salesperson. True, you can allow the salesperson the permission to take back ownership of the files; you could change his password, log on as the salesperson, and then take ownership of the files. However, the account password would have to be changed, so the salesperson would know something had been going on.

Let the sales manager explain it to the salesperson, and keep your head down.

Configuring Auditing On Folders And Files

The sales manager complains that someone keeps deleting his sales figures from the Sales_info folder. Boy, this guy's a real pain. He has asked all of the sales team, and they insist they're not doing it. It's up to you to find out what's going on and why. You decide to configure auditing for deletion of the sales figure. Once again, this is a job for Windows NT Explorer:

1. Click Start|Programs|Windows NT Explorer.

2. Locate the relevant file using the Explorer, and right-click on it. From the pop-up menu, select Properties. From the Properties window, click the Security tab, then the Auditing button.

3. The Auditing window is displayed. Click the Add button to add the user or groups whose events you want to audit. In this case, because you don't know who is deleting the files, you need to add the group Everyone, which is the group that all users are assigned to when their accounts are created. Click the Everyone group, and then the Add button. The Everyone group is placed in the Add Names window. Click OK.

4. You are returned to the Auditing window. In the Events To Be Audited pane, select both the Success and Failure checkboxes. Click OK. You might receive a message informing you that auditing is not enabled in this domain or system. You will correct this with the next step. If you don't receive this message, you still need to perform the next task to make sure the correct events are being audited.

5. Click Start|Programs|Administrative Tools. Select Domain User Manager, or User Manager if this is a workgroup configuration.

6. In the Policies menu, select Audit. Make sure that the Audit These Events box is selected, as shown in Figure 4.19. Now, select the File and Object Access Success and Failure checkboxes. Click OK, and exit the User Manager.

When the sales manager tells you the file has been deleted, you can use the Event Viewer to find out who deleted the file. The Event Viewer is covered in detail in Chapter 8, but here are the basic steps:

1. Click Start|Programs|Administrative Tools|Event Viewer.

2. In the Log menu, select the Security option if isn't already selected. The Security Log is displayed. Locate the approximate time the deletion took place, and look for an

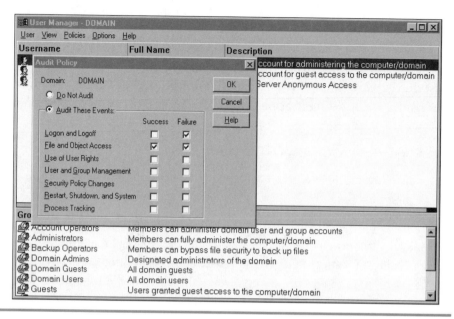

System Audit Policy window.
Figure 4.19

object access event. Double-click on the event to obtain a more detailed view. The user who has deleted the file in question is displayed at the top of the event record.

Now you can keep the sales manager happy by giving him a name of someone he can now take to task.

Compressing Volumes, Folders, And Files

You're running short of free space on several data volumes. These volumes contain legacy data that isn't used that much but still needs to be kept online. So, why not compress it? The small performance overhead incurred by using compressed data won't matter, since the data is not in day-to-day use. It's back to the trusty Windows NT Explorer:

1. Click Start|Programs|Windows NT Explorer.

2. Locate the object in question, and right-click it. From the pop-up menu, select Properties. From the General tab, select the Compression box. Click OK. That's it. The object is compressed.

Users and applications can use the compressed objects directly; they don't need to decompress them first. However, if in the future you decide to decompress any object, just deselect the Compression box under the General tab.

Remember, compression is only available with NTFS volumes.

Disabling The 8.3 Short File Name Creation

The users in your marketing department really like using the long file names that can be used with NTFS volumes and now have very descriptive file names. Unfortunately, they often choose very similar names which causes NTFS to spend quite a bit of its time generating unique 8.3 short names. As you have just managed to remove the last of the DOS applications from your company, hooray, you don't need these short names to be generated any more. So, let's make life easy for NTFS and disable their creation.

There are two tools that can be used to disable the short names. Both tools make changes to the same registry entry. The first tool that can be used is the System Policy editor contained with the Administrative Tools menu:

1. Click Start|Programs|Administrative Tools|System Policy Editor.

2. The System policy editor window is displayed. Click File|Open Registry. The Local Registry window appears. Double-click the local system icon. The local system registry window will appear.

3. Double-click Windows NT System|File System. Select the Do Not Create 8.3 Name checkbox.

4. Click OK. Exit from the system policy editor. Click Yes to save the registry change. All files now created will only have long file names.

The registry edit tool regedt32 could also be used disable the short name creation:

1. Click Start|Run. Click Browse, and select the regedt32 tool; it is contained in the system root subfolder system32.

2. Select the HKEY_LOCAL_MACHINE window. Double-click System|Current Control Set|Control|File System.

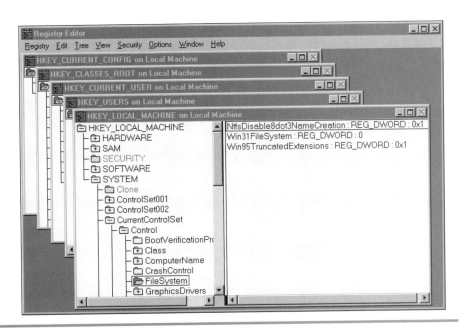

The registry.
Figure 4.20

3. The right pane of the window will display the NtfsDisable8dot3NameCreation parameter, as shown in Figure 4.20. This parameter needs to be set to 1 to disable short name creation. Double-click the parameter, and enter 1 in the dialog box. Click OK, and the change will go into effect.

Considerable care should be taken when using the registry editor tool. Do not make any changes to the registry if you don't fully know what the outcome of the change will be. It is possible to prevent Windows NT from starting by making incorrect changes to registry entries.

Quick Reference Specifications

The following are the bare-bones facts and figures.

- *Boot partitions can be mirrored or duplexed, but not striped.*

- *Mirror sets are comprised of two partitions on separate physical disks, available with Windows NT Server only. Mirroring is also known as a RAID 1 configuration.*

- *Duplex sets are connected to separate disk controllers, available with Windows NT Server only.*

- *Stripe sets combine free space on 2 through 32 separate disks into one single logical area. Stripe sets are also known as a RAID 0 configuration.*

- *Stripe sets with parity combine free space on 3 through 32 separate disks into a logical area and also provide fault tolerance. Stripe sets with parity are also known as a RAID 5 configuration.*

- *Volume sets combine free space on 1 through 32 disks into a single logical area.*

- *NTFS volume sets can be extended without reformatting.*

- *When you move objects between folders on the same volume, the object's attributes, such as permissions and compression state are retained.*

- *When copying or moving objects to a different volume, the objects inherit the attribute of the target parent folder.*

- *Only NTFS volumes have local security.*

Utilities To Use

The utilities used in this chapter and their functions are listed in this section. Consider this section to be a memory aid for the busy system administrator.

Disk Manager

- Creating and formatting partitions, volumes, and stripe sets.
- Creating and formatting stripe sets with parity.
- Establishing and breaking mirror/duplex sets.
- Assigning drive IDs.

Windows NT Explorer

- Managing folders and files.
- Viewing and setting object permissions.
- Taking ownership of folders and files.
- Configuring auditing on files and folders.

User Manager Or User Manager For Domains

- Establishing system- or domain-wide audit policies.

Event Viewer

- Viewing audit events logged in the security event log.

Chapter 5

- Creating A User Account
- Setting The Expiration Date On A User Account
- Setting Workstation Logon Restrictions
- Setting Restrictions On Logon Hours
- Renaming A User Account
- Copying A User Account
- Disabling A User Account
- Deleting A User Account
- Changing The Rights Assigned To A User
- Creating A Group And Adding Members To The Group
- Viewing And Removing Group Members
- Adding Rights To A Group
- Removing Rights From A Group
- Changing User Passwords
- Setting The Password Expiration Date
- Enabling The Password History
- Setting The Minimum Password Age
- Setting The Number Of Allowed Bad Logon Attempts
- Clearing A Locked Account
- Defining A User's Home Directory
- Creating And Assigning A Profile
- Returning A User's Personal Profile Back To Default
- Creating A Domain-Wide User Policy
- Adding A User-Specific Policy To An Existing Configuration
- Deleting A User Policy

The User Environment

Administrator's Notes...

Chapter 5

Administrating the user environment in any reasonably large Windows NT installation is something with which the Windows NT administrator quickly becomes proficient. When creating user accounts, you should give careful consideration to the user environment. Assigning appropriate properties during the creation of user account templates is considerably more productive than creating accounts and then configuring the required properties, especially as the number of accounts increases.

User Accounts

For NT workstations configured as a workgroup, user accounts are managed with the User Manager administration tool. For NT servers in a domain, the User Manager For Domains tool is used. Shown in Figure 5.1, User Manager For Domains is identical to User Manager, with a few additional features.

Windows NT user accounts are identified by the username, which may be up to 20 characters long. Letters, numbers, and some special characters may be used in the username. Each user account may be assigned a password of up to 14 characters, or the password may be blank, if the account policy is configured to allow this. Passwords may be constructed of letters, numbers, and some special characters. Windows NT can be configured to retain a password list of up to the last 24 passwords used so that users are unable to keep reusing the same passwords when forced to change them by the account policy.

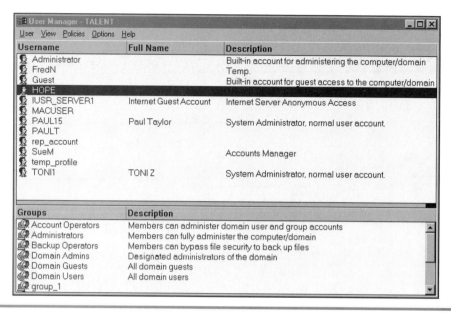

The User Manager For Domains tool.
Figure 5.1

When a user account is created, a Security ID, or *SID*, is assigned to the account. This is used by Windows NT internally to identify the user accounts. Windows NT creates the SID by using a hashing algorithm based on three 32-bit numbers generated from the following information:

- Computer name.

- System time on the computer.

- User mode execution time of the process used to create the SID.

Using this method ensures a unique SID is generated for each account.

Once generated, the SID is never changed, so if a user account is renamed, the account will still be recognized by Windows NT and retain its rights and permissions. However, if the user account is deleted and then added using the same username and password, the account would have a different SID than the original, so it would not gain the permissions or rights of the original account. In this case, the required permissions and rights would have to be re-created. To avoid this headache, always make sure that a user account will not be required at a later date before deleting it.

Account Policies

User account configurations are set by the account policy in force for either a specific computer in a workgroup or for the entire domain. The domain account policy has several more options available than the workgroup. Figure 5.2 shows the Account Policy dialog box for a Windows NT domain. The following section explains the policies and the differences between the two configurations.

Groups

By adding users who need to perform the same functions to groups, assigning rights and permissions becomes simpler. In other words, it's easier to administrate and assign rights to 20 groups than for the 1,000 accounts these groups might contain.

Windows NT creates and uses a number of default groups. Table 5.1 shows these groups, along with their corresponding rights, for Windows NT Workstation; and Table 5.2 shows them for NT Server. Appendix C contains a full description of both the basic and advanced rights. It is not advisable to remove any of the rights assigned to the default groups. The rights that have been set for these groups are the correct

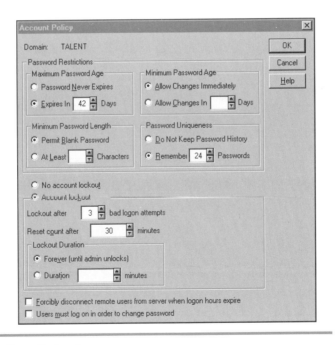

The Account Policy dialog box.
Figure 5.2

Rights	Administrators	Backup Operators	Power Users	Users	Guests
Access This Computer From Network	X	–	X	–	–
Back Up Files And Directories	X	X	–	–	–
Change The System Time	X	–	X	–	–
Force Shutdown From A Remote System	X	–	X	–	–
Load And Unload Device Drivers	X	–	–	–	–
Log On Locally	X	X	X	X	X
Manage Auditing And Security Log	X	–	–	–	–
Restore Files And Directories	X	X	–	–	–
Shut Down The System	X	X	X	X	–
Take Ownership Of Files And Other Objects	X	–	–	–	–

Table 5.1   Windows NT Workstation default groups and rights.

rights for Windows NT to function properly; changing them could inhibit Windows NT's performance.

With Windows NT Workstation, the Everyone group, which contains all Windows NT users, is also created. The Everyone group does not appear in the group list; however, the rights assigned to the group can be displayed. This group has the Access This Computer From Network, Log On Locally, and Shut Down The System rights. This means that all users will receive these rights along with the rights associated

| Rights | Administrators | Operators | | | |
		Account	Backup	Print	Server
Access This Computer From Network	X	–	–	–	–
Add Workstation To Domain	–	–	–	–	–
Backup Files And Directories	X	–	X	–	X
Change The System Time	X	–	–	–	X
Force Shutdown From Remote System	X	–	–	–	X
Load And Unload Device Drivers	X	–	–	–	–
Log On Locally	X	X	X	X	X
Manage Auditing And Security Logs	X	–	–	–	–
Restore Files And Directories	X	–	X	–	X
Shut Down The System	X	X	X	X	X
Take Ownership Of Files And Other Objects	X	–	–	–	–

Table 5.2 Windows NT Server default local groups and rights.

with any other group they may be a member of. In addition, a Replicator group exists, which is used in the replication of data between computers. This group has no members or rights assigned to it.

Windows NT Server also creates the Everyone group, which contains all Windows NT users. This group does not appear in the group list; however, as with Workstation, the rights assigned to the group can be displayed. This group has the Access

This Computer From Network rights. Like Workstation, a Replicator group exists, which is used in the replication of data between computers. This group has no members or rights assigned to it. A Guests Local group will also be created which has the Domain Guests group as a member but no rights assigned to it.

Windows NT Server has two types of groups: local and global. The differences between the two are explained in the following lists. Three global groups are created with Windows NT Server Domain: Admins, Domain Guests, and Domain Users. Windows NT Workstation only has the local group.

Windows NT Workstation Local Group

- Used to assign permissions to local Windows NT Workstation resources.

- Members of the group may include local workstation users, global groups from the local domain, and global groups from a trusted domain.

- Local groups cannot be members of other groups.

Windows NT Server Local Group

- Used to assign permissions to local domain resources. A local group may be assigned permissions for resources located on any server in the domain.

- Members of the group may include local domain users, trusted domain users, local domain global groups, and trusted domain global groups.

- A domain local group cannot be a member of any other group.

Windows NT Server Global Group

- Primarily used to organize domain users by assigning users to the global group and by making the group a member of a local group that contains the required permissions.

- Members of the group may include local domain users.

- Global groups cannot contain local groups or other global groups.

- Global groups may be made members of Windows NT Workstation local groups that are in the same domain or in a trusting domain.

- Global groups be made members of domain local groups in the same domain or in trusting domains.

Unlike usernames, groups cannot be renamed. For example, if you had a group called sales1 that you wanted changed to sales2, the sales1 group would have to be deleted, a new group called sales2 created, and the relevant members added to the group.

User Profiles

Windows NT uses user profiles to store the desktop and working environment for each user who logs on. The information contained in the profile includes such items as screen colors, printer settings, network share connections, and much more. Because the profile information is saved on a per-user basis, it allows multiple users to use the same workstation and set the desktop to their preferences. Shown in Figure 5.3, the System Properties utility contained in the Control Panel is used to manage the profiles.

Three types of profiles are used by Windows NT: local personal, roaming personal, and mandatory. Their features are:

- *Local Personal Profiles*—Used when Windows NT is being used in a non-domain configuration or if the user logged on specifically to the local host, by selecting the computer name, instead of the domain name, in the Logon box. Local profiles are created automatically for users upon logon.

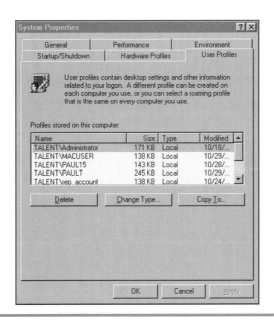

The System Properties User Profiles display.
Figure 5.3

- *Roaming Personal Profiles*—When using Windows NT Server, it is possible to establish a *roaming personal profile* on the server that follows the user. Then whenever the user logs on to the domain from a Windows NT workstation, the user will receive his or her profile. If a user logs on to Windows NT and no preconfigured roaming profile exists, the default user profile will be copied to a new user profile. This new profile will be used to store any configuration changes the user might make to the desktop and user environment.

- *Mandatory Profiles*—These profiles are server-based. When a user's account is configured to use a mandatory profile, no changes made to the user environment by the user will be saved to either the desktop or user environment. The mandatory profile can be used by the system administrator to preset the user environment, which can then be assigned to all users, giving a common look and feel to the working environment.

Personal profiles are given the .USR extension and mandatory profiles the .MAN extension. Renaming a personal profile with a .MAN extension makes it a mandatory profile, which appears as read-only to the user.

By default, any user account is capable of creating a user profile. If you want to assign a common profile to users, you can create a test account to define a profile and then use the administrative tools to assign this profile to the relevant users. An example of this procedure is given in the Practical Guide later in this chapter.

 User profiles can also be used with Windows 95, if Windows 95 has been configured for them.

System Policy Editor

The local computer configuration information is combined with the user profile and stored in the Registry to provide the total working environment. The local computer registry information can be managed by using the System Policy Editor. Using this tool allows you to set up either a domain-wide or a computer- or user-based configuration.

As shown in Figure 5.4, the System Policy Editor can be used to provide some control of the user environment without having to resort to the total restrictions of the mandatory profile. Only items specifically set by the policy will be enforced; users will still be able to use their personal profiles to store settings not set by the policy.

The System Policy Editor.
Figure 5.4

Table 5.3 shows the user property items that can be configured. Because they are too numerous, the computer properties are not listed; however, you can view them with the System Policy Editor.

Policy	Available Settings
Control Panel I Display	Deny access to display icon. Hide Background tab. Hide Screen Saver tab. Hide Appearance tab. Hide Settings tab.
Desktop	Wallpaper. Color scheme.
Shell I Restrictions	Remove Run command from Start menu. Remove folders from Settings on Start menu. Remove taskbar from Settings on Start menu. Hide drives in My Computer. Hide Network Neighborhood. No Workgroup contents in Network Neighborhood. Hide all items on desktop. Disable Shutdown command. Don't save settings at exit.
System I Restrictions	Disable Registry editing tools. Run only allowed Windows applications.

continued

Table 5.3   System Policy Editor user properties.

(continued)

Policy	Available Settings
Windows NT | Custom Folders	Custom Program folder. Custom Desktop folder. Hide Start menu subfolders. Custom Startup folder. Custom Network Neighborhood. Custom Start menu.
Windows NT | Restrictions	Only use approved shell extensions. Remove common group from Start menu.
Windows NT System	Parse Autoexec.bat. Run logon scripts synchronously.

Table 5.3   System Policy Editor user properties.

With Windows NT 4, the terms folder *and* subfolder *have been introduced as replacements for* directory *and* subdirectory. *However, not all of the Administration tools have caught up with this new naming convention. One such example is the Home Directory. The Home Directory is used as a default folder for all undirected file operations. The Home Directory can be either local or a network share.*

Logon Scripts

Logon scripts are an optional logon configuration technique. These scripts can perform user configuration tasks, such as creating network connections and starting applications. One advantage of using logon scripts instead of user profiles is that logon scripts can be changed to make a new network connection upon logon. This connection would be made automatically the next time the user logs on. If a user profile was used, the user would have to first log on and then manually make the network connection. When writing logon scripts, various logical parameters can be used in the script. The parameters will be evaluated by Windows NT when the scripts are run and can be used to customize the scripts for users and groups as required. Table 5.4 lists these parameters, and Table 5.5 shows some uses for them.

Logon scripts are obtained from whichever server in the domain validates the logon. Therefore, you should use the Replicator service to make sure that these logon scripts are available on all domain validating servers. This is done by holding a master set of

Parameter	Function
%HOMEPATH%	Full path to the user's home folder.
%HOMEDRIVE%	Drive letter associated with the user's home folder on the user's local workstation.
%HOMESHARE%	Share name containing the user's home folder.
%OS%	Operating system running on the user's workstation.
%PROCESSOR_ARCHITECTURE%	Type of processor the user's workstation is using.
%PROCESSOR_LEVEL%	The processor level of the user's workstation.
%USERDOMAIN%	The domain that contains the user's workstation.
%USERNAME%	User's logon account name.

Table 5.4 Logon script logical parameters.

Command	Function
net use * \\server1\%username%	Connects to a network share controlled by server1 with the same name as the user account; e.g., the share UNC name could be \\server1\pault.
net use * \\server1\%os%	Connects to a network share controlled by server1 with the share that matches the workstation operating system. Can be used to make sure the workstation connects to the correct location for its version of server-based software.

Table 5.5 Example logon script logical parameters.

logon scripts in \%systemroot%\System32\Repl\Export\scripts, then importing them into all servers.

Further description of the **net use** command can be found in Chapter 7.

User Environmental Variables

User environmental variables are configured by using the System utility contained in the Control Panel. Unique to each user who logs on, user environmental variables are used to configure the parameters for the temporary file storage and path locations. The System Properties Environment window is shown in Figure 5.5.

In addition to user environment variables, system variables are located in the System utility and are system-wide variables that only administrators are able to change.

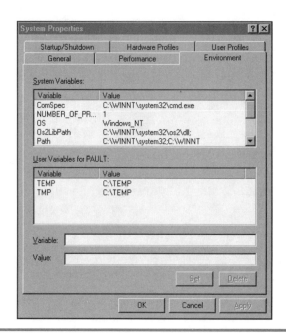

The System Properties Environment window.
Figure 5.5

Practical

Guide To

Administering

The User

Environment

The following section provides real-life examples and step-by-step instructions on how to successfully administrate the Windows NT user environment. For these examples, User Manager For Domains is used. (As mentioned earlier, User Manager is used in the same way but does not have all the features of the domain version.) Refer to the text earlier in this chapter for more information on the differences between these two administrative tools.

Creating A User Account

A new employee has joined your department on a temporary basis. You want to put her to work right away so you can get back to the important things in life—like planning your next vacation. So, first things first. Let's set up a user account.

1. Select Start|Programs|Administrative Tools|User Manager For Domains. The User Manager For Domains window appears.

2. Choose User|New User. The New User window appears, as shown in Figure 5.6.

3. Enter the username and password for the new user account. A full name and description box is available for optional information. By default, the user must change her password on the first logon, although this can be modified if required.

4. At this point, you can perform additional configurations on the account. You can add the account to various groups, set the required profile, restrict logon hours, and so on. These extra administration tasks won't be done in this example but are covered in other examples in this section. Click the Add button. The account is created, and you are returned to a blank New User window. At this stage, you can add more accounts if you need to. Click Close when done.

When the user logs on for the first time with the password supplied by you, the Change Password window will appear, and the user will be forced to change her password before continuing.

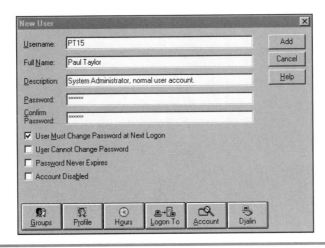

The New User window.
Figure 5.6

 Usernames must be unique. They can be up to 20 characters long and are not case sensitive. Passwords can be up to 14 characters and are case sensitive.

Setting The Expiration Date On A User Account

You've planned your vacation and just can't wait to sample some of that sun, sea, and.... When the calendar comes back into focus as you return to reality, you realize that the temporary employee's contract will end while you're away. With you gone, who's going to disable the user account at the appropriate time? That's right, no one. Let's put in the expiration date now, so you can relax.

1. Choose Start|Programs|Administrative Tools|User Manager For Domains. The User Manager For Domains window appears.

2. Select the required user in the username list. Then double click the username, or press Enter, or choose User|Properties. The User Properties dialog box appears.

3. Click the Account button. The Account Information dialog box appears, as shown in Figure 5.7. Click the End Of option in the Account Expires pane, and set the required date. Click OK. You will be returned to the User Properties dialog box. Click Close.

If the user attempts to log on using this account past the End Of date, the logon will be refused. To re-enable this account at a later date:

1. Choose Start|Programs|Administrative Tools|User Manager For Domains. The User Manager For Domains window appears.

2. Double click the required user in the username list. The User Properties dialog box appears.

3. Click the Account button. The Account Information dialog box appears. Change the End Of date in the Account Expires pane to a more suitable date. Click OK. You are returned to the User Properties dialog box. Deselect the Account Disabled box, and click OK.

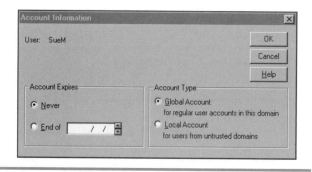

The Account Information dialog box.
Figure 5.7

Setting Workstation Logon Restrictions

For various political reasons, all having to do with money, of course, it has been decided that all users can only log on to their own department's workstations. To create workstation logon restrictions:

1. Choose Start|Programs|Administrative Tools|User Manager For Domains. The User Manager For Domains window appears.

2. Double click the required user from the username list. The User Properties dialog box appears.

3. Click the Logon To button. The Logon Workstations dialog box appears.

4. Choose the User May Log On To These Workstations option. The workstation selection boxes are highlighted. Enter the computer name of each workstation where the user is permitted to log on, as shown in Figure 5.8. Click OK. You are returned to the User Properties dialog box. Click Close.

The computer name referred to in the User Manager is the NetBIOS name. You can view the name by using the Network utility contained in the Control Panel as follows: Log on to the workstation in question, and choose Start/Settings/Control Panel. Double click the Network icon. The Network Identification window will appear, and the computer name will be shown.

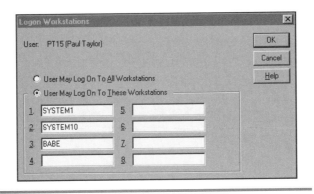

The Logon Workstations dialog box.

Figure 5.8

Setting Restrictions On Logon Hours

You have some students working for your company over their summer vacation. These two are really on the ball. It makes you wonder if you shouldn't start thinking about hanging up the old mouse and riding off into the sunset....

Just as you return from your reverie, the boss storms in with the bill from your Internet service provider and wants to know what's going on. It appears the bill is twice as much as usual, and he's not happy. It doesn't take much digging to find out that the students have been coming into work on weekends and amusing themselves on the Internet at the company's expense. Restricting the students' logons to working hours would be an excellent idea.

1. Choose Start|Programs|Administrative Tools|User Manager For Domains. The User Manager For Domains window appears.

2. Double click the user on the username list. The User Properties dialog box is displayed.

3. Click the Hours button. The Logon Hours dialog box appears. On this window, the filled-in blocks indicate the hours the user is authorized to log on. The clear blocks indicate when the user is not allowed to log on. By default, no hour logon restrictions are configured. Figure 5.9 shows settings that permit the user to log on only between the hours of 6 a.m. and 6 p.m., Monday through Friday.

4. To restrict a user to the same access shown in Figure 5.9, click the Sunday button to select the whole day. Then click the Disallow button to clear the selected blocks. Repeat the process for Saturday.

5. To clear the hours on each weekday, click the start time you wish to clear and drag to the stop time—for instance, click Midnight and drag to 6 a.m. Then, click the Disallow button to clear the selected blocks. Repeat for each workday, and click OK. You are returned to the User Properties window. Click Close.

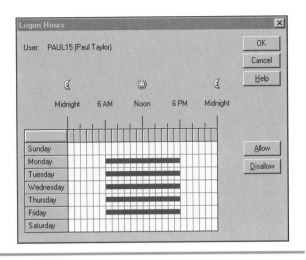

The Logon Hours window.
Figure 5.9

Although the user in Figure 5.9 is restricted to certain hours, if the user is still connected when logon hours expire, the user will be able to continue to work. However, if the user logs out and then tries to log on again, he or she would be refused access. If you prefer, you can configure the Account Policy to forcibly disconnect users from the server when their logon hours have expired. To do this:

1. Choose Start|Programs|Administrative Tools|User Manager For Domains. The User Manager For Domains window appears.

2. Choose Policy|Accounts. The Account Policy dialog box appears. Select the Forcibly Disconnect Remote Users From Server When Logon Hours Expire option. Click OK.

Now the users will be disconnected from the server when the time expires.

Renaming A User Account

One of the users in the accounts department has left the company and a replacement has been hired. The replacement starts today and will need an account. The new employee needs the same access as her predecessor, so reusing the existing account makes sense. Two options spring to mind: force the new employee to change her name (not a bad plan) or rename the user account (not as much fun, but probably more practical).

1. Choose Start|Programs|Administrative Tools|User Manager For Domains. The User Manager For Domains window appears.

2. Select the required user from the user list. Choose User|Rename. The Rename dialog box appears, as shown Figure 5.10.

3. Type the new username in the Change To box, and click OK. The account is renamed, and you are returned to the User Manager For Domains window.

The renamed user account retains the original SID, so it will have the same user rights and permissions assigned.

The Rename dialog box.
Figure 5.10

Copying A User Account

The marketing department hired a new executive and wants you to create an account that matches another executive's account. (*That* account took you about six months to get just perfect.) No problem, we've got this covered.

1. Choose Start|Programs|Administrative Tools|User Manager For Domains. The User Manager For Domains window appears.

2. From the username list, select the user whose account you want to copy. Choose User|Copy, or when the required user is selected, press the F8 key. The Copy window appears.

3. You'll need to set a new username and password, as shown in Figure 5.11. If you want to make any changes to the new user account configuration, you can do so at this point or make the changes once the account is created. Click the Add button. The account is created, and you are returned to the Copy window. Click Close.

The user account that was copied will not be affected by this copy operation. The new account will receive its own SID.

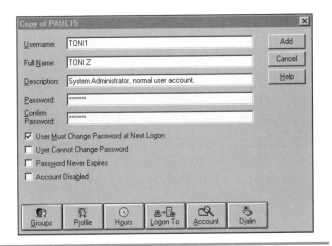

The Copy window.
Figure 5.11

Disabling A User Account

Juicy news on the company grapevine: A company hotshot had a blazing argument with the boss and told him where to stick his company. Not very creative for someone from the marketing department, was it? Your experience with hotshot executives is that they never say what they mean. So, there's no way you're deleting this account until you're sure it's no longer needed. Instead, you decide to disable the account.

1. Choose Start|Programs|Administrative Tools|User Manager For Domains. The User Manager For Domains window appears.

2. Double click the user in the username list. The User Properties window appears.

3. Select the Account Disabled box, and click OK. No more logons using this account will be validated.

The account has only been disabled; no other changes will have been made to it.

Deleting A User Account

Well, the hotshot is history after all. He did come back, but only to clear out his desk. The boss has ordered all traces of this ex-employee removed. Just to make sure that he really was gone, you wisely put off the account deletion for an extra month. But you might as well do it now.

1. Choose Start|Programs|Administrative Tools|User Manager For Domains. The User Manager For Domains window appears.

2. Select the user from the username list and choose User|Delete or press the Delete key.

3. A User Manager For Domains warning message appears, as shown in Figure 5.12. This warning is very important and is designed to make you check your actions. Once an account is deleted, there is no way to reproduce the same account again due to the unique way the SID is produced. Make sure you really want to delete this account, then click OK. You will be asked to confirm the deletion. Click the Yes button, and the account will be deleted.

Only the SAM record for this account will have been deleted. No user files or profiles will have been removed.

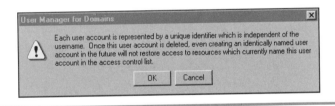

The warning message that displays when deleting user accounts.
Figure 5.12

Changing The Rights Assigned To A User

A new security officer at the company wants to be able to administrate the Windows NT security logs and asks you to give him an Administrator account. No way. The first rule of network security is to only give people what they really need. Assigning the Manage Auditing And Security Log right will do.

1. Choose Start|Programs|Administrative Tools|User Manager For Domains. The User Manager For Domains window appears.

2. Click Policies|User Rights. The User Rights Policy dialog box appears.

3. Use the Right selection box to select the right you want to assign. The right will be displayed in the Right box, and the Grant To box will show who the right has been granted to.

4. Click the Add button. The Add Users And Groups dialog box appears. By default, only groups are displayed in this window. To also display users, click the Show Users button. Select the user to whom you want to grant the right, and click the Add button. The user will be added to the Add Names box, as shown in Figure 5.13. Click OK. You are returned to the User Rights Policy dialog box. Click OK again, and the right will be granted.

If the user is currently logged on, the user won't receive the user right until he logs off and back on. This is because the Security Access Token is only generated on logon. The Security Access Token is explained further in Chapter 2.

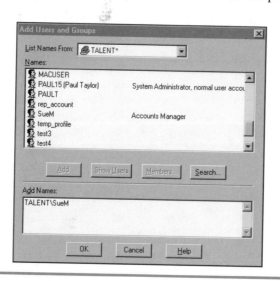

The Add Users And Groups window.
Figure 5.13

Creating A Group And Adding Members To The Group

You have the chance to install a new Windows NT setup at a site that presently doesn't have any existing Windows NT. The company can be broken down into neat divisions and departments. (This is just too good to be true. There has to be a catch...they probably won't pay you.) Using groups at this site has to be the way to go. Some planning now will save a lot of work later, so once you have worked out who goes where, you can create the groups as follows:

1. Choose Start|Programs|Administrative Tools|User Manager For Domains. The User Manager For Domains window appears.

2. Choose User|New Local Group. The New Local Group dialog box appears, as shown in Figure 5.14.

3. Enter the group name into the dialog box and, if you require, a description. Click the Add button. The Add Users And Groups dialog box appears. Select the user or group you want to add to this group and click Add. The selected items are displayed in the Add Names pane. Repeat for all the items you want to add to the group, and click OK.

4. You are returned to the New Local Group dialog box, and the users or groups you have just added are shown in the Members pane. Click OK, and the group is created.

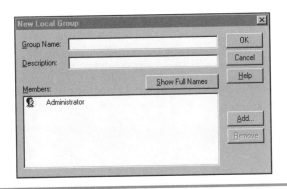

The New Local Group dialog box.
Figure 5.14

Viewing And Removing Group Members

That's progress for you. Because the new Windows NT setup is just so productive, half of the users have been canned. (Anyone know a back road out of town?) So all your carefully created and arranged groups now have to be reconfigured. I'm sure you kept a detailed plan as to what users were in what group, but just to help you out, here's how you view and remove group members:

1. Choose Start|Programs|Administrative Tools|User Manager For Domains. The User Manager For Domains window appears.

2. Double click the group you want to administrate. The Local Group Properties window appears. The group members are displayed in the Members pane. To remove a member from the group, select the member, and click the Remove button. The group member will be removed from the Members pane. Click OK to initiate the changes.

Adding Rights To A Group

Your company has now expanded the security team from one to five. You have decided that at this rate, it would be a good idea to have these guys in a security group and assign the correct rights to that group. (Do you know how many security officers it takes to change a lightbulb? Me neither. Apparently it's a secret.) Here's how you set rights for a group:

1. Choose Start|Programs|Administrative Tools|User Manager For Domains. The User Manager For Domains window appears.

2. Choose Policies|User Rights. The User Rights Policy dialog box appears.

3. In the Right selection box, select the right you want to add to the group. Click the Add button. The Add Users And Groups dialog box appears.

4. Select the group from the Names list, and click the Add button. The group is displayed in the Add Names pane. Click OK, and you are returned to the User Rights Policy window. Click OK again to initiate the changes. You are returned to the User Manager For Domains window.

Removing Rights From A Group

You've heard that the security team has been making up system administrator jokes. Well, we'll see who's laughing after their rights have been trimmed down. Actually, they've been demanding more rights than they will ever need, anyway. The rule is: If the group is not important, tell them to get lost. If they are important, *politely* tell them to get lost. If they start making a fuss, give them the right, then recover it very quietly at a later date. They'll probably never know (just don't blame me if you get caught).

1. Choose Start|Programs|Administrative Tools|User Manager For Domains. The User Manager For Domains window appears.

2. Choose Policies|User Rights. The User Rights Policy dialog box appears.

3. In the Right selection box, select the right you want to remove from the group.

4. The Grant To window lists the users and groups who currently have this right, as shown in Figure 5.15. Select the group you want to remove the right from, and click the Remove button. The group is removed from the Grant To window. Click OK. You are returned to the User Manager For Domains window.

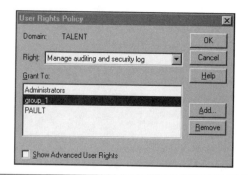

The User Rights Policy dialog box.
Figure 5.15

Changing User Passwords

It's been a holiday weekend, and everyone has been off having lots of fun. You can tell because your phone hasn't stopped ringing with users asking for their passwords to be changed. (Well, it did stop ringing for the 45 minutes you had the phone off the hook.) Oh well, there is quite a pile of users who need their passwords changed, so it really should be done.

1. Choose Start|Programs|Administrative Tools|User Manager For Domains. The User Manager For Domains window appears.

2. Double click the user in the username list. The User Properties dialog box appears.

3. Select the Password box, and remove the asterisks representing the password. Enter and confirm the new password. The User Must Change Password On Next Logon option will be selected by default; this can be changed if required. Click OK, and the password will be changed.

 Always remind users when changing their passwords that passwords are case sensitive.

Setting The Password Expiration Date

In an effort to increase security at your site and prevent users from using each other's accounts, it has been decided that all passwords will expire after 30 days. Of course, such decisions don't affect you, do they? Yes, they do. If there is one account a hacker would like to access, it's yours. If you don't follow the rules, how can you expect the users to?

1. Choose Start|Programs|Administrative Tools|User Manager For Domains. The User Manager For Domains window appears.

2. Choose Policies|Account. The Account Policy dialog box appears.

3. In the Password Restrictions pane, use the Maximum Password Age selection box to set when the password will expire. When users log on after the expiration date, they will be forced to change the password before completing the logon process.

Remember, all policies are either system-wide, as in a workgroup configuration, or domain-wide. If you don't want the password to expire on certain accounts, select the Password Never Expires option on the User Properties dialog box.

Enabling The Password History

You have a feeling that some of the users are using the same password each time the Account Policy forces them to change it. This really is a typical user trick. Why do they think you're making them change their password in the first place? Okay, they've asked for it. Let's turn on Password History and see if that slows them down.

1. Choose Start|Programs|Administrative Tools|User Manager For Domains. The User Manager For Domains window appears.

2. Choose Policies|Account. The Account Policy dialog box appears. The Password Restriction pane from this dialog box is shown in Figure 5.16.

3. Under Password Uniqueness, choose the Remember option, and select the number of passwords you want to be retained; up to 24 passwords may be retained, but 8 is a typical number to set. Click OK, and the password history will be operational.

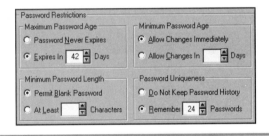

The Password Restrictions pane.
Figure 5.16

Setting The Minimum Password Age

Well, the password history stopped the users from using the same passwords over and over again for a while. That is, until one of them discovered that the maximum number of passwords in the history list is eight; the office grapevine did the rest. Now when forced to change their password, they change it eight times and then set it back to the original. The password history could be increased to retain 24 passwords, but they would get around this too. All right, if they want to play dirty, that's it. Dig in, and set the minimum password age.

1. Choose Start|Programs|Administrative Tools|User Manager For Domains. The User Manager For Domains window appears.

2. Choose Policies|Account. The Account Policy dialog box appears. By default, in the Minimum Password Age pane, the Allow Changes Immediately option will be selected.

3. Select the Allow Changes In option, and set the number of days between password changes. Click OK.

The minimum password age must be set to be less than the maximum password age.

Setting The Number Of Allowed Bad Logon Attempts

As the saying goes, youth is wasted on the young, and the youth in the shipping department is really wasted. After a liquid lunch, he thought it would be fun to try and hack into the boss's account and send threatening emails to his soon-to-be ex-colleagues. Well, let's hope he had fun, because he is history, and the boss has decided that after three bad logons to any account, the account will be locked. (Monday mornings are going to be such fun.)

1. Choose Start|Programs|Administrative Tools|User Manager For Domains. The User Manager For Domains window appears.

2. Choose Policies|Account. The Account Policy dialog box appears. The Account Lockout pane is used to configure the number of bad logon attempts allowed before the account is locked. By default, no account locking takes place.

3. Select the Account Lockout option. The default Account Lockout options will be selected, along with the default parameters for these options, as shown in Figure 5.17. Change these settings as required. Click OK.

When a user causes the account lockout to be triggered by entering bad passwords, an information message is displayed advising them that the account is locked and to contact the system administrator. It's worth balancing your security needs against the administrative overhead. Setting the account lockout to 1 may be very secure, but it will generate a lot of locked user accounts.

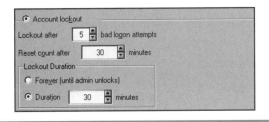

The Account Lockout options.
Figure 5.17

Clearing A Locked Account

The boss has just been caught by his own trap. Still half asleep this morning, he managed to get his password wrong so many times the account got locked out. Better unlock it so he can read his email and play some solitaire (one of these days he's going to see those bouncing cards).

1. Choose Start|Programs|Administrative Tools|User Manager For Domains. The User Manager For Domains window appears.

2. Select the relevant user, and double click to display the User Properties dialog box. The Account Locked Out option will be selected, as shown in Figure 5.18.

3. Clear the Account Locked Out option, and click OK. The account is now available for use.

If the account lockout duration time is in use—in other words, the Forever Locked option is not used—the account will be cleared automatically at the end of the duration time. As shown in this example, a manual clear can be used to speed things up.

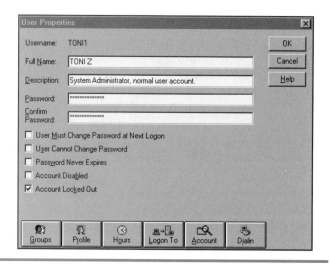

The User Properties dialog box, with Account Locked Out selected.
Figure 5.18

Defining A User's Home Directory

As staff leave your sunny outpost, it is getting increasingly difficult to identify which files they were using. To overcome this, you decide to allocate home directories for each user. Then, hopefully, when someone leaves, it should be easier to see which files are no longer required.

1. Choose Start|Programs|Administrative Tools|User Manager For Domains. The User Manager For Domains appears.

2. Select the relevant user, and double click to display the User Properties dialog box.

3. Click the Profile button. The User Environment Profile dialog box appears. Enter either the local path to the home directory or the Connect To Share in the Home Directory pane. Click OK, and you are returned to the User Properties dialog box. Click Close.

Creating And Assigning A Profile

You have several new users starting to use Windows NT today. Because they are all going to be trained at the same time, it would be a nice idea if they started off with the same environment. They'll change them in a couple of days, of course, but that's life.

The first step is to create a user account with the profile you want to assign. You could use your own account, but it would involve messing up your working environment just to create someone else's.

1. Choose Start|Programs|Administrative Tools|User Manager For Domains. The User Manager For Domains window appears.

2. Click User|New User. The New User dialog box is displayed. Enter the username of the profile template account—for instance, Profile_template—and then enter and confirm the password. Click Add and then Close.

3. Log on using this template account and configure the working environment as required—for example, set screen colors, drive and printer mappings, and so on. Then, log out from this account. When you log out, the environment changes that you made are saved in the personal user profile.

Now that you've created the profile template, you'll need to establish a profile share, if one is not already available. This is demonstrated in the next example, along with how to create a subfolder to hold the user profile. Using your Administrator account now instead of the template user, perform the following steps:

4. Choose Start|Programs|Windows NT Explorer. The Windows NT Explorer window appears.

5. Indicate that you want to establish the profile share in an existing folder, or create a new folder by clicking File|New|Folder and entering the folder name. Press the Enter key.

6. Select and right-click the folder. Choose Sharing from the pop-up menu. The Folder Properties Sharing dialog box appears.

7. Click the Shared As button, then click OK. The share will be established.

8. Create a subfolder of the share with the username as the folder name—for instance, PaulT.

9. Choose Start|Settings|Control Panel.

10. Double click the System icon. The System Properties sheet appears. Select the User Profiles tab. Select the template user profile that you created earlier from the Profiles Name list; the profile name will be the same as the user account name.

11. Click the Copy To button to access the Copy To dialog box.

12. Click the Browse button in the Copy Profile To pane, and in the Browse window, locate the subfolder you have created for the user (PaulT, in our example). Click OK. You are returned to the Copy To dialog box.

13. Click the Change button in the Permitted To Use pane. The Choose User window appears.

14. Click the Show User button to display usernames, in addition to group names. Select the user you want to receive the profile from the username list, and click the Add button. The username will be displayed in the Add Name window. Click OK. You are returned to the Copy To dialog box, as shown in Figure 5.19. Click OK again.

Now you need to configure the user account record for the relevant user to use the new profile.

15. Choose Start|Programs|Administrative Tools|User Manager For Domains. The User Manager For Domains window appears.

16. Double click the relevant user from the username list. The User Properties dialog box appears. Click the Profile button, and the User Environment Profile dialog box is displayed, as shown in Figure 5.20.

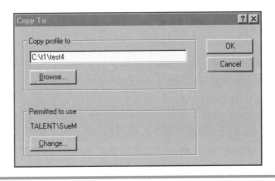

The Copy To dialog box.
Figure 5.19

17. Enter the full UNC name path to the profile in the User Profile Path dialog box. The pathname will take the form *servername**sharename**username* (in our example, \\server1\profiles\PaulT). Click OK. You are returned to the User Properties dialog box. Click OK again, and the user account database will be updated.

When the user logs on to the domain, the profile that has just been set up will be used. This profile is a roaming profile that follows the user to each workstation. The profile will be cached locally on each workstation the user uses. This cached copy will be used if the server copy is unavailable for any reason.

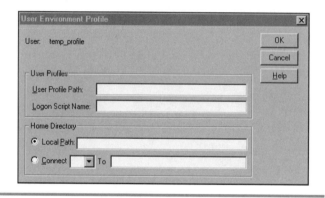

The User Environment Profile dialog box.
Figure 5.20

Returning A User's Personal Profile Back To Default

One of your more annoying users (you know the type) thinks he knows everything. He has changed so much of his desktop environment that he now says it's unusable. So, of course, this is now your problem, and he wants you to sort it out right away. Oh, yes, I forgot to mention, his problems are much more important than anyone else's. It's nearly lunchtime, so I think he should wait till after lunch, don't you?

After you've had a nice lunch, do the following:

1. Choose Start|Settings|Control Panel.

2. Double click the System icon. The System Properties sheet appears.

3. Choose the User Profiles tab. Select the User Profile in question (the default naming convention for user profiles is to use the username as the profile name), and click the Delete button. Click Yes to confirm the deletion of the profile. You are returned to the System Properties sheet. Click OK.

Next time this user logs on, the default profile will be supplied, and he can start messing with it again.

Creating A Domain-Wide User Policy

The corporate colors are to be used on all users' desktops in order to present a unified corporate image. The users are sure to revolt over this one (just like the time the company tried to introduce a company uniform, and everyone walked around all day saying, "Do you want fries with that?"). Since you only need to set the color scheme, you can use the System Policy Editor.

1. Choose Start|Programs|Administrative Tools|System Policy Editor. The System Policy Editor window appears.

2. Choose File|New Policy. Double click the Default User icon. The Default User Properties dialog box appears. Double click the relevant book icon to expand, and view the current settings—for instance, Desktop.

3. Select the setting you want to enforce. Let's choose Color Scheme under Desktop. A Settings For Color Scheme dialog box appears in the Default User Properties window, as shown in Figure 5.21. Set the required color scheme. When all required policy settings have been made, click OK.

4. You are returned to the System Policy Editor window. Now you'll need to save the policy in the NetLogon folder of the PDC. Choose File|Save As. Locate the PDC logon share—for instance, \\server1\netlogon—and save the file as Ntconfig.POL.

In addition, this file will need to be replicated to all the domain BDCs so that it's available when the domain logon is validated. All users will now use this policy. They will still be able to save settings in their personal profile for items not specified by the policy.

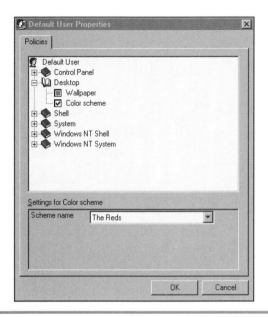

The Default User Properties Policies window.
Figure 5.21

Adding A User-Specific Policy To An Existing Configuration

It seems that having the corporate color scheme has upset a few of the more senior personnel, so the IT manager has relented somewhat and allowed certain key people to set their own color schemes. Come the revolution, all will be equal. But for now, you'll need to do as you're told.

1. Choose Start|Programs|Administrative Tools|System Policy Editor. The System Policy Editor window appears.

2. Choose File|Open Policy. The Open Policy File window appears. Use this to locate the required policy. Click Open.

3. The System Policy Editor window will now show the icons associated with this policy. Choose Edit|Add User. The Add User dialog box appears, as shown in Figure 5.22. Click the Browse button. The Add Users dialog box for the current domain appears.

4. Select the required user from the Names list, and click the Add button. The user name will be displayed in the Add Names pane. Click OK. You are now returned to the System Policy Editor window, and an icon has been created for the user.

5. Double click the User icon and make the required configuration changes to it. Click OK. You will be returned to the System Policy Editor window. Choose File|Save, and the policy will be updated.

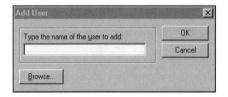

The Add User dialog box.
Figure 5.22

Deleting A User Policy

One of the important users who was allowed to change his color scheme has fallen out of favor, so he is being demoted back to the ranks. This is quite easy to change. By deleting the user-specific policy, the user will then be forced to use the default user policy, just like everyone else.

1. Choose Start|Programs|Administrative Tools|System Policy Editor. The System Policy Editor window appears.

2. Choose File|Open Policy. Select the policy using the Policy Open dialog box.

3. The policy is displayed. Select the user icon for the user you want to remove. Choose Edit|Remove. Click Yes to confirm. Choose File|Save to save the changes you have made to the system policy. Exit the System Policy window.

It's worth remembering that when a user account is deleted from the SAM by using the User Manager For Domains Administration tool, the profiles are not removed. This is an extra administrative task that needs to be performed.

Quick Reference Specifications

The following are the bare-bones facts and figures.

- *Usernames can be up to 20 characters long and must be unique in the domain.*

- *Usernames are not case sensitive. They can include letters, numbers, and some special characters.*

- *Passwords can be up to 18 characters long.*

- *Passwords are case sensitive. They can include letters, numbers, and some special characters.*

- *The Security ID, or SID, is unique and cannot be re-created.*

- *Windows NT Workstation uses local groups.*

- *Windows NT Server uses local and global groups.*

- *Group names can be up to 14 characters long.*

- *Windows NT has three types of profiles: local personal, roaming personal, and mandatory.*

- *User policies can be configured to offer more flexibility than mandatory profiles.*

Utilities To Use

The utilities used in this chapter and their functions are listed in this section. Consider this as a memory aid for the busy system administrator.

Administrator User/Administrator User For Domains

- Create, copy, rename, and delete user accounts.
- Set and change user passwords.
- Create and add users to groups.
- Set account and user rights policies.
- Set account logon hours and workstation restrictions.
- Define paths for profiles and logon scripts.

System Policy Editor

- Create domain-wide system policies.
- Create domain-wide user policies.
- Create user- and system-specific policies.

System

- Copy user profiles.
- Delete user profiles.

Windows NT Explorer

- Create folders and subfolders.
- Create profile shares.

Chapter 6

Printing

Administrator's Notes...

Chapter

6

The Windows NT print system is a straightforward system to administrate and use. However, a number of points must be taken into consideration by the system administrator. One is that the terminology used by Microsoft to describe the print system can sometimes be confusing, especially if you have administrated other operating systems. Another potential problem area is that Windows NT printer drivers are processor- and version-dependent, which can cause some administrative problems.

Windows NT Printing Terminology

This section provides an overview of the main terms used to describe the Windows NT print system and points out where the confusion with these terms often occurs. The most important points are covered in more detail later in this chapter.

- *Print device*—The print, or printing, device is the actual physical hardware that produces the print output. In most other operating systems, and in day-to-day life, this is known as the printer. This is not the case with Windows NT.

- *Printer*—The printer is the Windows NT software component that connects Windows NT to the print device. This is generally known in other operating systems as the print queue.

- *Print spooler and spooling*—The print spooler schedules, distributes, and controls print jobs. Spooling refers to the process of writing print jobs to a file, known as a *spool file*, where they wait to be printed. If the system fails, the print job is preserved in the spool file and can be printed when the system restarts. The print spooler can be controlled by using the Services icon in the Control Panel.

- *Print server*—The print server is a computer or network device that connects to print devices and makes them available for use on the network. It can be either a Windows NT Workstation or Server, as well as a print device directly attached to the network.

- *Creating a printer*—Creating a printer means to connect to either a network or locally attached printing device and installing the relevant print driver.

- *Connecting to a printer*—Connecting to a printer means to connect to a printer being shared by a Windows NT print server.

- *Printer drivers*—Printer drivers provide the necessary driver codes for a particular manufacturer's printing device.

- *Print router*—The print router is responsible for locating the printers, obtaining the correct printer driver for the client system, and routing print jobs to the correct spooler.

- *Print processor*—The print processor converts the application print data into raw printable data that can be sent to the printer. If the data is already in this state—for example, in ASCII—no conversion is needed.

Administrating Printing

The print system is administrated by using the Printers window, as shown in Figure 6.1. Contained within this window is the Add Printer icon used to invoke the Add Printer Wizard, which guides you through the steps needed to create and connect to printers. Also displayed are icons of other, if any, printers that have already been created. Double-clicking these icons invokes the Printer Server window for the printer. Both the printer and print documents can be managed from this window.

Printer Security

One of the fundamental design policies of Windows NT is to treat all software components as objects. This also holds true for the print system. Because full security and auditing can be enabled on all Windows NT objects, the Windows NT administrator is provided with a flexible, secure print system. Table 6.1 shows the permissions that

The Printers window.
Figure 6.1

can be configured for printers and the functions this access allows. Not listed in this table is the No Access permission, which, as the name implies, is a blocking permission that overrides assigned permissions.

The Print Operators group is defined in a Windows NT domain to manage the printers. By default, this group has no members.

Printer Drivers

Printer drivers can be a troublesome area for the Windows NT administrator. Often the printer driver is the first component that needs to be upgraded if any printing problems occur. Unfortunately, print devices are frequently the last computer resource to be upgraded and may be required to function for years. You might well

Function	Print	Manage Documents	Full Control
Print documents	X	X	X
Manage own print jobs	X	X	X
Manage all print jobs		X	X
Share a printer			X
Change printer permissions			X
Delete printers			X

Table 6.1   Printer permissions.

find that a printer driver is not supplied with Windows NT for your particular print device. In that case, you'll need to obtain a driver from the hardware manufacturer.

Printer drivers are not compatible among different processor type. For instance, a printer driver for an Intel x86 platform will not work on a RISC-based system, and vice versa. At first glance, this might not seem to be much of a problem, because you wouldn't need to use an Intel printer driver on a RISC box. However, as we examine more closely the way Windows NT handles remote printing, you will see where the problem occurs.

The Print Process

To help you understand the actual print process, the following steps explain how Windows NT produces print jobs. The printing device in this example is connected to a remote Windows NT print server, and the print job is from a standard Windows application.

1. The print driver is loaded. If the driver is not found locally, it will be downloaded from the print server. This means that the print server must contain the correct processor type and software version of the driver for this client. If the client does have a locally installed driver, it will be compared to the print server driver version. If the print server is a later revision than the driver already on the client, it will be downloaded. If it isn't, the local driver will be used.

2. The application print output file is used with the print driver to generate an output journal file.

3. The journal file is sent to the spooler, which passes it on to the appropriate print processor.

4. The print processor uses the journal file to produce the raw print data.

5. The spooler on the client computer takes the raw data file and routes it to the spooler on the print server. (This step is not needed if the printer is locally attached.)

6. The spooler on the print server sends the raw data file to the print monitor.

7. The print monitor sends the file to the relevant port to be printed.

Print Monitors

Print monitors are used with the Windows NT print system to control the connection to the I/O port to which the actual print device is connected. This port could be

Monitor	Function and Uses
DECPSMAN.DLL	Digital network-attached print devices; can use either the TCP/IP or DECnet protocol. DECnet is not supplied with Windows NT.
HPMON.DLL	HP JetDirect network adapters; uses the DLC protocol only.
LOCALMON.DLL	Local I/O ports; e.g., LPT1 or COM1.
LPRMON.DLL	LPD print servers; usually Unix hosts.
NWMON.DLL	Pserver print devices; usually used in NetWare configurations.
PJLMON.DLL	Printer job language monitor; used to monitor the status of the print device.
SFMMON.DLL	AppleTalk network-attached printers.

Table 6.2   Print monitors.

a local, remote, or network port. Table 6.2 shows the default print monitors and their functions.

Print Separator Files

Print separator files, often called flag, burst, or banner pages, are used to separate print jobs. Windows NT includes three default separator files, which are located in the %systemroot%system32 folder. These files contain the necessary codes for switching HP printing devices between PCL (Printer Control Language) and PostScript. The files can be used as templates to create your own separator files. Table 6.3 shows some of the most useful escape codes that can be placed in separator files.

The following separator escape codes can be used to produce a simple separator page containing the username, the job number, and the date when the job was submitted.

- FLAG1.SEP\
- \Luser name = \N\0
- \Ljob number = \I\0
- \Ldate = \D\0
- \E

Escape Code	Function
\	Must be the only character on the first line of the separator file.
\x	Line feeds x number of lines. Line feed of 0 moves printing to next line.
\D	Prints the date when the job is printed.
\E	Indicates the end of a separator file, and ejects the page.
\Hxx	Sends the ASCII escape sequence to the printing device.
\L	All characters following this command are printed. Command turned off when any other escape code is reached.

Table 6.3 Separator escape codes and functions.

Printer Pools

An unlimited number of print devices can be combined into a *printer pool*. The printer pool is seen by users as a single printer to which they submit their print jobs. The print spooler will take care of routing the print jobs to every available print device in the pool. Because the print devices are seen as a single printer, they must all be the same device type.

Printer Scheduling And Priorities

Printer scheduling can be used to set the hours a printer is available. However, unlike the Hours function provided with User Manager For Domains, which allows the days as well as hours to be set, printer scheduling is restricted to hours only. The default is for the printer to be available at all times.

Printer priorities can be configured on an individual printer basis from 1 to 99, with the lowest priority being 1. When two printers are configured to use the same print device, frequently one printer is configured at a higher priority than the other. Print priorities can be used so that priority print jobs receive preferential access to the print device.

Both printer scheduling and printer priorities are configured by using the Printer Properties Scheduling page, as shown in Figure 6.2.

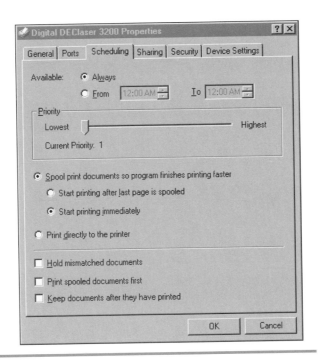

The Printer Properties Scheduling page.

Figure 6.2

Print Forms

Print forms are defined on a per-print server basis—a print server in this case is either a Windows NT Workstation or Server. Print forms are defined by using the Server Properties window accessed from the Printers window. These forms define the basic print area. The paper width and height can also be defined, as well as the left, right, top, and bottom margins.

A large number of predefined print forms are provided for all standard paper and envelope sizes. If required, these can be used as templates for creating your own specific forms. Print forms must be assigned to the correct print device paper tray, which is done by using the Printer Properties Device Settings tab. An example of configuring print forms is given in the Practical Guide.

Practical

Guide To

Printing

The following section provides real-life examples and step-by-step instructions on how to administrate and use the Windows NT print system. The print system is administrated by using the Printers window. This window can be accessed in several ways, including via the My Computer icon or the Control Panel. Although the following examples access this window from the Start button, any method is valid.

Creating A Printer Attached To A Parallel Port

You have managed to get your dirty little hands on a very high-quality ink jet printer, originally intended for some big cheese who never actually started working for the company. It's got great print quality and is very quiet, so it won't hurt too much on Monday mornings.

1. Choose Start|Settings|Printers. The Printers window appears.

2. Double-click the Add Printer icon, and the Add Printer Wizard window is displayed, as shown in Figure 6.3.

3. As this is a locally attached printer, select the My Computer option. Click the Next button. The available ports appear. Select the port box that has the printer attached to it—for instance, LPT1. Because this is a parallel port, no further port configuration is required.

4. Click the Next button. The Add Printer Wizard displays the manufacturers who have provided drivers for Windows NT.

5. Select the printer manufacturer in the left-hand pane and the printer model in the right-hand pane. Click the Next button. A Printer Name dialog box appears.

6. Enter the printer name; this is the name that this printer will be known by under Windows NT. Also, select whether this printer is to be set as the default print device for Windows applications. Click the Next button.

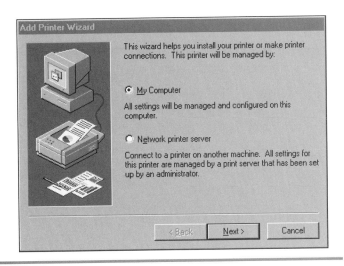

The Add Printer Wizard.
Figure 6.3

7. The Add Printer Wizard displays the Network Share window. This printer is not going to be shared at the moment, so click the Next button.

8. The Add Print Wizard inquires if a print test page should be sent to the printer. Because this is a recommended procedure, it is the default setting. Click the Finish button, and the printer will be created.

Creating A Printer Attached To A Serial Port

You have recovered an old printer from the back of a cupboard and have decided to use it on a Windows NT workstation for some local printing.

1. Choose Start|Settings|Printers. The Printers window appears.

2. Double click the Add Printer icon to access the Add Printer Wizard window.

3. Because this is a locally attached printer, select the My Computer option. Click the Next button. The available ports are displayed. Select the port that has the printer attached to it—for instance, COM2.

4. Click the Configure Port button. The list of available ports is displayed. Select the relevant port, and click the Settings button. The Settings dialog box appears, as shown in Figure 6.4.

5. Select the required communications settings, and click OK. You are returned to the Ports window. Click Close, and you are returned to the Add Printer Wizard window.

6. Click the Next button. The Add Printer Wizard displays the manufacturers who have provided drivers for Windows NT.

7. Select the printer manufacturer in the left-hand pane and the printer model in the right-hand pane. Click the Next button. A Printer Name dialog box appears.

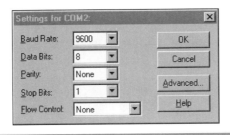

The Settings dialog box.
Figure 6.4

8. Enter the printer name; this is the name that the printer will be known by under Windows NT. Select whether this printer is to be set as the default printing device for Windows applications. Click the Next button.

9. The Add Printer Wizard displays the Network Share window. This printer is not going to be shared at the moment, so click the Next button.

10. The Add Print Wizard will inquire if you want to print a test page. Because this is a recommended procedure, it is the default setting. Click the Finish button, and the printer will be created.

Creating A Network-Attached Printer

On a ridiculously tight deadline, your department must print out the annual customer reports. The only trouble is that one of your print devices has just broken down. Looks like it could be a long night unless some print capacity is found. You then remember the four delivery guys struggling to get a huge Digital printer installed in manufacturing. I think it's time to get connected and go home.

1. Choose Start|Settings|Printers. The Printers window appears.

2. Double click the Add Printer icon. The Add Printer Wizard window appears. Select the My Computer option, and then press Next.

3. Select the Add Port button, and the Printer Ports window appears, as shown in Figure 6.5. Select the required printer port from the list, and select New Port.

4. Click the Add Ports button. The Add Port window appears, as shown in Figure 6.6. This is where the protocol used to communicate with the printer is defined—either TCP/IP or DECnet.

5. Click TCP/IP, and enter the port name. The port name is used to uniquely identify the printer port on the actual network printer and must match the name assigned on the printer network device. Click OK, and confirm the location of the Windows NT source software.

6. Click Continue. You are returned to the Printer Ports window. Click Close, and you are returned to the Add Printer Wizard window.

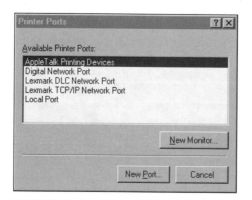

The Printer Ports window.
Figure 6.5

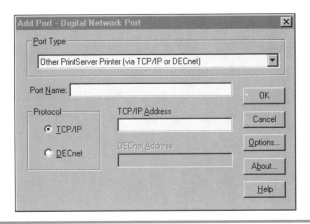

The Add Port window.
Figure 6.6

7. The Digital printer server is displayed as an available port in the port list. Select this port if it isn't already selected, and click the Next button.

8. The Add Printer Wizard displays the manufacturer list and printer model list. From the left-hand panel, select the manufacturer—in our example, Digital—and from the right-hand panel, select the model—for instance, DEClaser 3200. Click the Next button.

If the manufacturer or type of printer you are configuring doesn't appear in the displayed list, you will need to obtain a Windows NT driver disk for your printer from the printer manufacturer and use the Have Disk button to load the driver. In addition, if you want to use DECnet as the protocol to communicate with the print server, this will have to be obtained separately from Digital. The DECnet protocol is not supplied with standard Windows NT software distribution.

9. Now you'll need to configure the printer name. The default name is the printer model type, but this can be changed if required. Select whether this printer is to be set as the default printing device for Windows-based applications. Click the Next button. The Add Printer Wizard share window appears, as shown in Figure 6.7.

10. Select the Shared option. In the Share Name dialog box, enter the share name.

11. From the operating system list, select all the operating systems that will be printing to this printer. Click the Next button.

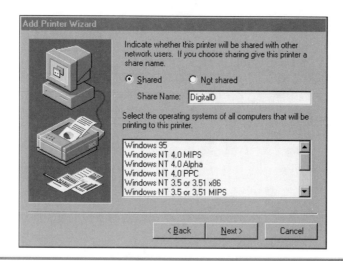

The Add Printer Wizard share window.
Figure 6.7

12. The Add Printer Wizard inquires whether a test page should be sent to the printer. Click the Finish button for the printer to be created, and confirm whether the test page has been received.

Pausing A Printer

The general print device has started to produce faded output. Looks like it's time for a new print cartridge. The only trouble with replacing the cartridge is that this print device is constantly producing output. (So much for the paperless office.) Pausing the printer is the only way you're ever going to have a chance to change the cartridge.

1. Choose Start|Settings|Printers. The Printers window appears.

2. Double click the icon of the printer you want to pause. The Printer Server window appears, as shown in Figure 6.8.

3. The documents waiting to be printed are displayed in the document list. Choose Printer|Pause Printing. The printer will be paused, as indicated by the status bar at the top of the window.

4. The printer will still accept documents to be printed, but they will be held until printing is resumed. To resume, choose Printer|Pause Printing again.

When a printer is selected in the Printers window, the management functions for this printer can be accessed via the File menu. To view the document list for a selected printer, from the Printers window, choose File/Open.

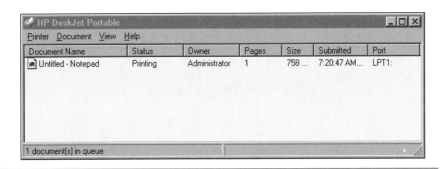

The Printer Server window.
Figure 6.8

◆ Connecting To A Printer

The graphics department recently installed a new top-of-the-line color printer. It just so happens that you have a few pictures on disk that would brighten up the office wall. You printed them out in monochrome, but they really need color to do them justice. The graphics department personnel are so friendly, they're sure not to object.

1. Choose Start|Settings|Printers. The Printers window appears.

2. Double click the Add Printer icon to display the Add Printer Wizard. Select the Network Printer Server option. Click the Next button. The Connect to Printer window appears.

3. In the Shared Printers pane, select the required printer. The printer's UNC share name appears in the Printer box, as shown in Figure 6.9. Click OK. You are returned to the Add Printer Wizard window.

4. Select whether this printer should be made the default printer for Windows applications. Click the Next button. Click the Finish button. The printer is created, and an icon is added to the Printers window.

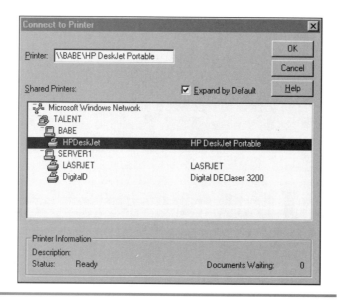

The Connect to Printer window.
Figure 6.9

Changing The Windows Default Printer

One of the users has complained that her Windows default printer is situated at the end of the office from her. Being the nice person you are, you decide to redefine which printer is the default on her Windows NT workstation.

1. Choose Start|Settings|Printers. The Printers window appears.

2. Select the Printer icon for the printer you want to make the default. Click File|Set As Default. All Windows print documents that aren't directed to a specific printer will now be directed to this new printer.

Deleting Print Documents From The Printer

Someone (who will remain nameless) has managed to send a huge print job to the printer. Nearby users say the printer has been spitting out paper for a good 20 minutes so far. I know we recycle, but what a waste. Let's delete the document before the print device shakes itself to bits.

1. Choose Start|Settings|Printer. The Printers window appears.

2. Double click the icon for the printer that has the document you want to delete. The Printer Server window appears.

3. Select the document you want to delete from the document list. Choose Document|Cancel, and the document will be removed.

After selecting the document, you can also press the Delete key to remove the document.

Purging A Printer Of All Documents

The general print device has been out of operation for a couple of hours. Users have been printing their documents elsewhere in the company, but there is a long list of documents no longer required. The print device is about to be restarted, and you don't really want these unwanted documents hogging the resources. You could delete each document individually, but that would be time-consuming. A purge of all documents is required.

1. Choose Start|Settings|Printers. The Printers window appears.

2. Double click the relevant printer icon, and the Printer Server window appears.

3. Choose Printer|Purge Print Documents. All waiting print documents will be removed from the printer.

Using Separator Pages

You have a large-capacity, high-speed printer that is used by most people in the company. You find that users are continually picking up the wrong print documents; usually they take the first couple of pages of the next job, which gets to be very frustrating for the next user. You decide to enable separator pages on this printer.

1. Choose Start|Settings|Printers. The Printers window appears.

2. Double click the relevant printer icon, and the Printer Server window is displayed.

3. Choose Printer|Properties to display the Printer Properties sheet, as shown in Figure 6.10.

4. On the General page, click the Separator Page button. The Separator Page dialog box appears. Click the Browse button and locate the separator page you want to use. By default. the .sep file extension is used to identify separator files.

Now, before each print document, a separator page will be printed. Further information on the default separators provided with Windows NT is provided earlier in this chapter.

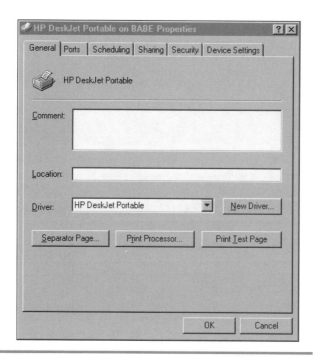

The Printer Properties sheet.
Figure 6.10

Chapter 6: Practical Guide

Scheduling Printing

Your company produces lots of printed reports for large companies. These reports don't have to be provided instantly to clients, and you usually have a couple of days to get them done. However, whenever you start these jobs, the users complain about having to wait for their print jobs. So, you decide that sending these jobs to a printer scheduled to run only overnight is a good idea. (Plus, it will probably spook the security guard when the print device just starts working, which might make him nicer the next time you forget your security pass.)

1. Choose Start|Settings|Printers. The Printers window appears.

2. Double click the relevant printer icon, and the Printer Server window appears. Click Printer|Properties to access the Printer Properties sheet.

3. Choose the Scheduling tab to access the Scheduling page. Choose the Available From option, and set the hours that the printer can be used by using the two selection boxes—for instance, 6:00 p.m. to 6:00 a.m., as shown in Figure 6.11. By default, no restrictions

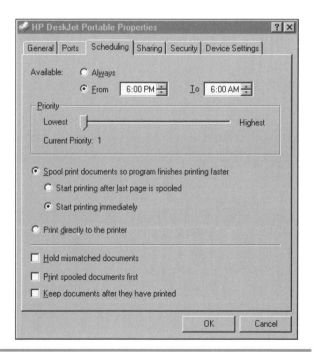

Setting the printer schedule.
Figure 6.11

are placed on printer availability. When the required restriction times have been set, click OK.

Users will be able to send documents to this printer at any time, but the actual print documents will not be sent to the printing device until the schedule allows it.

 Remember, with Windows NT printing, the printer is the software that controls the printing. The print device is the physical printer that produces the document output.

Printing Security

The company check print device has been used for printing documents other than checks. At first, this didn't sound like a problem, until you heard that the checks are sometimes left loaded in the print device. A dozen checks had to be destroyed because someone printed a Word document over them. It could have been worse, of course; someone could have actually counterfeited some checks. Setting the security on this printer sounds like a wonderful idea.

1. Choose Start|Settings|Printers. The Printers window appears.

2. Select the relevant printer, and choose File|Properties. The Printer Properties sheet appears.

3. Choose the Security tab. Click the Permissions button to display the Printer Permissions dialog box.

4. As shown in Figure 6.12, the group Everyone has print permissions as default. To remove this permission, select the group from the list, and click the Remove button.

5. To add the Accounts Managers group permissions, click the Add button. The Add Users and Groups dialog box appears.

6. Select the Accounts Managers group from the list, and click the Add button. The group is displayed in the Add Names pane, as shown in Figure 6.13.

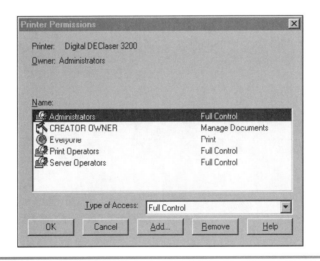

The Printer Permissions dialog box.
Figure 6.12

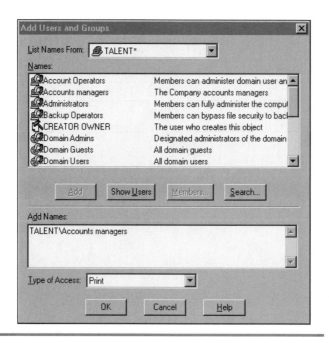

The Add Users and Groups dialog box.
Figure 6.13

7. Use the Type Of Access box to select the permissions required. The default permission is Print, which is correct for this example. Click OK to update the printer permissions. Now click OK to exit the Printer Properties window.

Printer Auditing

The graphics department has complained about unauthorized use of their color printer. Apparently, this printer has a really high page cost. The head of graphics wants to know who is using the printer. Auditing can be enabled on printers just like any other object, and audit events can then be logged in the event log. So, here goes:

1. Choose Start|Settings|Printers. The Printers window appears.

2. Select the relevant printer icon, and choose File|Properties to display the Printer Properties sheet.

3. Choose the Security tab. Click the Auditing button. The Printer Auditing dialog box appears.

4. Click the Add button to access the Add Users And Groups dialog box. From the list of names, select the Everyone group, and click the Add button. The Everyone group will be displayed in the Add Names pane. Click OK. You will be returned to the Printer Auditing dialog box.

5. The Everyone group will now be shown in the Name pane, as shown in Figure 6.14. In the Events To Audit pane, select the Success and Failure checkboxes to the right of Print. Click OK. You will be returned to the Properties window. Click OK to exit.

Although the auditing has been configured on the printer, you need to configure the audit policy before any audit events are logged.

6. Choose Start|Programs|Administrative Tools|User Manager For Domains. The User Manager For Domains window appears.

7. Click Policies|Audit to display the Audit Policy dialog box. If it is not already selected, select Audit These Events. To the right of File And Object Access, select the Success and Failure checkboxes. Click OK.

The printer audit events will be recorded in the security event log, which can be viewed by using the Event Viewer under the Administrative Tools menu.

8. Choose Start|Programs|Admininstrative Tools|Event Viewer. The Event Viewer window appears.

9. Choose Log|Security. The Security Event log is displayed. Double clicking an entry in this log will provide a detailed view of it.

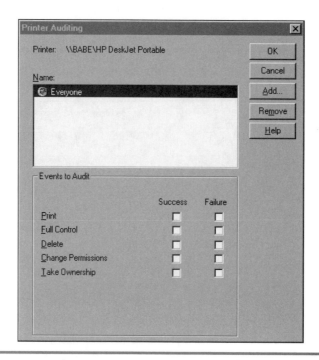

The Printer Auditing dialog box.
Figure 6.14

Configuring Print Forms

You're helping the marketing department send out a brochure to all your company's clients. The trouble is, the front cover of this brochure needs to have the address printed on it and there isn't a standard print form that matches the cover size. Not to worry, it won't take you long to get things underway. (Just don't volunteer to help stuff the envelopes.)

1. Choose Start|Settings|Printers. The Printers window appears.

2. Choose File|Server Properties. The Print Server Properties dialog box appears, as shown in Figure 6.15.

3. Select a form in the form list that most closely matches the one you need to create. Select the Create New Form option. Enter a form name in the Form Description pane. Change the paper size and margins as required. Click the Save Form button. Click OK, and you are returned to the Printers window.

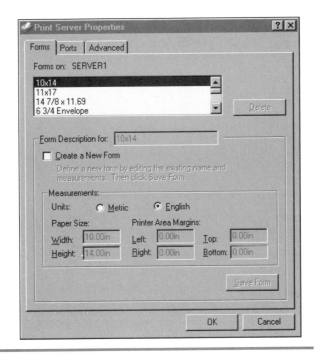

The Print Server Properties dialog box.
Figure 6.15

The new print form is now available for use, but it will have to be associated with a print tray on the relevant printing device.

4. Select the relevant printer in the Printer window. Choose File|Properties to access the Properties sheet.

5. Select the Device Settings tab. The Printer Device Settings page appears, as shown in Figure 6.16.

6. Select the relevant paper tray in the top part of the window, and then select the required form in the Change pane. Click OK. The form assignment is set.

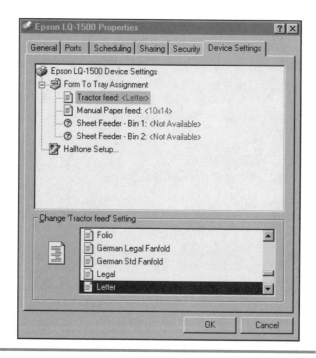

The printer Device Settings page.
Figure 6.16

Configuring A Printer Pool

In the main sales office, there are quite a few printers, and the users are always getting confused as to where their print jobs have been sent. In addition, the print device by the coffee machine is the most heavily used (why is that, I wonder?). If the print devices were physically located by the coffee machine and a printer pool was configured, the load on the print device and the number of lost print jobs would be lessened.

1. Choose Start|Settings|Printers. The Printers window appears.

2. Double click the Add Printer icon to display the Add Printer Wizard.

3. Select the Enable Printer Pooling option. You can then select multiple ports for the printer, as shown in Figure 6.17. Click the Next button.

4. The Add Printer Wizard displays the manufacturers who have provided printer drivers for Windows NT.

5. Select the printer manufacturer in the left-hand pane and the printer model in the right-hand pane. Click the Next button. A Printer Name dialog box appears.

6. Enter the printer name; this is the name that this printer will be known by under Windows NT. Also, select whether this printer is to be set as the default printing device for Windows applications. Click the Next button.

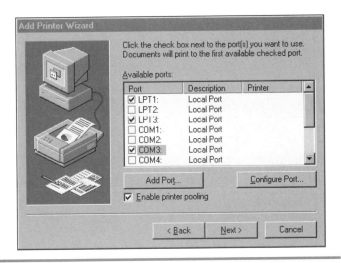

Enabling printer pooling.
Figure 6.17

7. The Add Printer Wizard displays the Network Share window. Click the Shared option to create a network share for this printer, and enter the required share name. Click the Next button.

8. The Add Print Wizard inquires if a print test page should be sent to the printer. This is a recommend procedure, so it appears as the default setting. Click the Finish button, and the printer will be created.

Although Windows NT treats the pool as a single printer, the documents are sent to the first available printer in the port list. Therefore, to get the best print through-put, always have the fastest printing device connected to the first port in the list.

Configuring Multiple Printers On One Print Device

You are in the process of changing all the printer names to meet the new corporate naming convention. You have 200 print devices and 2,000 clients to reconfigure—this is not a five-minute job. You realize that if you rename a printer, some clients won't be able to use the print device. You decide to create a second printer for the same print device and gradually migrate the clients across to this new name.

1. Choose Start|Settings|Printers. The Printers window appears.

2. Double click the Add Printer icon to display the Add Printer Wizard window.

3. Because this is a locally attached printer, select the My Computer option. Click the Next button. The available ports are displayed. Select the port that has the printer attached to it—for instance, LPT1.

4. This port is a parallel port, so no further port configuration is required. Click the Next button. The Add Printer Wizard displays a list of manufacturers who have provided a printer driver for Windows NT.

5. Select the printer manufacturer in the left-hand pane and the printer model in the right-hand pane. Click the Next button. A Printer Name dialog box appears. Set this to a different name than the existing printer configured on this port.

There will now be two different printers configured for the same print device. The printers can be treated as different objects by Windows NT and have unique security, scheduling, and priority configurations. (More detail on the parameters that can be configured is provided earlier in this chapter.)

Configuring The Printer Priority

You have two printers both printing to the same print device. The first printer is used for general-purpose printing and the second is the help desk hotline printer for printing fault reports. At the moment, both these printers have the same priority, so print jobs are treated equally. This means that some urgent print jobs are getting delayed. Of course, buying another print device would take care of the problem, but you're tired of going through the usual hoops for budget approval. Instead, you decide to increase the priority of the hotline printer.

1. Choose Start|Settings|Printers. The Printers window appears.

2. Select the relevant printer. Choose File|Properties to display the Properties sheet.

3. Select the Scheduling tab. Printer priority is controlled by the slider in the Priority pane, shown in Figure 6.18. Move the slider to the right to increase the printer priority. Click OK. You are returned to the Printers window.

Setting the printer priority.
Figure 6.18

Connecting To A Printer From The Command Line

You keep having to reconfigure users' profiles as they change departments, and they object to having to walk to adjacent buildings to pick up their print jobs. (Yes, the users should be able to reconfigure their own profiles, but, as usual, they want you to do it.) Okay, using logon scripts to make the printer connections would be good. That way, you could just assign the correct script and the connections would be established the next time users log on.

1. Locate the relevant logon script, and open it using a text editor—for instance, Notepad.

2. Now enter the **net use** command into the logon script that will make the connection to the relevant network share—for instance, **net use lpt3: \\server1\hpprinter**. Exit and save the logon script.

Installing Alternate Printer Drivers

As Windows NT slowly starts to take over your company (Bill will be pleased), the different versions of Windows NT and different processors' architectures are starting to cause problems. Not big problems, but at least once a day you get calls from users saying that they can't connect to a particular printer because the driver is not available. Just installing the additional driver will take care of the situation; however, if this is a regular problem, installing all of the additional drivers for all the printers might not be a bad idea.

1. Choose Start|Settings|Printers. The Printers window appears.

2. Select the required printer, and choose File|Properties to display the Printer Properties sheet.

3. Choose the Sharing tab. The available alternate drivers are displayed at the bottom of the window, as shown in Figure 6.19.

4. Select the required driver, and click OK. The driver is installed, and you are returned to the Printers window.

The client will now be supplied with the correct printer drive.

Windows NT 4 has printer drivers for x86, MIPS, Alpha, and PPC available as alternate printer drivers. Support is also provided for Windows NT 3.1, 3.5, and 3.51. Support for the PPC is not available until 3.51. In addition, printer drivers for Windows 95 are also supplied.

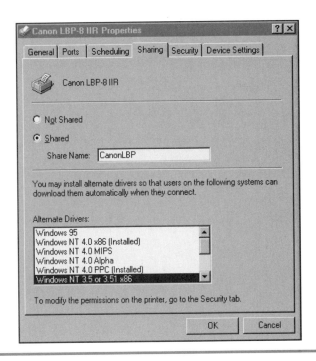

Alternate printer drivers.
Figure 6.19

Quick Reference Specifications

The following are the bare-bones facts and figures.

- *The print device is the physical printer.*

- *The printer is a printing software component.*

- *Printer pools combine separate print devices into a single printer.*

- *Printer drivers are processor- and version-dependent.*

Utilities To Use

The utilities used in this chapter and their functions are listed in this section. Consider this as a memory aid for the busy system administrator.

Add Printer Wizard

- Create printers.
- Connect to printers.

Printer Properties Window

- Set printer permissions.
- Set printer auditing.
- Configure separator page.
- Configure printer scheduling.

Print Server Properties Window

- Configure print forms.

User Manager For Domains

- Configure printer audit policy.

Chapter 7

Networking

Administrator's Notes...

Chapter 7

The networking facilities provided with Windows NT are extensive. The multiple standard networking protocols help make the integration of Windows NT into existing networks relatively straightforward. Windows NT is a protocol-independent operating system and will function with whichever protocols best suit your requirements.

Key Network Components

The following lists the key network components of Windows NT. Each is discussed in detail in this chapter.

- PDCs, BDCs, and servers
- Browsers
- Replicator service
- Protocols (NWLink, NetBEUI, TCP/IP, AppleTalk, and DLC)
- Domain Name System
- Windows Internet Naming Service
- NetWare Gateway Service
- Remote Access Service
- Macintosh services

Network Utility

The Network utility contained in the Control Panel is where virtually all network software components are installed from and configured. The majority of changes made to the network software components require you to restart the system before these changes take effect. When making any network protocol-related changes, you will see that Windows NT automatically reconfigures the network bindings, either when you exit the Network utility or when you select the Bindings tab. *Bindings* are the communication connections between the networking subsystem—for instance, the adapter card, protocols, and services. The Network utility management window is shown in Figure 7.1.

The Domain Model

Windows NT networks can be constructed in one of two ways: around a workgroup or around a domain model. (Chapter 1 provides more detail regarding the differences between these two configurations.) From a networking point of view, we will

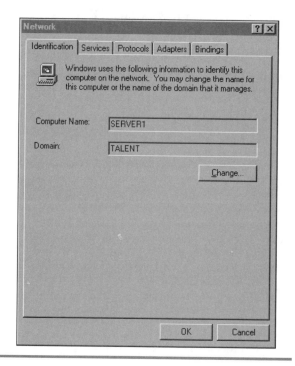

The Network utility management window.
Figure 7.1

concentrate on the domain model and the additional steps required to administrate and support this model. Workgroup administration, on the other hand, is more concerned with the administrative overhead of supporting multiple security account databases.

The key issue to understand about the domain model is that a single security database is used to validate the security and logons for the whole domain. Keeping this database available and synchronized is our main concern. When computers are added to the domain, a user account for each computer is created in the domain Security Account Manager database. Server Manager under Administrative Tools can be used to add or remove systems from the domain.

Primary Domain Controller (PDC)

The PDC is used to hold the domain Security Account Manager database, or SAM, which contains all the domain account security information. Here is where all updates are made to the database. There should only ever be one PDC per domain. In addition, the PDC can be used to validate domain logons.

Backup Domain Controllers (BDCs)

The BDCs hold read-only copies of the domain database. There can be multiple BDCs in a domain. BDCs can validate domain logons and, in doing so, reduce the load on the PDC. The BDC copies of the domain databases are automatically synchronized with the PDC. In addition, the system administrator can force this synchronization to take place immediately.

BDCs should be carefully placed in your network design to ensure that the domain logons are validated evenly across the network. Also, wherever possible, the validation should not take place across slow wide-area links.

The BDC is only synchronized automatically with the PDC at 15-minute intervals. A situation could arise where a user changes his or her password at the PDC, logs out of the domain, and then logs back on. If that logon is handled by a BDC that hasn't yet synchronized the password change with the PDC, the logon would be invalid. When the BDC can't validate a logon, it passes the logon to be validated by the PDC, and the user would gain access to the domain.

 To move either a PDC or BDC between domains, you will need to reinstall Windows NT.

Any BDC has the potential of being promoted to a PDC. When a BDC is promoted, the existing PDC is automatically demoted to a BDC.

Servers

Servers take no part in the validation of domain logons and do not hold copies of the domain database. The computers designated as servers are often used for mission-critical applications, and their resources are required in running the application instead of validating domain logons.

 The role a system plays in the domain is designated upon installation. If the system has been designated as a server, that system cannot be promoted to either a BDC or PDC. To allow servers to be promoted, you must reinstall Windows NT. To move servers between domains, no reinstallation is necessary.

The relationship between the PDC, BDCs, and servers is shown in Figure 7.2, along with the validation of domain logons.

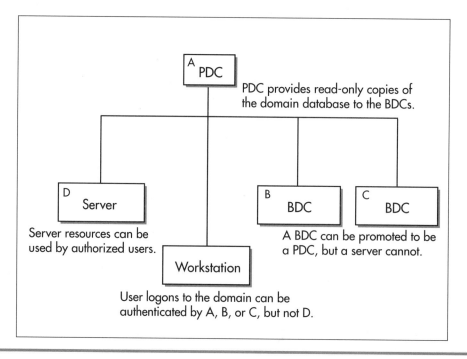

Domain and server relationships.
Figure 7.2

Domain Trusts

In large or complex networks, there can often be multiple domains. By default, no relationship exists between these domains; users can only log on from systems in their own domain. With personnel becoming increasingly mobile, this limitation presents problems.

If a *domain trust* is established between two or more domains, however, users will be able to log on across domains just as if they were on a computer in their own domain. Trusts can be established either as one- or two-way relationships. In a one-way trust, one domain is the trusting and the other the trusted. In other words, domain A trusts domain B; therefore, users of domain A can use the resources of domain B. When the users of domain A log on from a system in domain B, they'll find that domain A is listed in the Domain selection box on the Logon Information window. In this one-way trust example, the users of domain B would not be allowed to log on from domain A. In fact, domain B would not appear in the Logon window of domain A computers.

If the trusts had been configured on a two-way basis, both sets of users would be able to log on from either domain. A two-way trust relationship is shown in Figure 7.3. When the trusts are configured, an initial trust password is provided by the system

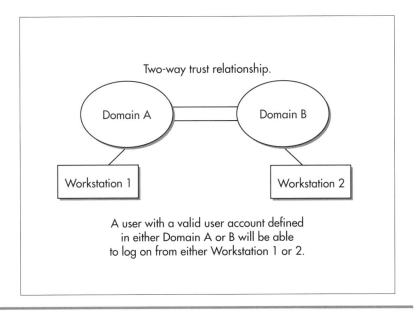

A two-way domain trust.
Figure 7.3

Administrator. This password must be entered in both domains and is used to initially verify the domain trust. Once the trust relationship is established, a new trust password is established and used by Windows NT; there is no way for the administrator to find out what this password is.

Browser Service

The Browser service is used to aid in the location of network resources. The browser builds a list of available network resources, which is built from the computer and domain announcement messages that are sent out at regular intervals.

One system on the network is elected as the master browser and is responsible for the creation and maintenance of the browse list. The system that assumes the role of master browser is elected based on various system parameters. However, in the domain model, because the PDC is given the highest priority, it will assume the role of master browser for the domain.

Backup browsers are used to hold copies of the browse list obtained from the master browser. All Windows NT Servers in a domain will act as backup browsers for the domain, and no Windows NT Workstations will act as backup browsers.

In a Windows NT Workstation workgroup configuration, one workstation will be elected as the master browser, and a second workstation will act as a backup browser. For every additional 32 workstations, there is an additional backup browser. If the master browser is unreachable for any reason, the backup browser that discovers this will force a browser election to elect a new master browser. Backup browsers update their browse lists every 15 minutes.

Due to the way the browse list is established by the master domain controller, and because a computer or domain is not considered unavailable until it has failed to announce itself for up to 3 announcement periods, it can take up to 36 minutes for a computer and 45 minutes for a domain to be removed from the browse list.

The browse list is passed to the browsers from the master browser. This list can be accessed by any network-ready system.

Replicator Service

The Windows NT Replicator service is used to replicate folders and files between both Windows NT Servers and Workstations. Because a domain logon validation may be done by either the PDC or one of several BDCs, the Replicator service is useful to keep the logon scripts and profiles available on all systems that validate logons. By default, Windows NT will attempt to locate these scripts on the host that validates the logon in the \Import\Scripts folder. The replication of files occurs only after they have been modified and closed. This replication can be configured to take place immediately after the file is closed or after a file settle-down period has expired. The subfolders' structure of the Export folder will automatically be created in the Import folder. No files will be deleted by the Directory Replication service, even if they are deleted from the Export folder.

Windows NT Servers can both export and import folders and files, but Windows NT Workstations can only import. The Manage Exported Directories dialog box is shown in Figure 7.4.

 When replicating logon scripts from the PDC Export folder, you must import the scripts back to the PDC so they are available in the \Import\Scripts folder for logon validations performed by the PDC.

Universal Naming Convention (UNC)

All network resources in a Windows NT network can be accessed either by browsing the relevant network resource or by using its UNC to directly access the resource. When creating logon scripts, you can use the UNC to establish the correct shares required for a particular user or group. The UNC of a particular share can be seen in the Share Properties dialog box, but it takes the format of *server**share**subfolder*. The UNC can be used to access all network shares, whether they are folders or printers.

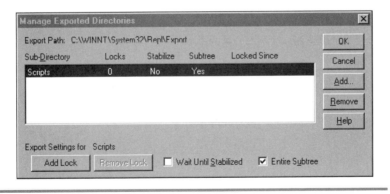

The Manage Exported Directories dialog box.
Figure 7.4

To use UNC to access network resources, both workstation and server services need to be running on the computer where the resource is located and where the computer is making the connection. Both the workstation and server services are run on Windows NT Workstation and Server.

Network Protocols

The network protocols supplied with Windows NT are shown in Table 7.1, along with their key features and specifications. Figure 7.5 shows the Protocols tab within the Network utility. These and other protocols are covered in more detail in the next section.

NetBEUI

An acronym for NetBIOS Extended User Interface, NetBEUI is based on the original IBM LAN Manager protocol. NetBEUI is often used in small networks, because it is the easiest to install and use. One reason for NetBEUI's ease of installation is that it has no conception of areas and, therefore, is not routeable. NetBEUI relies on the computer name to locate and use network resources.

NWLink

In addition to integrating Windows NT to NetWare, in networks containing large numbers of NetWare systems, the network administrator frequently decides to standardize on a single network protocol, even if there is no communication between the NetWare and Windows NT systems. The native protocol of IPX/SPX can be used for this purpose. IPX/SPX is a routeable protocol, and NWLink is its Windows NT implementation.

Protocol	Routeable	Key Features
NetBEUI	No	Very good for small networks. Easy to set up.
IPX/SPX	Yes	NetWare networks.
DLC	No	IBM mainframe- and HP network-attached printers.
AppleTalk	Yes	Provides Macintosh integration.
TCP/IP	Yes	Corporate networks and Internet connections.

Table 7.1 Network protocol features.

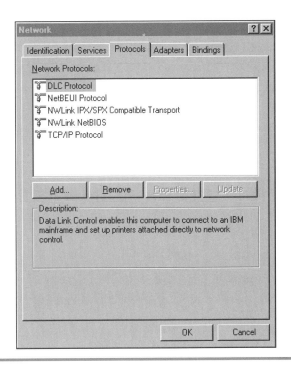

The Protocols page.
Figure 7.5

DLC

The DLC (Data Link Control) protocol is used for connectivity with either IBM mainframes using 3270 emulation or with Hewlett-Packard printers that are directly connected to the network using NetJet interface cards.

AppleTalk

AppleTalk is the Apple Computer proprietary network protocol. It can be used to effectively integrate Windows NT Servers with Macintosh computers and networks.

TCP/IP

TCP/IP (Transmission Control Protocol/Internet Protocol) is the protocol of choice for many corporate networks. Also used to access Internet resources, TCP/IP is too complex to be fully explained in a few short paragraphs. This section, however, should give you an understanding of the basics of TCP/IP. Tables 7.2 and 7.3 are provided as a memory aid for the Windows NT administrator.

TCP/IP is routeable and very robust. Originally developed for low-speed serial links, this protocol is ideal for long-distance network communications. It is also the most difficult of the Windows NT protocols to configure, because it requires a basic understanding of how the protocol works. Once you have achieved this understanding, TCP/IP is probably the most flexible of the protocols and is certainly the protocol usually used in communicating with different types of computer systems.

Each network device using the TCP/IP protocol—for instance, your Windows NT workstation—will have an IP address assigned to each of its network adapters. The IP address is a 32-bit address divided into 4 fields, which are separated by a period. Each field contains a number up to 255. The network device will also have a subnet mask assigned to it. The *subnet mask* is used by receiving hosts to identify which part of the IP address indicates the unique address of the host and which part is the general network area address.

Three classes of IP address are available. The class determines how many hosts you can allocate for each address. Table 7.2 shows the relationship between subnet masks, the IP address, and the IP address's breakdown.

Each class has a range of addresses that can be allocated for the first field of the network address. This is shown in Table 7.3, along with the maximum number of hosts and the networks available with each class.

Class	Default Subnet Mask	Network Part of Address (x), Host Part (y)
A	255.0.0.0	x.y.y.y
B	255.255.0.0	x.x.y.y
C	255.255.255.0	x.x.x.y

Table 7.2 IP address class subnet masks.

Class	Address Range for First Network Field	Available Networks	Number of Hosts per Network
A	1-126	126	16,777,214
B	128-191	16,384	65,534
C	192-223	2,097,151	254

Table 7.3 IP address class.

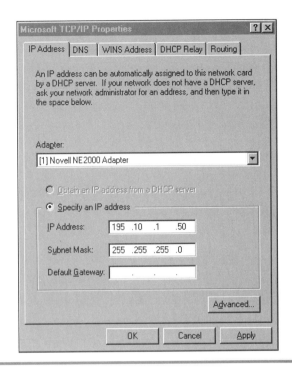

The TCP/IP Properties window.
Figure 7.6

If you are connecting your computer to the Internet, your Internet service provider will allocate a unique IP address to your system. Figure 7.6 shows the Network utility's TCP/IP Properties sheet.

To clarify, let's draw an analogy between how the phone system works and TCP/IP addressing. For example, if the IP address of your Windows NT workstation is 195.10.1.50, and the subnet mask is 255.255.255.0, this would be a Class C network address, with .50 being the unique part of the address for your workstation in this network. If you consider the IP address of 195.10.1.50 to be your telephone number, the subnet mask is used to indicate which part of your number is the area code. Therefore, the subnet mask, or 255.255.255.0, tells you that 195.10.1 is the area code, leaving .50 as the unique part of your telephone number. So just as you and your neighbors share an area code, your workstation and others on your network share a part of the IP address.

Domain Name System (DNS)

Because TCP/IP network devices are addressed using their IP addresses, when the size of the network increases, remembering the particular IP address of a host becomes increasingly difficult. In addition, when you're in a hurry, it's easy to type in the wrong IP address. DNS provides a host name to the TCP/IP address lookup function, making TCP/IP easier to use.

When accessing network resources, you can use the host name, and DNS will translate the name into the relevant TCP/IP address for the Network tool. All host names and IP addresses have to be manually configured into DNS. DNS expects the host and IP names to remain static, so the Dynamic Host Configuration Protocol (DHCP) is not supported.

Dynamic Host Configuration Protocol (DHCP)

DHCP is used to simplify the management of TCP/IP addresses. This protocol maintains a central pool of TCP/IP addresses that are used when required. Because the TCP/IP address is supplied by the DHCP server, the configuration on the host will be considerably simplified. When the Obtain An IP Address From A DHCP Server box is selected, the rest of the TCP/IP options will be grayed out.

When a Windows NT Server or Workstation is started using DHCP, it will request a TCP/IP address from the DHCP server. This address will be leased to the system for a set period of time, determined by the lease time-out period. If the address leased to a particular system is not used within the lease time-out period, it will be made available for reassignment by the DHCP server. However, if the address is in constant use, it will remain with that host and never be reassigned.

Using DHCP avoids the common mistake of having doubly allocated IP addresses, which can cause all sorts of network problems. The DHCP server must have a statically assigned IP address and can not assign itself one or obtain one from another DHCP server. Both Windows NT Workstations and Servers can obtain their TCP/IP addresses from DHCP servers, but only Windows NT Server provides the DHCP server service.

Other Tools

Windows Internet Naming Service (WINS)

Like DNS, the Windows Internet Naming Service is used to provide a computer name to the IP address lookup function. Unlike DNS, WINS uses the NetBIOS name rather than the host name. This name can be viewed and changed with the Network utility contained in the Control Panel.

A WINS server is used to hold the names and IP addresses of computers on the network, and the WINS client systems automatically register themselves with the server when they start the TCP/IP protocol. Because the systems are automatically registered, WINS will not let two systems with the same name register.

WINS supports DHCP and provides the same dynamic functionality. Figure 7.7 shows a WINS client registered when viewed via the WINS Manager.

HOSTS And LMHOSTS

HOSTS and LMHOSTS are local name-to-IP lookup tables that must manually be updated on each Windows NT Workstation or Server using them. The HOSTS file is used to provide a local lookup table for host names and the LMHOSTS file for WINS names. Both files are located in the \systemroot\System32\Drivers\etc folder. A typical lookup entry would be formatted as follows:

197.100.20.1   SERVER1

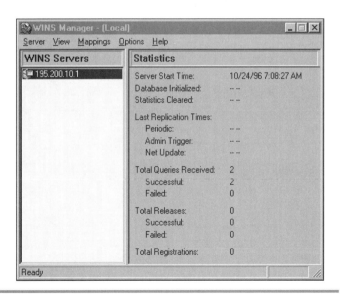

The WINS Manager.
Figure 7.7

TCP/IP Command Prompt Tools

A host of configuration and test tools are available from the Windows NT command prompt and are shown in Table 7.4. Some of the Windows NT TCP/IP commands are not currently two-way implementations, so the commands can only be issued from the Windows NT end.

Most of the TCP/IP commands have a wide selection of configuration switches. Help can be accessed by following the command with -? (for instance, **netstat -?**). Following is

Tool	Function
arp	IP-to-adapter hardware address lookup.
finger	Displays information about a specified user on a remote host.
ftp	File transfers to and from remote hosts.
hostname	Displays the name of the current host.
ipconfig	Displays the TCP/IP configuration details.
lpq	Obtains status of print queue running LPD servers.
lpr	Prints a file to a host running on an LPD server.
nbstat	Displays protocol statistics for NetBIOS over TCP/IP.
netstat	Displays protocol statistics for TCP/IP.
ping	Verifies host connectivity.
rcp	Copies files between systems running the RSH server.
rexec	Runs a command on the remote host.
route	Manages the network routing table.
rsh	Runs a command on the remote host.
telnet	Provides terminal emulation to the remote host.
tftp	Transfers files to and from the remote host.
tracert	Determines the route taken to reach a remote host.

Table 7.4   TCP/IP command prompt tools.

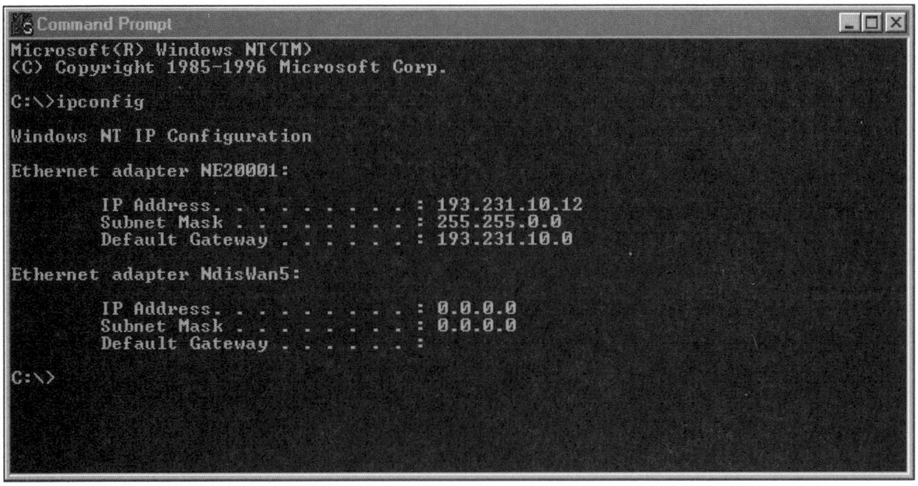

The output of ipconfig.
Figure 7.8

more detailed information on the more useful connectivity and diagnostics commands:

- **ipconfig**—Displays the TCP/IP network configuration details, including those parameters configured by a DHCP server. Figure 7.8 shows the range of information provided by this tool.

- **netstat**—Displays protocol statistics and current network connections. The **nbstat** command provides similar information but is restricted to the NetBIOS over TCP/IP protocol.

- **ping**—Verifies host connectivity by sending out echo packets to the remote hosts and listening for the echo reply. By using the IP address and host name with the **ping** command, host-to-IP address resolution problems can be detected.

- **telnet**—Provides a terminal emulation connection to a remote host that has been configured as a Telnet server.

- **tracert**—Traces the route taken to a destination host.

Network Shares

Network shares can be established for printers and folders located on any of the Windows NT-supported file systems. These shares can have permissions assigned to them to provide security on both a user and group basis.

Windows NT Explorer can be used to create and manage network shares. Figure 7.9 shows the permissions being configured on a new network share. Multiple network shares can also be created for the same object, and each share can be given a different share name and uniquely assigned permissions. When accessing a network share contained on an NTFS volume, you need to consider two sets of permissions: share and NTFS. The effective permissions used will be the most restrictive. For example, if you have read/write permissions assigned via NTFS permissions, but only read via the network share, and you are accessing the data through the network share, the effective permissions will be read only.

You can create invisible network shares by appending the share name with **$**, e.g., **unseen$**. This invisible share won't show up when you're browsing the network, but you can connect to it if you specify the full share name.

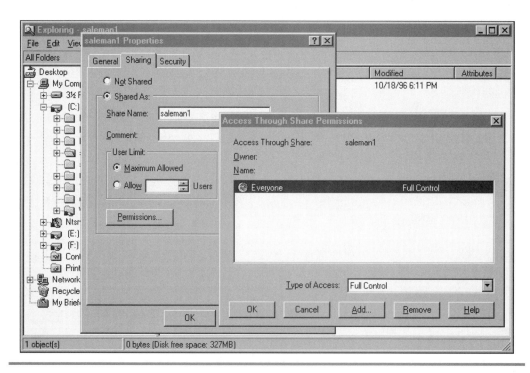

The Access Through Share Permissions dialog box.
Figure 7.9

NetWare Gateway Service

To use NetWare resources—for example, accessing NetWare volumes and printers—Windows NT clients must use the NetWare Gateway Service in conjunction with the NWLink protocol. This gateway service is a one-way service, so Windows NT clients can access NetWare resources, but NetWare clients cannot access Windows NT resources.

The NetWare Gateway Service is NDS-aware, so it can fully integrate with NetWare 4 systems. It can also use the Bindery in earlier versions of NetWare. When the gateway is used with a NetWare 4 server, the NetWare password will automatically be updated each time the Windows NT password is changed. However, when the gateway is used with NetWare 2/3 systems, users must manually change their passwords from the Windows NT command prompt by using the **setpass** command.

NetWare Migration Tool

Available only with Windows NT Server, the NetWare Migration Tool can be used to migrate user accounts, groups, volumes, files, and folders from a NetWare server to a Windows NT server. The Migration Tool can also be used to run *trial migration*, which produces a log file indicating what would happen if the actual migration was run. This allows any potential problems to be highlighted and resolved.

A NetWare server can be migrated to a Windows NT server configured as either a PDC or BDC. The actual migration can be made to either the server you are running the NetWare Migration Tool on or to a remote server. When migrating NetWare volumes to Windows NT volumes, you should use the NTFS file system to allow the NetWare security to be migrated. Figure 7.10 shows the Migration Tool For NetWare window.

Remote Access Service (RAS)

To gain transparent access to a remote Windows NT network, Microsoft clients can use the Remote Access Service. Once the RAS connection has been established to the remote network, the resources of that network can be used by the standard administration tools just as though the connection had been made to a local network resource.

RAS is available with both Windows NT Workstation and Server, although Workstation is limited to only one inbound RAS connection. Server supports up to 256 connections, if the additional hardware to support 256 connections is available.

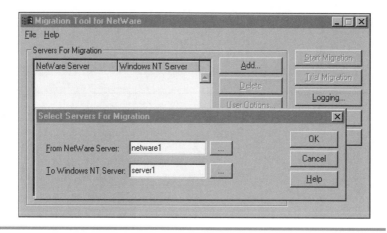

The Migration Tool for NetWare window.
Figure 7.10

As with any remote access to your network, RAS security must be carefully considered. RAS access can be assigned on a per-user or per-group basis. Other security features include dial-back security and data encryption.

Provided with RAS is a template logon script that can be used to construct the script required to connect to your Internet service provider. Figure 7.11 shows a sample logon script.

RAS Protocol Overview

The actual remote access connections are established by using either the Serial Line Internet Protocol (SLIP), Point-to-Point Protocol (PPP), or Point-to-Point Tunneling Protocol (PPTP):

- SLIP provides support for TCP/IP connections to be established over low-speed serial lines.

- PPP is an enhancement to the original SLIP specifications and supports many protocols over low-speed serial lines. The Windows NT implementation of PPP can be used to support TCP/IP, IPX, and NetBEUI.

- PPTP provides the capability to create virtual networks over the Internet. It does this by routing PPP packets over the IP-based Internet. Any PPP-supported protocols may be used with PPTP.

```
pipe - Notepad
File  Edit  Search  Help

; Sample Logon for pipe internet service provider.
;==============================================================
[pipe]

; Start communication with remote host.
    COMMAND=<cr>

; Wait until remote host requests login username.
    OK=<match>"ogin:"
    LOOP=<ignore>

; Send username to remote host.
    COMMAND=solpt1<cr>

; Wait until remote host requests password.
    OK=<match>"assword:"
    LOOP=<ignore>

; Send Passord to remote host.
    COMMAND=testpassword<cr>

; Wait until remote host requests protocol type.
    OK=<match>"otocol:"
    LOOP=<ignore>

; Send protocol type of PPP.
    COMMAND=PPP<cr>

; Ignore final response from remote host.
    OK=<ignore>
```

A sample logon script.
Figure 7.11

Internet Explorer

The Internet and Internet Explorer are vast areas that rightly have a huge number of books dedicated to them. Windows NT Workstation and Server both come with Internet Explorer. In addition to accessing the Internet, many corporations use Internet Explorer to access their internal Web servers (intranets). To this end, the Microsoft Internet Server is available with Windows NT Server.

Macintosh Services

The Macintosh services available with Windows NT Server provide file and print services to Mac users using the standard Macintosh AppleShare software. Mac clients are treated as equal clients by Windows NT. The Macintosh client connections and

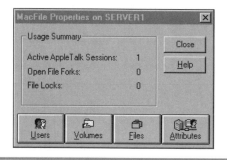

The MacFile Properties window.
Figure 7.12

resources can be viewed by using the MacFile utility in the Control Panel, as shown in Figure 7.12.

Macintosh-accessible volumes must be created on NTFS or CDFS volumes. These volumes can then be accessed either from Windows NT or from Mac clients. When viewed by Mac clients, files stored on the Macintosh volumes are represented by the standard Macintosh icons. When viewed from Windows NT, the file names are shown instead. Because Macintosh allows file names of up to 31 characters, if a file with a long name is copied to the Macintosh volumes, the Macintosh will use the short 8.3 name to access it.

Windows NT Services for Macintosh use the domain account database, so any valid domain user account can be used to access Macintosh servers. In addition, the Guest Account facility can be used. The permissions set on the NTFS Macintosh volumes are automatically translated into their equivalent Macintosh permissions for access via the Macintosh server's software. Passwords on individual Macintosh volumes can also be set so that when a particular volume is accessed by Macintosh services, the user will have to supply the password.

The AppleTalk passwords are sent over the network in plain text format, presenting a security risk, since the data packet could be captured and the password seen. Windows NT Services for Macintosh provides a facility to use encrypted passwords to overcome this issue.

The Print Server for Macintosh service enables Mac clients to print to Windows NT printer devices and PC clients to print to printers attached to the AppleTalk network.

Command Prompt Networking Commands

The Windows NT command prompt has several useful network-related commands that can be used in scripts to perform network administration tasks. Table 7.5 lists the most useful.

The **net use** command is most commonly seen in logon scripts to establish the connections to the shares. The command takes the basic form of *net use\\computername\sharename*. Table 7.6 shows some uses of this command. Help can be obtained on any of the Windows NT net commands by using a **net help** command, such as **net help use**.

Command	Function
net share	Creates, deletes, or displays shared resources.
net session	Lists users currently connected to the server.
net use	Used to connect and disconnect from network resources. These resources can be either folders or printers.
net view	Lists either servers or resources being shared by a server.

Table 7.5   Network commands.

Command	Function
net use * \\server1\data1	Establishes a connection to a network share located on server1 with a share name of data1; the next available drive letter will be assigned to the connection.
net use E: \\system1\data1 /user:pault	Establishes a share connection using the drive ID of E, and makes the connection using the user account pault.
net use E: /delete	Deletes the established drive share, connected as drive E.
net use *: \\system1\data1 /home	Makes a connection as the home directory; the directory will be used to save all data when a specific location is not specified.

Table 7.6   net use command examples.

Practical

Guide To

Networking

The following section provides real-life examples and step-by-step instructions on how to successfully administrate your Windows NT network. Keep in mind that many of the changes made to the networking components of Windows NT require the system to be restarted before the changes will take effect.

Installing Network Adapters

Your trusty old 8-bit network card really does seem a bit underpowered. Each time the server has gotten upgraded, it just seems to have been forgotten. (See? Quietly getting on with the job never gets you noticed. You've got to be loud and flashy if you want to get ahead.) So this time when the server has its annual upgrade, it's getting an all-singing, all-dancing, 32-bit wonder card. Don't worry about the old-timer though—old network cards never die, they just get reused in less-important computers (like the CEO's, maybe?).

The network cards are configured by using the Network utility in the Control Panel. It's worth getting to know this utility; as a Windows NT administrator, you're going to use it a lot.

1. Choose Start|Settings|Control Panel.

2. Double click the Network icon. The Network sheet appears. Choose the Adapters tab.

3. Click the Add button. The Select Network Adapter dialog box is displayed. If the adapter you wish to install is on this list, select it, and click OK. If it isn't, you'll need a driver disk from the adapter manufacturer. In this case, click the Have Disk button to select the driver from the disk.

4. Depending on the hardware type of the card, you might need to enter some hardware configuration details, as shown in Figure 7.13. Confirm the details, and click OK. Confirm the location of the Windows NT source software, and click Continue. The necessary adapter software will be installed. Click Close, and the software bindings will be reconfigured.

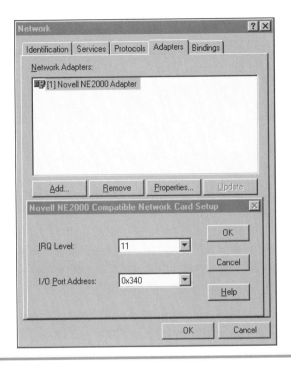

Network card setup.
Figure 7.13

5. Depending on the protocols in use on your computer, you might be prompted to enter protocol configuration information at this point. You'll need to restart the computer for the network adapter to be available.

Sharing A Folder

A common data folder has been created for all employees to access. This folder holds such items as the disciplinary procedure (boo), the holiday roster (yay), and the company mission statement (what's that?).

Although it's available to all employees, it needs to be read-only when accessed via the share. The folder is on a FAT volume, but that's not a problem because the security can be set on the share. So, first create the share, then set the permissions and test its soundness.

1. Choose Start|Programs|Windows NT Explorer.

2. Right click the folder you want to share, and select Sharing from the pop-up menu. The Folder Sharing window appears. Select the Share As option. The Share name will automatically be constructed from the folder name, as shown in Figure 7.14; however, a different share name can be used if required.

The share permissions will now need to be configured. In this example, we need to specify a read-only configuration for all users.

3. Click the Permissions button. The Everyone group will have full control. To achieve our required permissions, select Read-only from the permission list, and click OK.

4. You are returned to the Share window. Click OK, and the share will be created.

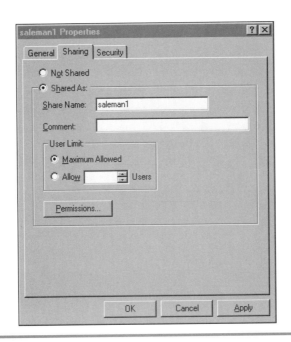

Sharing a folder.
Figure 7.14

 Who's Accessing The Server?

You're working alone, late at night. (What's that noise? Are those footsteps? Be quiet, you watch too many late-night horror movies.) But you do notice that the Windows NT Server's disk access lights are flashing away. You know the backup finished a few hours ago, so what's going on? Let's check it out just in case it's the phantom programmer, rumored to access systems overnight and plant bugs in clean code.

1. Choose Start|Programs|Administrative Tools|Server Manager. The Server Manager window appears.

2. Double click the relevant server from the Computer list. The Properties dialog box appears.

3. Click the Users button. The list of connected users appears, as shown in Figure 7.15. The number of files each user has open is also displayed. To close the connection for a particular user, select the user from the list, and press the Disconnect button. To close all connections to the server, press Disconnect All.

 The Server Manager utility in Administrative Tools is only available with Windows NT Server by default. If you want to have the domain version of Server Manager on your workstation, install the Network Client Management tools. An example of how to do this is given later in this chapter. The domain version of Server Manager can be used to check the status of all networked Windows NT systems. Contained within the Control Panel is the Single System Server Manager, which provides information on the local system only. This tool is available with both Windows NT Workstation and Server.

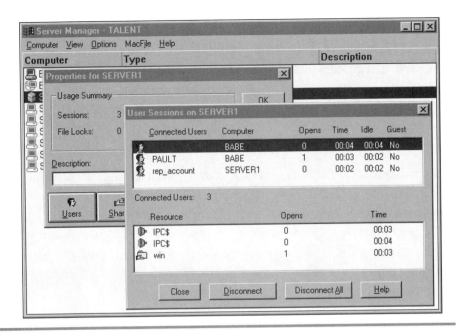

The User Sessions dialog box.

Figure 7.15

Changing Workgroup Workstations To Domains

You support a small workgroup of five Windows NT workstations (well, you don't want to support a large workgroup, do you?). A user complains that when he tries to connect to a coworker's computer, a dialog box appears, prompting him for a username and password. This never used to happen. The user has tried entering the username and password he uses to log on to his system, but it still doesn't work. Obviously, the guy needs help.

The most probable cause of this is that the user has changed his password on his local system, which of course now doesn't match the password contained on his coworker's computer. So, the quick fix is to get the passwords back in synch. The real fix, however, is to get these workstations into your domain. If you don't, it's a sure thing that the user will be back in 30 days, or whenever your security policy dictates, with the same problem. To reconfigure the Windows NT workstations:

1. Choose Start|Settings|Control Panel.

2. Double click the Network utility, and click the Change button on the identification sheet. The Identification Changes dialog box appears, as shown in Figure 7.16. Choose the Domain option in the Member Of pane. Enter the name of the domain you want to join in the Domain box.

3. Choose the Create A Computer Account In The Domain box. Enter a valid domain username and password with the right to add computers to the domain in the relevant dialog box. Click OK, and the computer will join the domain. Click Close. The change will take effect upon restarting the computer.

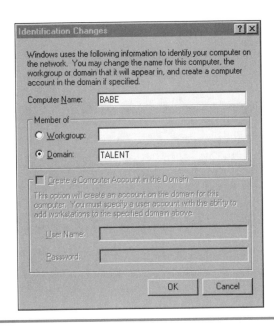

The Identification Changes dialog box.
Figure 7.16

When users log on at this computer, you'll need to tell them to select the domain in the From box as the local SAM database will still contain the account information that existed before the computer joined the domain. If this is used to validate the logon, the user would not be accessing the domain SAM, so they wouldn't gain access to domain resources.

Changing The System Name

The CEO just got a new system, and it's been configured beautifully by you. Job well done! (I thought I'd say it, since no one else will.) But you know what they say about absolute power...he's not happy with the computer name BIGKAHUNA and wants something more respectful.

1. Choose Start|Settings|Control Panel.

2. Double click the Network icon. On the Network window, click the Change button. The Identification Changes dialog box appears. Select the computer name, and type in the new name. You will get a warning message about system name changes in domains. Acknowledge the message, and click OK.

 If this system had already been used in the domain, it would now need to have its domain account deleted and added because this computer would no longer be recognized by the domain.

Installing And Configuring NetBEUI

You have a small LAN configured using NetBEUI. You have relocated a server from another network in your organization and need to configure NetBEUI as the common protocol, because this poor server had been forced to talk to that strange protocol called IPX/SPX.

1. Choose Start|Settings|Control Panel.

2. Double click the Network icon. Select the Protocols tab, as shown in Figure 7.17.

3. Click the Add button. Select NetBEUI from the protocols list. Click OK. Confirm the location of the Windows NT source CD. Click Continue, and the protocol will be installed.

4. Click Close. The changes to the adapter bindings for NetBEUI will be made. You'll need to restart the computer before NetBEUI can be used.

Once the changes have been made, no further configuration is required. In fact, if you select the NetBEUI protocol in the Network Protocol window, the Properties button will be grayed out.

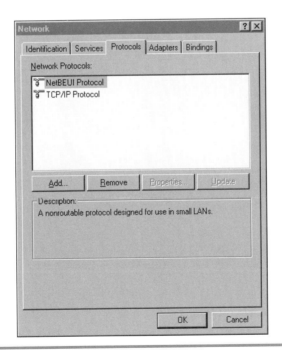

The Protocols page.
Figure 7.17

Installing And Configuring IPX/SPX

After much political infighting, you have finally managed to get a Windows NT server installed at the northern area branch office. You managed to get your way by pretending to make a great sacrifice and installing IPX/SPX as the network protocol. This is obviously no great sacrifice, but the plan worked in any case.

1. Choose Start|Settings|Control Panel.

2. Double click the Network icon. In the Network utility sheet, select the Protocols tab. Press the Add button. The Select Network Protocol dialog box appears, as shown in Figure 7.18.

3. Select NWLink IPX/SPX Compatible Transport from the protocol list. Click OK. Confirm the location of the Windows NT source software, and click Continue. The IPX/SPX protocol will be installed.

4. Click Close. The changes to the adapter bindings for IPX/SPX will be made upon restarting the system.

At this point, the IPX/SPX protocol will require configuring.

5. Choose Start|Settings|Control Panel.

6. Double click the Network icon. Select the Protocols tab. Select NWLink IPX/SPX Compatible Transport from the protocol list. Click the Properties button. The NWLink IPX/SPX Properties window appears, as shown in Figure 7.19.

The IPX/SPX network number and frame type will need to be configured. The *network number* is the area to which this server is assigned. For instance, all servers attached to this physical LAN might have been configured to be in area 42. (The CNE will be able to tell you what the NetWare servers are configured for.) The *frame type* is the actual construction of the network data packets. NetWare can use two different types: 802.2 or 802.3. (Again, the CNE should be able to help. If not, Windows NT can autodetect the frame type currently in use on the network.)

7. Select the Internal Network Number box, and type in your network (area) number.

8. Set the frame type being used by either entering it manually or by clicking the Auto Frame Type Detection box. Click OK. The Network utility sheet will be redisplayed. Click Close. You will need to restart the computer for the reconfiguration to take effect.

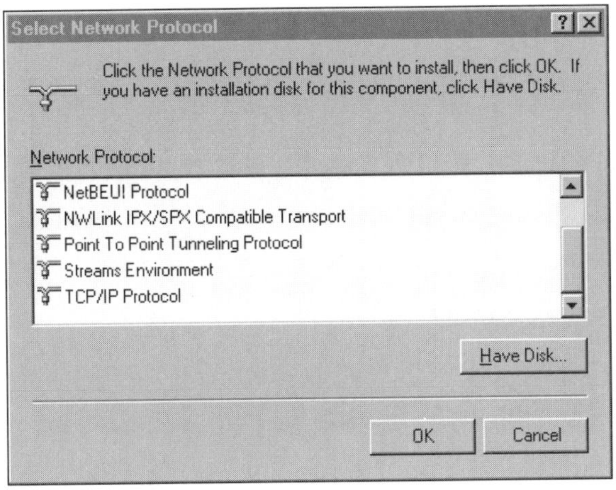

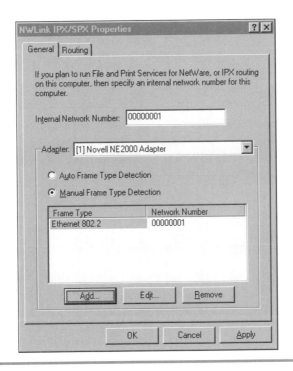

The Select Network Protocol dialog box.

Figure 7.18

The NWLink IPX/SPX Properties window.

Figure 7.19

Installing And Configuring TCP/IP

The networking team has decreed that your corporate network supports a single network protocol: TCP/IP. Well, it's all right for them to sit in their ivory tower and make these decisions; they don't have to do the system reconfigurations....

Now that you have cooled off a bit, you realize that it does make good sense to run with a single protocol. So, smile, take the money, and get on with it.

1. Choose Start|Settings|Control Panel.

2. Double click the Network icon. Select the Protocols tab. Click the Add button. Select TCP/IP Protocol from the protocol list. Click OK.

3. You will be asked if there is a DHCP server on your network. If so, click the Yes button; the TCP/IP software will only have to be installed, and no addressing information will have to be added. If not, the TCP/IP properties will have to be configured.

4. Confirm the location of the Windows NT source software. Click the Continue button. The TCP/IP protocol will be added to the system. Click Close, and the adapter bindings will be reconfigured. The TCP/IP Properties window appears, as shown in Figure 7.20.

5. Select the IP Address box, and enter a unique IP address. (Remember, each network adapter will require a unique IP address.) Select Subnet Mask, and enter the subnet mask address.

Many more TCP/IP parameters can be configured under Windows NT, but the IP address and subnet mask will be enough information to get basic connectivity going for LAN computers.

6. Click OK, and restart the computer.

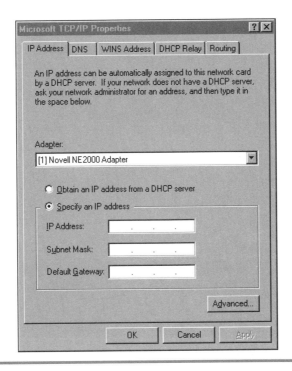

The TCP/IP Properties window.
Figure 7.20

◙ Checking TCP/IP Connectivity

You have been asked to look at a system that has been set up by a colleague. She's unable to connect to any shares using the TCP/IP protocol. TCP/IP has been installed on the local system and looks to be configured correctly, so you're not too sure if it is a network or a local host problem. Figure 7.21 shows an example **ping**, first to the local host and then to a remote host that is not currently reachable.

1. Choose Start|Programs|Command Prompt.

2. Using the **ping** command, first try TCP/IP connectivity to yourself and then to a remote host to which a connection can't be established. For the remote host, try both the host name and the IP address in case a DNS server has been incorrectly configured, e.g., ping 195.10.100.1 or ping server.

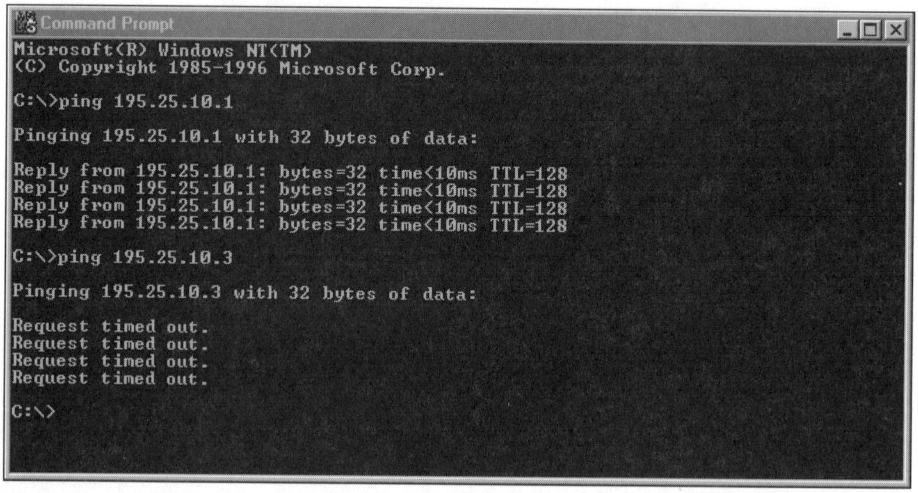

```
Command Prompt                                                    _ □ ✕
Microsoft(R) Windows NT(TM)
(C) Copyright 1985-1996 Microsoft Corp.

C:\>ping 195.25.10.1

Pinging 195.25.10.1 with 32 bytes of data:

Reply from 195.25.10.1: bytes=32 time<10ms TTL=128
Reply from 195.25.10.1: bytes=32 time<10ms TTL=128
Reply from 195.25.10.1: bytes=32 time<10ms TTL=128
Reply from 195.25.10.1: bytes=32 time<10ms TTL=128

C:\>ping 195.25.10.3

Pinging 195.25.10.3 with 32 bytes of data:

Request timed out.
Request timed out.
Request timed out.
Request timed out.

C:\>
```

*The **ping** command.*
Figure 7.21

Installing And Configuring A DHCP Server

Now that you have a corporate LAN that only uses TCP/IP as its protocol, you have decided to install and use a DHCP server to simplify the allocation of TCP/IP addresses. Because everyone keeps playing musical desks, you need to reconfigure their TCP/IP addresses. First, you have to install the DHCP server. This is only available with Windows NT Server.

1. Choose Start|Settings|Control Panel.

2. Double click the Network icon. Select the Services tab. Click the Add button.

3. Select DHCP Server from the services list. Click OK, and confirm the location of the Windows NT source software. Click Continue.

4. An information message appears, stating that the TCP/IP address for the adapters on this server will need a static address and not rely on a DHCP server to provide them. Click OK. Click Close. The binding configuration takes place once the system is restarted.

Now the DHCP server needs to be configured, starting with the DHCP Manager scope. (The *scope* is the range of addresses that are assigned to this DHCP server for allocation to DHCP clients.)

5. Choose Start|Programs|Administrative Tools|DHCP Manager. The DHCP Manager window appears, as shown in Figure 7.22.

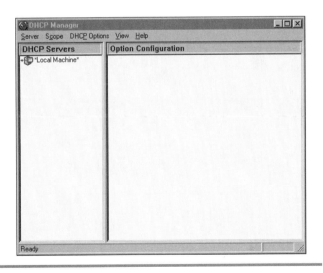

The DHCP Manager window.
Figure 7.22

6. Select the Local Machine in the DHCP Servers list. Choose Scope|Create. The Create Scope dialog box appears, as shown in Figure 7.23.

7. Enter the start and end TCP/IP addresses and the subnet mask. Any excluded addresses can also be added here. Excluded addresses could be already statically allocated or managed by another DHCP server. You can also set the lease duration in this window.

 The lease duration is the length of time that an IP address will remain allocated to the computer when that address is not being used. Once the lease duration time expires, the address will be available for reassignment by the DHCP server.

8. Click OK. The scope will then be created, and you will be asked whether you want to activate this scope now. Click Yes.

The DHCP server will now be ready to assign TCP/IP addresses. Now you'll need to reconfigure the TCP/IP clients to use the DHCP server. If all the TCP/IP addresses available in the DHCP scope are allocated, no more DHCP clients will be able to lease addresses. If TCP/IP is the only protocol running on these clients, they will not be able to access any of the domain resources.

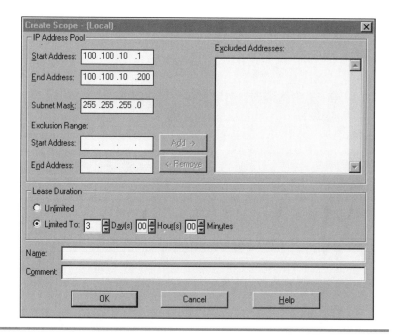

DHCP scope configuration.
Figure 7.23

Configuring Clients To Use The DHCP Server

Since you have spent the time setting up a DHCP server, you might as well go ahead and use it. Now users can move their own systems around, because you won't need to make any configuration changes.

1. Choose Start|Settings|Control Panel.

2. Double click the Network icon. Select the Protocols tab. Select TCP/IP from the protocol list, and click the Properties button. The TCP/IP Properties window appears.

3. Select the Obtain An IP Address From A DHCP Server option. Acknowledge the information message stating the DHCP server address will override the TCP/IP information on the property page. You are returned to the TCP/IP Properties window. Click Close, and restart the system.

Configuring And Using WINS

You decide to simplify the reconfiguration work you have to do each time you move one of your Windows NT workstations by using WINS in conjunction with DHCP.

1. Choose Start|Settings|Control Panel.

2. Double click the Network icon. The Network utility window is displayed. Select the Services tab.

3. Click the Add button on the Services page. The Select Network Service dialog box appears, as shown in Figure 7.24.

4. Select Windows Internet Name Service, and click OK. Confirm the location of the Windows NT source software, and click Continue.

5. The Windows Internet software will be installed. Click Close, and the necessary binding will be made. You'll need to restart the computer to implement WINS.

Now, you'll need to configure the Windows NT workstations to become WINS clients.

6. Choose Start|Settings|Control Panel.

7. Double click the Network icon. Select the Protocols tab. Select TCP/IP from the Protocols list, and click the Properties button.

8. Select the WINS Address tab, and enter the TCP/IP address of the primary WINS server—in other words, the one just created. Click OK. You'll need to restart the system to use WINS.

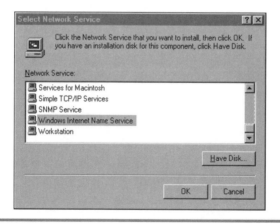

The Select Network Service dialog box.
Figure 7.24

Configuring And Using DNS

You're networking a few Windows NT systems into a large Unix setup. You have convinced the head Unix guy that running DNS on your Windows NT Server will make his job easier.

1. Choose Start|Settings|Control Panel.

2. Double-click the Network icon. The Network utility window is displayed. Choose the Services tab. Click the Add button. The Select Network Services dialog box appears.

3. Select Microsoft DNS Server from the services list, and click OK. Confirm the location of the Windows NT source software, and click Continue. The software will be installed, and you are returned to the Services window.

4. Click Close. The binding reconfigurations will take place. You'll need to restart the system to use DNS.

Now, you will need to configure the DNS server by using the DNS Server Management tool in the Administrative Tools menu.

5. Choose Start|Programs|Administrative Tools|DNS Manager. The DNS Manager window appears.

6. Choose DNS|New Server. The Add DNS Server dialog box appears, as shown in Figure 7.25. Enter the IP address or name of the DNS Server. Click OK.

7. Choose DNS|Create Zone. Select the Zone Type in the Zone Type pane. Click Next. Enter the Zone name and the Zone file (this will default to the zone name). Click Finish to create zone. When creating the new zone for the DNS server, keep in mind that the zone name is the domain name—for instance, microsoft.com or coriolis.com. Also, make sure that the Windows NT server where the zone is to be created has an IP address, host, and domain name configured for it.

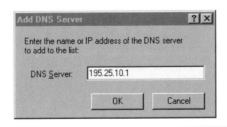

The Add DNS Server dialog box.
Figure 7.25

Which DHCP Client Is Using What TCP/IP Address?

The network team has a problem (don't they always?). They claim that a certain network device is broadcasting garbage on the network. No, we're not talking about Three Stooges reruns here; we're talking bad data packets.

The network team knows you have some wizzy way of dynamically allocating IP addresses, so they're a bit doubtful that you can tell where the problem is located. So just click your heels together three times, and follow me.

1. Choose Start|Programs|Administrative Tools|DHCP Manager. The DHCP Manager window appears.

2. Double click the Local Machine icon and select the TCP/IP address for the relevant DHCP Server.

3. Choose Scope|Active Leases. The IP addresses currently leased are displayed, as shown in Figure 7.26. This list shows the leases that have been assigned by this DHCP server and the host to which they've been assigned.

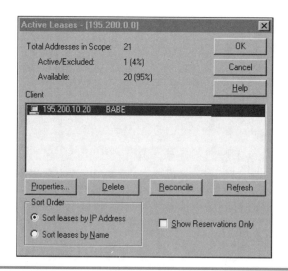

Active leases.
Figure 7.26

Installing And Configuring Gateway Services For NetWare

The two worlds of Windows NT and NetWare have just collided with a huge crash. The CEO has recently attended a Windows NT road show and discovered that he doesn't actually need to copy all his files onto a floppy to move them from NetWare to Windows NT (he did need the exercise though).

So the word of the day from the CEO office is *integration*. (Hang on a minute, I'm still trying to downsize everything from that last seminar he went to. Things sure ran a lot smoother when the CEO was a technophobe.)

1. Choose Start|Settings|Control Panel.

2. Double click the Network icon. The Network utility window appears. Select the Services tab. Click the Add button.

3. From the Network Service list, select Gateway (And Client) Services For NetWare. Click OK, and confirm the location of the Windows NT source software.

4. The gateway software will be installed. Click Close. The necessary binding reconfiguration will take place when you restart the computer.

 If the IPX/SPX protocol hasn't already been installed, it will be automatically installed once you install the gateway services for NetWare. The configuration needed for IPX/SPX should be done the same way as in the preceding "Installing and Configuring IPX/SPX" example.

When users log on after the computer has restarted, they will be asked to select either their preferred server or the tree and context to connect to. The preferred server is set for NetWare 2/3 servers or NetWare 4 servers running in Bindery Emulation mode. Tree and context is used for NDS configuration with NetWare 4.

The Windows NT account information will be used to perform the account validation on NetWare. When used with NetWare 2/3 servers, the passwords are not automatically synchronized and must be kept in step manually by the user. NetWare 4 servers, however, are automatically synchronized.

The NetWare Gateway icon will have been added to the Control Panel during installation. This icon can be used to configure NetWare volumes as Windows NT shares.

Remote Access Service

The boss tells you he wants to access some data held on the Windows NT server from home this weekend. What he doesn't want is excuses. He knows it can be done because his golf partner (there's always one, isn't there?) told him so. It's getting late in the day, and you have a hot date tonight. And what with your fashion sense, you were hoping to cut out on time to get ready.

Okay, first let's configure the Windows NT server; then, if you can pry that very expensive executive toy known as a laptop away from the boss, we can get that configured, too.

1. Choose Start|Settings|Control Panel.

2. Double click the Network icon. Select the Services tab. Click the Add button, and select Remote Access Service from the service list. Click OK.

3. Confirm the location of the Windows NT source software. Click Continue, and the RAS software will be installed. If no modems have previously been configured, the modem wizard will appear. Use this to select the correct modem type. There is also an auto configure option which can be used that will allow Windows NT to search for your modem. The Add RAS Device window will appear.

4. Select the required RAS device—in other words, your modem—from the selection box, and click OK. The Remote Access Setup window will appear.

5. RAS will automatically be configured to allow connections over all installed protocols and to allow dial-in connections only. If you need to change this configuration, click the Network button. Click Continue. The Network Configuration dialog box appears.

6. Indicate whether a protocol is restricted to this server or if the RAS client can gain access to the entire network. Click OK. You are returned to the Remote Access Setup window.

7. Click Continue. Depending on the protocols installed, additional protocol-related questions might be asked. You are now returned to the Network window. Click Close. Once the computer is restarted, the bindings will be reconfigured.

Now, you'll need to assign permissions to the users or groups who need to use RAS. This is done with the Remote Access Administrator utility.

8. Choose Start|Programs|Administrative Tools|Remote Access Admin. The Remote Access Admin window appears.

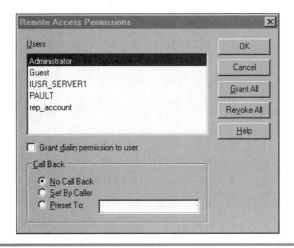

The Remote Access Permissions dialog box.
Figure 7.27

9. Choose Users|Permissions. The Remote Access Permissions dialog box appears, as shown in Figure 7.27.

10. Select the relevant user from the user list, and select the Grant Dial-In Permission To User checkbox. Click OK, and you are returned to the Remote Access Admin window.

Now the RAS client needs to be configured, so grab the laptop and here goes:

11. Choose Start|Programs|Accessories|Dial-Up Networking. The Dial-Up Networking Install window appears.

12. Click the Install button. The software will be installed, and a list of RAS capable devices will appear.

13. Choose Add Modem to install a modem. The Install Modem window appears. Here you can set the system for either automatic or manual modem detection. To perform a manual selection, choose the Don't Detect My Modem; I Will Select It From A List option.

14. Select the required modem and communication port. Click the Add button. You will be returned to the Add RAS Device window.

15. From the Add RAS Device window, select the required modem and port from the RAS-capable device list, and click OK. The Remote Access Setup window will appear.

16. Click the Configure button. The Configure Port Usage window will appear. Select the Dial-Out Only option, and click OK. Click OK again, and you are returned to the Remote Access Setup window. Click the Continue button. Remote access service will be installed. Again, you'll need to restart the computer.

Now you can enter the phone entry, which defines the connection to your Windows NT Server.

17. Choose Start|Programs|Accessories|Dial-Up Networking. A Dial-Up Networking window appears, advising that the Phonebook is empty.

18. Click OK. The new Phonebook entry wizard will enter the phone number and other information for the dial-up connection to your server. The phonebook entry is displayed, as shown in Figure 7.28. When the Dial button is clicked, the user will be prompted for a valid username and password. When entered, the dial-up connection will be established.

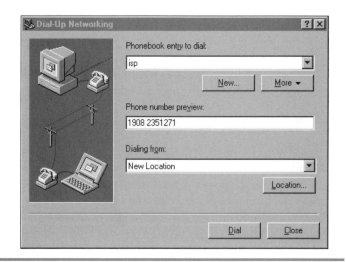

The dial-up connection.
Figure 7.28

Replicator Service

You have discovered more by accident than deduction that the domain logon scripts need to be on the server that validates the logon. You *had* considered playing a new game called "Guess the Server," but it does seem to be a bit on the difficult side.

Oh well, you'll have to use the conventional method and replicate the logon scripts to BDCs from the PDC. First, you'll need to create a user account for the Replicator service to use, then configure the PDC to export the logon scripts.

1. Choose Start|Programs|Administrative Tools|User Manager For Domains.

2. Choose User|New User, and enter the username and password of the account you want to create. Make sure the account is configured so that the password never expires and the user is not forced to change the password at the next logon.

3. Select the Groups button. Using the Add button, add the replicator user you have just created to the following groups: Backup Operators, Replicators, and Domain Users. Click OK. Click the Add button. The user account will be created. Click Close, and exit User Manager For Domains.

4. Choose Start|Settings|Control Panel.

5. Double click the Services icon. Select the Directory Replicator service, and if it is currently running, click the Stop button.

6. Click the Startup button, and set the Startup Type to Automatic. Choose the Browse button in the Log On As pane, and select the account you have just added. Choose the Add button. Click OK, and the username will be added to the This Account box.

7. Enter and confirm the account password. Click OK. The account will be granted the Logon As A Service right. Click OK. Click the Start button to start the Replicator service. Click Close to exit the Services window.

8. Choose Start|Settings|Control Panel. Double click the Server icon. The Server window appears.

9. Click the Replication button to display the Directory Replication dialog box, as shown in Figure 7.29. Select the Export Directories option. Select the directory to export. Click the Add button, and from the Select Domain dialog box, select either the domain or computer to which you want the directory exported. Click OK. You are returned to the Directory Replication dialog box. Click OK.

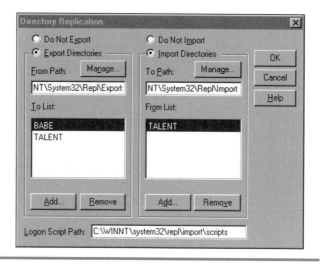

The Directory Replication dialog box.
Figure 7.29

On the BDCs, the Replicator service will need to be configured to import the logon scripts.

10. Choose Start|Settings|Control Panel.

11. Double click the Services icon. Select the Directory Replicator service, and click the Startup button. Set the Startup Type to Automatic.

12. Click the Browse button, and select the replicator account you just added to the server. Click the Add button, then click OK. Enter and confirm the account passwords. Click OK, and click Close to exit the Services window.

13. Choose Start|Settings|Control Panel.

14. Double click the Server icon. The Server window appears.

15. Click the Replication button. The Directory Replication dialog box appears. Select the Import Directory option. Select the directory import path. Click the Add button, and select either the domain or computer for the directory to be imported. Click OK.

This example illustrates replicating data between computers in the same domain. If you want to replicate between domains, make sure you create the same user account in both domains.

The initial release of Windows NT 4 contains a bug that inhibits the Directory Replicator Service from functioning. This is due to the incorrect permissions being set on a Registry key. This bug can be identified by a system error 5 for the Replicator service being logged in the system event log. To overcome this problem, the permissions on the relevant Registry key need to be changed on the export server.

1. Choose Start|Run. The Run dialog box will be displayed.

2. Use the Browse button to select the Registry editor REGEDT32. Click OK. Select the HKEY_LOCAL_MACHINE hive.

3. Select SYSTEM|CurrentControlSet|Control|SecurePipeServers|winreg. From the Registry Editor menu, choose Security|Permissions, and the Registry Key Permissions dialog box will be displayed. Click Add, and the Add Users And Groups dialog box will appear.

4. Click Show Users, and select the Replicator user created earlier in this example. Click Add, and the user will be added to the Add names list. Select Full Control in the Type Of access box. Click OK. You will be returned to the Registry Key Permissions dialog box. Click OK. Close the Registry Editor. The system will need to be restarted for the change to take effect.

Locating The PDC And The BDCs

The Windows NT administrator at one of your company's divisions has failed to return from her skiing trip in Vermont. You're a well-respected administrator, so the company has shipped you to the division until she returns (everyone's money runs out sooner or later). Because you have never seen this domain before, it's probably a good time to locate all of the important network systems.

1. Choose Start|Programs|Administrative Tools|Server Manager. The Server Manager window appears, giving you a list of systems and their roles in the domain.

2. Double click a computer you want to learn more about. This brings up the Properties window.

Promoting A BDC To A PDC

The power is going to be turned off to the communications room on the first floor in about 10 minutes. This has been scheduled for a week, but you now remember that the primary domain controller for your corporate domain is housed in this room. Better get a backup domain controller promoted fast or that corner office will never be yours.

1. Choose Start|Programs|Administrative Tools|Server Manager. The Server Manager window appears.

2. Select the BDC that you want to promote. Choose Computer|Promote To Primary Domain Controller. The server manager warning message will appear, as shown in Figure 7.30. Click Yes to acknowledge the change. The NetLogon services on both systems will be stopped, the roles of the systems changed, and the NetLogon services restarted.

 Promoting a BDC to a PDC will cause all network connections to both systems to close while the change takes place.

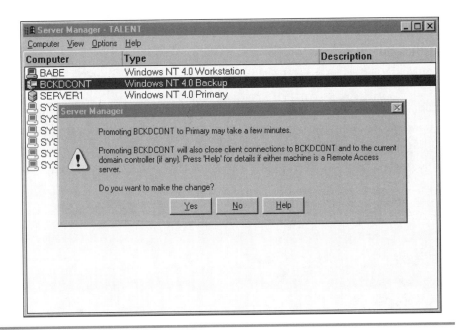

Promoting a BDC to a PDC.
Figure 7.30

Promoting A BDC To PDC When The PDC Is Down

It's pouring down rain, and you couldn't find a parking space. You finally get into the office to find a small crowd gathered around your desk. Quick, run! Too late...they've seen you. There's only one thing to do—walk tall and maintain eye contact. If they smell fear, they'll rip you apart.

So, the story is that a maintenance crew member unplugged the PDC, heard the disks spin down, realized his mistake, and quickly plugged it back in, which caused the PDC to emit a loud bang, then die. You need to promote a BDC because with this bad weather, there's no telling how long it will be before the engineer gets here.

1. Choose Start|Programs|Administrative Tools|Server Manager. The Server Manager window appears.

2. Select the BDC that you want to promote. Choose Computer|Promote To Primary Domain Controller. The Server Manager will warn you that it can't contact the PDC and that this could cause problems when the original PDC comes online. Because there's not much you can do about that until the PDC is fixed, go ahead and promote the BDC.

When the engineer has fixed the PDC and the system has been restarted, it will attempt to join the domain as the domain PDC; however, you have already promoted a BDC to take its place. Figure 7.31 shows how the Server Manager window appears when this event occurs. When the original PDC starts, it will discover that a PDC is already available in the domain. Because there can only ever be one PDC in a domain, the original PDC will stop its NetLogon service and take no part in the validation of domain logons. Use the Server Manager to demote the original PDC down to a BDC. Wait a while for the domain to stabilize, and then if you want, you can repromote the system to take over as the PDC.

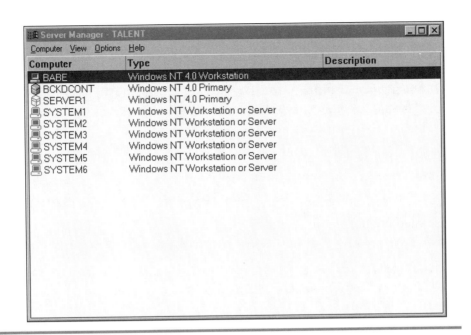

Server Manager view of two PDCs.

Figure 7.31

Synchronizing The Domain

The network link between your branch office and the corporate headquarters has been down all weekend. For certain political reasons, the PDC is located at headquarters (not that they would know a PDC if it bit them). Your BDC is holding down the fort pretty well, but the link has just come back up, and you want everything resynchronized as soon as possible—certainly before the 9:00 a.m. logon rush.

The domain will, of course, synchronize itself over time. As the administrator, however, you can force either your BDC to synchronize with the PDC or all BDCs to synchronize. You have onward links to other BDCs from your office, therefore it's probably a good idea to synch the whole thing.

1. Choose Start|Programs|Administrative Tools|Server Manager.

2. Select the PDC from the list of systems. Choose Computer|Synchorize Entire Domain. Click Yes to confirm. The domain synchronization and information message is shown in Figure 7.32.

If you can't see the PDC displayed in the list of systems, click View, and check that the view currently displayed is correct.

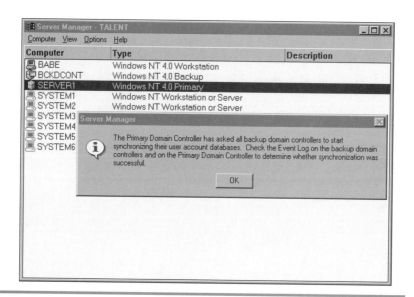

Synchronizing the domain.
Figure 7.32

Configuring Domain Trusts

Your company has just acquired a small manufacturing plant, and your mission, should you choose to accept it (actually, it's your mission regardless), is to integrate their Windows NT domain with yours. You have been given the Administrator password for the remote domain, and the necessary wide-area communication links have been put in place. Because personnel will be moving back and forth between the two offices—especially during the initial integration period—all users need to be able to log on anywhere. This can be done easily by establishing a two-way domain trust.

Okay, on your local domain PDC:

1. Choose Start|Programs|Administrative Tools|User Manager For Domains. The User Manager For Domains Window appears.

2. Choose Policies|Trust Relationships. The Trust Relationships dialog box appears. This is going to be a two-way trust relationship, so you'll need to add the remote domain as both a trusted domain and a trusting domain, as shown in Figure 7.33.

3. Click the Add buttons to add the domain names. A password will need to be entered. This password is used to establish the trust relationship and must be set the same for both domains. This password is automatically changed once the trust relationship has been established.

You'll need to repeat this process on the remote domain; however, this time, you add your domain name as both a trusting and trusted domain. The User Manager For

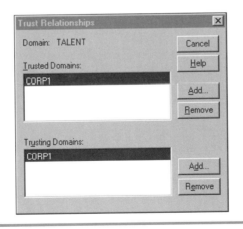

Adding domain names.
Figure 7.33

Domains tool has a Select Domain option accessed via the User menu. You will be prompted for a valid username and password on the remote domain when the connection is established.

Once the two-way trust is established, users from either location will be able to log on to the domain by using the Domain Selection box in the Logon window to select the domain where their account is located.

 Care must be taken when setting up two-way trust relationships between domains. The administrator of the remote domain must be trusted, because poor security in the remote domain could compromise your domain.

Removing Computers From A Domain

A whole department within your company has now been moved to a new division, so providing them network resources is no longer your problem. All the users have been moved to the new domain, but you are left with 20 computers in your Server Manager display that are no longer required. Each one of these systems will have a corresponding SAM account that was created to allow the computer access to the domain. These accounts were created automatically when the computer first joined the domain and can now be removed.

1. Choose Start|Programs|Administrative Tools|Server Manager. The Server Manager window appears.

2. Select a computer you want to remove from the server manager list. Choose Computer|Remove From Domain. A warning message is displayed, as shown in Figure 7.34, advising that the removed system will not be able to authenticate domain logons. Click Yes to remove the computer.

If one of the computers removed from your domain was then moved back into your domain, the computer would need to be deleted and re-added, because the computer would no longer be identified with the original account created for it.

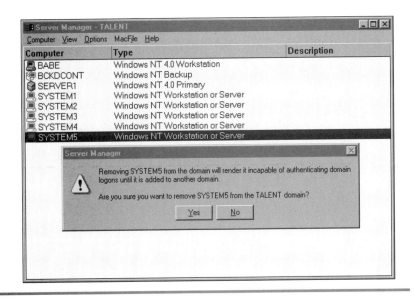

Removing computers from the domain.
Figure 7.34

Managing A Domain From A Windows NT Workstation

All the Windows NT servers have now been installed in their nice, new computer room. So, each time a user forgets his or her password, are you really going to the computer room to change it? No, of course not. Instead, you'll install the Network Client Administration tools.

1. Choose Start|Programs|Administrative Tools|Network Client Administrator Tools. The Network Client Administrator window appears, as shown in Figure 7.35.

2. Select the Copy Client-Based Network Administration Tools option, and click the Continue button. The Share Client-Based Administration Tools window appears. You can use the default settings or, if required, create the share with a different name or on a different volume. Click OK.

3. The relevant files and folders are copied from the Windows NT source software, and the share is established. Click OK to acknowledge the successful share. You are returned to the Network Client Administrator window. Click Exit.

Now, from the client from which you want to manage the domain, do the following:

4. Choose Start|Programs|Windows NT Explorer. The Windows NT Explorer window appears.

5. Choose Tools|Map Network Drive. From the Map Network Drive window, select the Client-Based Administration Tools share by using the Browse window. Click OK. You are returned to the Windows NT Explorer window.

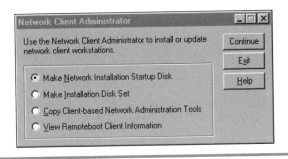

The Network Client Administrator.
Figure 7.35

6. Refresh the display by pressing the F5 key. Using Explorer, locate the Winnt subfolder on the network client share. Double click the setup program in this folder, and the Network Administrator tools will be added to your computer.

If the Network Neighborhood icon was used to locate and run the setup program, the installation will fail because the installation cannot be done from a remote network location. In other words, a drive mapping needs to be established.

Sending A Message To A Remote Computer

An engineer has arrived to take a look at one of the Windows NT workstations that has been crashing a couple of times a day. You don't want to leave your desk, because you're expecting an important phone call. You have tried phoning the user, but he's on the phone (even users have friends). Using the Server Manager Message function would probably be a good idea at this point.

1. Choose Start|Programs|Administrator Tools|Server Manager. The Server Manager window appears.

2. From the list of available computers, select the system you want to send the message to. Choose Computer|Send Message. The Send Message dialog box appears, as shown in Figure 7.36. Type your message in the message box and click OK.

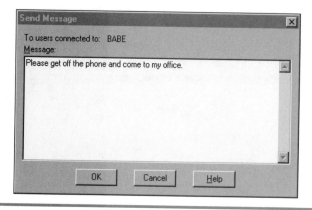

The Send Message dialog box.
Figure 7.36

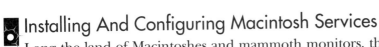

Installing And Configuring Macintosh Services

Long the land of Macintoshes and mammoth monitors, the graphics department has seen the light. Okay, to be totally honest, they have been told that if they want any more disk space, they have to use the available space on the Windows NT servers. So, you're going to have to do some work to keep these users happily pointing and clicking. You need to install Macintosh services, which is provided with Windows NT Server.

1. Choose Start|Settings|Control Panel.

2. Double click the Network icon. Choose the Services tab. The Network Services window appears.

3. Click the Add button. Select Services For Macintosh from the network services list. Click OK, and confirm the location of the Windows NT distribution software. Click Continue. The relevant software components will be installed. Click Close. The bindings will be changed for AppleTalk, the Macintosh network protocol, and the AppleTalk Properties window appears, as shown in Figure 7.37.

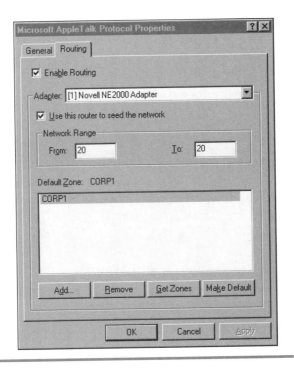

The AppleTalk Properties window.
Figure 7.37

If this is the first Macintosh server or router on the network, and if the Macintosh and Windows NT server are on the same LAN segment, Macintosh services can be used to seed the network. This provides the Macintosh systems with a network area number.

4. Select the Routing tab. Select Enable Routing. Select the Use this router to seed the network option. Enter the network range in the From and To boxes. If the network is a single LAN segment, this can be the same number in both boxes.

5. Click Add. The Add Zone box will appear. Enter the zone name (in effect, this is the AppleTalk domain name, and the seed number is the area).

6. Click OK. The system will have to be restarted before Macintosh services can be used.

Okay, all looks good at the server end. Windows NT will log an event in the system event log if a service fails to start. To test that Macintosh services are running correctly, we're going to have to use a Macintosh. (Does this mean I will be stripped of my Microsoft certification?)

7. Choose Apple|Control Panel|Network. The AppleTalk Connection window appears.

8. Select EtherTalk if it is not already selected, and confirm the switch. The current zone should change to indicate the Windows NT server zone.

9. Choose Apple|Chooser. Click the AppleShare icon. The file server list is displayed.

10. Select the Windows NT server, and click OK. The Logon window will be displayed for guest logons if enabled or for logons using a valid Windows user account. Logons and connections can be made to the Windows NT Macintosh volumes.

Configuring And Using Macintosh Print Services

The Macintosh users have discovered that they should be able to use the Windows NT printers, and of course, now they want to. They have got a point though, because they only have three Apple printers at the moment. Print Server for Macintosh, which is the service that provides the print integration, is installed with Macintosh Services. To enable permissions to be set for the Macintosh users, a generic print account needs to be created to run the print service.

1. Choose Start|Programs|Administrative Tools|User Manager For Domains.

2. Select Create User|New User, and create the user account to be used as the Macintosh print user—probably a name like "macprint" would work.

3. Enter and confirm the password for the account, and select the Password Never Expires box. Deselect the User Must Change Password On Next Logon box. Click the Add button, and the account is created. Click Close.

4. Choose Start|Settings|Control Panel. Double click the Services icon. The Services window appears.

5. Select Print Server For Macintosh from the service list and click the Startup button. The Service startup window is shown in Figure 7.38. Select the Startup Type as Automatic.

The Service startup window for Print Server For Macintosh.
Figure 7.38

6. Click the Browse button located in the Log On As pane. From the user list, select the Macintosh print user you have just created. Click the Add button, and the user will be shown in the Add name dialog box. Click OK, and the user will be added to the This Account box.

7. Enter and confirm the account password. Click OK. The user account will be granted the Log On As A Service right. Click OK. You are returned to the Services window. If currently running, click Stop to stop the service. Click the Start button to restart the Print Server For Macintosh Services.

On the Macintosh client:

8. Choose Apple|Chooser.

9. Click one of the printer icons in the Chooser window. The Windows NT available printing devices will be listed. Select the printer you want to use from the list, and click OK.

Creating And Using Macintosh Volumes

Well, the graphics team is just so pleased with the way you have integrated Windows NT with their Macintoshes that they want you to create data volumes for them on the server so they can store their graphics files online. (What's this? Converts? Don't trust them, they're up to something.) So after a pleasant lunch paid for by the graphics department, you're going to set up data volumes on Windows NT for them.

1. Choose Start|Programs|Administrative Tools|File Manager.

Yes, I know you discovered the first time that you sat in front of a Windows NT 4 system that File Manager had been replaced by Windows NT Explorer. But installing services for Macintosh brought it back. However, I don't suggest you use it for your day-to-day administration, because I don't think it's going to be available in future releases of Windows NT.

2. Select the folder you want to use as a Macintosh volume. Choose MacFile|Create Volume. The Create Volume window appears. The volume is a network share that can be accessed by Macintosh clients as well as from Windows NT. Confirm the volume name, and click OK.

 Permissions can be set for the Macintosh clients by using the MacFile/Permissions menu in File Manager.

To access the volume you have created from the Macintosh client:

3. Choose Apple|Chooser. The Chooser window is displayed.

4. Click the AppleShare icon. Select the Windows NT server from the file server list, and click OK. If you are already connected to this server, an information message will be displayed. If you are not, a Logon window will be displayed to allow you to log on. The Server Selection window will display available volumes. Select the relevant volume, and click OK. The connection is established, and a folder is created on the Macintosh desktop.

Configuring Macintosh Logon Messages

Your company has changed its security policy, and all users connecting to your network must be shown a logon message. Services for Macintosh provides an easy way to do this using the MacFile utility:

1. Choose Start|Settings|Control Panel.

2. Double click the MacFile icon. The MacFile Properties window appears.

3. Select the Attributes button. The MacFile Attributes window appears, as shown in Figure 7.39.

4. Enter the required logon message in the message box, and click OK. Click Close. All Macintosh users connecting to the Services For Macintosh will now have the logon message displayed when the connection is made.

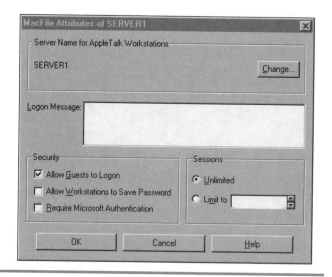

The MacFile Attributes window.
Figure 7.39

Using The Internet Via A Dial-Up Line

Well, the information superhighway has finally hit your small town. (Yes, I know you've been surfing the Net for years, but the boss has just woken up to the fact that people are actually doing business on the Web.) As a first brave step into this new world of virtual everything, the boss has decided that a single dial-up Internet account should be configured.

1. Choose Start|Programs|Accessories|Dial-Up Networking. The Dial-Up Networking Install window is displayed.

2. Click the Install button. The software will be installed, and a list of RAS-capable devices is presented.

3. Select Add Modem to install a modem. The Install Modem window appears. Here, you can set either automatic or manual modem detection. For this example, we'll select it manually by selecting the Don't Detect My Modem; I Will Select If From A List option.

4. Select the required modem and communication port. Click the Add button. You will be returned to the Add RAS Device window, as shown in Figure 7.40.

5. From the RAS Device window, select the required modem and port from the RAS-capable device list, and click OK. The Remote Access Setup window appears.

6. Click the Configure button; the Configure Port Usage window is displayed. Select the Dial-Out Only option, and click OK. Press the Network Configuration button, and select TCP/IP as the only protocol. Click OK, and you are returned to the Remote Access Setup window. Press Continue. Remote access service will be installed once the computer is restarted.

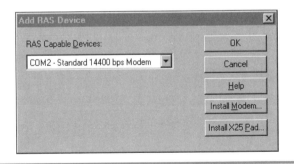

The Add RAS Device window.
Figure 7.40

Now, you'll need to set the dial-up configuration.

7. Choose Start|Programs|Accessories|Dial-Up Networking. A Dial-Up Networking window will appear, advising that the Phonebook is empty.

8. Click OK. The new Phonebook entry wizard will be displayed. Enter the configuration and communications detail for your Internet service provider.

9. Enter your Internet service provider's name, and click the Next button. The Server window appears. Here, you'll need to select all three boxes for many installation verification procedure (IVP) configurations. Select the appropriate settings, and click the Next button.

10. The Serial Line Protocol window appears. Choose either PPP or SLIP. (Your ISP will advise which is the right connection type for your connection.) Click the Next button.

11. The Logon Script window appears. This window configures the events that occur once the dial-up connection has been made with the ISP. One of three events can be scheduled:

    • nothing happens

    • a terminal window pops up to allow the connection username and password to be manually entered

    • a script can be run to automate the logon process

It's a good idea to run a test connection using the pop-up terminal so you can easily see what is happening with the connection process. This allows you to view the exact logon sequence for creating the correct logon script. To do this, select Use A Terminal on the Logon Script dialog box, and click the Next button.

12. The IP Address window is displayed. Enter the IP address that was provided to you by your ISP, and click the Next button.

IP addresses are unique for each network adapter. The modem isn't different from a network adapter, so the IP address you enter for your RAS connection must be different from the IP address you may have set up for your LAN network adapter.

13. The Name Server Address window appears. Enter the DNS address supplied by your ISP. Click the Next button. Click Finish to save the configuration you have just entered. The Dial-Up Networking window is displayed.

14. Click the Dial button. The connection is established. To change any of the Phonebook entries, click the More button, and choose Edit Phonebook Entry, shown in Figure 7.41.

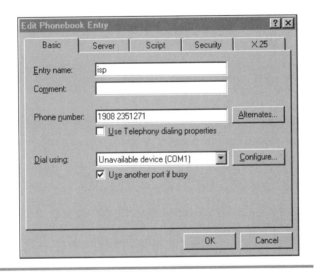

Modem properties.
Figure 7.41

Networking **295**

Quick Reference Specifications

The following are the bare-bones facts and figures.

- *Remote Access Server supports one incoming connection to Windows NT Workstation.*

- *Remote Access Server supports 256 incoming connections to Windows NT Server.*

- *One PDC per domain; the PDC contains the updateable copy of the SAM.*

- *There can be multiple BDCs in a domain; the BDCs contain read-only copies of the SAM.*

- *A BDC can be promoted to a PDC; the promotion will automatically demote the PDC.*

- *DHCP leases IP address to hosts.*

- *Systems designated as servers, as well as Windows NT workstations, do not hold copies of the SAM and take no part in domain logon validations.*

- *NWLink is the Windows NT implementation of IPX/SPX.*

- *WINS is used to resolve NetBIOS names to IP addresses.*

- *NetBIOS names can be up to 15 characters long.*

- *WINS name registration is dynamic.*

- *DNS resolves host names to IP addresses.*

- *DNS name registration must be done manually and cannot use DHCP.*

Utilities To Use

The utilities used in this chapter and their functions are listed in this section. Consider this as a memory aid for the busy system administrator.

Windows NT Command Prompt

- *TCP/IP connectivity test and information tools.*
- ***net*** *commands for command line connection and disconnection of shares.*

Dial-Up Networking

- *Defines phone entries.*
- *Connects to remote LANs using RAS and the Internet.*

DHCP Manager

- *Creates and manages the leased IP address range.*
- *Views which IP addresses are managed by which hosts.*

DNS Manager

- *Manages the DNS service.*

File Manager

- *Creates and manages Macintosh volumes.*

MacFile

- *Views, disconnects, and sends messages to Macintosh users.*
- *Views and closes client connection to Macintosh volumes.*
- *Views files opened by Macintosh clients and closes them.*

Network Icon

- *Changes domain, workgroup, or computer name.*
- *Adds or removes network services.*

➤ *Adds, removes, and configures protocols.*

➤ *Adds, removes, and configures network adapters.*

Network Client Administrator

➤ *Installs domain management tools on network systems.*

Remote Access Admin

➤ *Views and administrates RAS.*

➤ *Assigns user permissions for dial-up communications.*

Server Manager (Administrative Tools)

➤ *Manages domains.*

➤ *Adds and removes computers from domain.*

➤ *Sends messages to domain systems.*

➤ *Promotes BDC to PDC.*

➤ *Synchronizes domain controllers.*

➤ *Creates and manages Macintosh volumes.*

➤ *Sends messages to Macintosh users.*

Windows NT Explorer

➤ *Manages and establishes share connections.*

WINS Manager

➤ *Manages the WINS servers' replication functions.*

➤ *Views registered WINS clients.*

User Manager For Domains

➤ *Establishes domain trusts.*

Chapter 8

Event And System Monitoring Tools

Administrator's Notes...

Chapter 8

One of the biggest problems faced by the administrator of any multiuser, multitasking operating system is keeping track of what system events have occurred and what caused them. The Windows NT system administrator faces these same problems. Fortunately, NT provides some excellent system monitoring tools. Although the tools are easy to use, the interpretation of the results produced by these tools often causes the most problems, especially in the area of performance monitoring. This chapter hopes to provide you with enough information about these tools to point you in the right direction in tracking down your problems.

The Event Viewer

The Event Viewer is a system event log viewer accessed via the Administrative Tools menu. This tool provides a graphical management interface to view the contents of the system, security, and application logs. No special user rights are required to view the system and application logs; however, to view the security log, you must be a member of the Administrator group or have the relevant individual right assigned. All three logs can only be cleared down or have their log settings changed by an administrator. The Event Viewer is shown in Figure 8.1, and a description of the columns is listed in Table 8.1. The different functions of the three event logs are explained in Table 8.2.

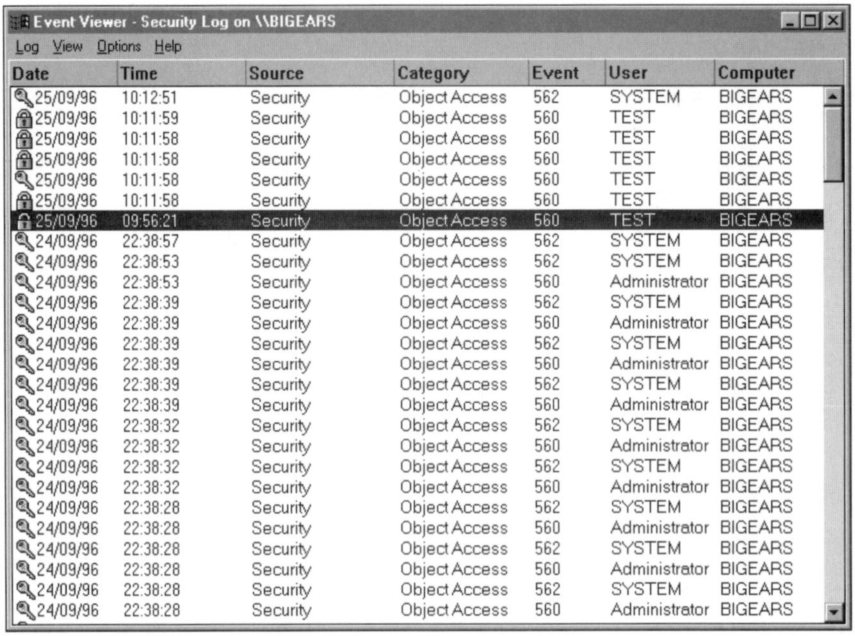

Event Viewer - Security Log on \\BIGEARS

Log View Options Help

Date	Time	Source	Category	Event	User	Computer
25/09/96	10:12:51	Security	Object Access	562	SYSTEM	BIGEARS
25/09/96	10:11:59	Security	Object Access	560	TEST	BIGEARS
25/09/96	10:11:58	Security	Object Access	560	TEST	BIGEARS
25/09/96	10:11:58	Security	Object Access	560	TEST	BIGEARS
25/09/96	10:11:58	Security	Object Access	560	TEST	BIGEARS
25/09/96	10:11:58	Security	Object Access	560	TEST	BIGEARS
25/09/96	09:56:21	Security	Object Access	560	TEST	BIGEARS
24/09/96	22:38:57	Security	Object Access	562	SYSTEM	BIGEARS
24/09/96	22:38:53	Security	Object Access	562	SYSTEM	BIGEARS
24/09/96	22:38:53	Security	Object Access	560	Administrator	BIGEARS
24/09/96	22:38:39	Security	Object Access	562	SYSTEM	BIGEARS
24/09/96	22:38:39	Security	Object Access	560	Administrator	BIGEARS
24/09/96	22:38:39	Security	Object Access	562	SYSTEM	BIGEARS
24/09/96	22:38:39	Security	Object Access	560	Administrator	BIGEARS
24/09/96	22:38:39	Security	Object Access	562	SYSTEM	BIGEARS
24/09/96	22:38:39	Security	Object Access	560	Administrator	BIGEARS
24/09/96	22:38:32	Security	Object Access	562	SYSTEM	BIGEARS
24/09/96	22:38:32	Security	Object Access	560	Administrator	BIGEARS
24/09/96	22:38:32	Security	Object Access	562	SYSTEM	BIGEARS
24/09/96	22:38:32	Security	Object Access	560	Administrator	BIGEARS
24/09/96	22:38:28	Security	Object Access	562	SYSTEM	BIGEARS
24/09/96	22:38:28	Security	Object Access	560	Administrator	BIGEARS
24/09/96	22:38:28	Security	Object Access	562	SYSTEM	BIGEARS
24/09/96	22:38:28	Security	Object Access	560	Administrator	BIGEARS
24/09/96	22:38:28	Security	Object Access	562	SYSTEM	BIGEARS
24/09/96	22:38:28	Security	Object Access	560	Administrator	BIGEARS

The Event Viewer.
Figure 8.1

Column	Description
Date	Date on system that event was logged.
Time	Time on system that event was logged.
Source	Software application or system component that logged the event.
Category	Source software-defined category for this type of event.
Event	Number assigned by the source software to identify events.
User	User name of the user logged on when the event occurred.
Computer	Computer name of the system where the event occurred.

Table 8.1 The Event Viewer column descriptions.

Log File	Description of Use
System	Used to log events generated by the operating system.
Security	System security events based on the Audit Policy setup are logged here.
Application	Both system and user application events are logged here.

Table 8.2 The event log file usage.

In addition to current log files, the Event Viewer can be used to view previously saved event files. This is of particular interest to high-security sites where saving security event files for several years is a normal practice.

The characteristics of the log files can be set on a per-log basis, and items that can be configured include the maximum log file size and how long events are kept before being overwritten. The defaults for the log settings are 512 K maximum size and 7 days before events are overwritten. Often, the first log setting to be changed is the security log overwrite time, because it is often advisable to keep a security audit trail for longer than a week. Events may be retained for a maximum of one year.

The basic one-line event message can be expanded to reveal more detail. The detail view not only provides a text description of the event record but sometimes includes additional hex data in the lower part of the event record. This data can be used by Windows NT support personnel to further diagnose the event. A sample detail record is shown in Figure 8.2.

Five different event types are used to categorize all events. These are shown in Table 8.3, along with a brief description of the audit events to which they are assigned. Event logs can be viewed on remote systems by using the Select Computer option from the Log menu. You must have administrator rights on the remote system to view the event logs.

As event logs become filled with data, locating a particular event becomes increasingly difficult. To help with this task, a search utility is included in the View menu. Also, you can set the order in which the events are displayed—for instance, oldest or newest first. In addition, you can filter the events, which is useful in removing irrelevant event records from the Viewer. This filter is only applied to the display and does not affect the actual log files.

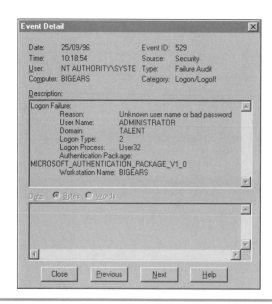

Detailed view of the event record.
Figure 8.2

The Event Viewer is static; no new event records will be added to the Viewer display as they occur. To display these new records, either use the View Refresh option or the F5 function key.

Event Type	Description
Error	Major error has occurred; used for the most serious errors.
Warning	Warning of impending problems or non-critical errors.
Failure Audit	Failed audit event has been received; logon failures generate this event.
Information	Used to indicate the successful conclusion of a system event.
Success Audit	Success audit event has been received; successful logons generate these events.

Table 8.3 Audit event types and descriptions.

Event log files can be saved for future use in one of three formats:

- *Event file format*—This is the native Event Viewer file format. When files are saved, the Event Viewer can be used to view these files directly.

- *Text file format*—Files in this format can be viewed in applications such as word processors.

- *Comma-delimited text file format*—Log files in this format can be viewed in applications such as spreadsheets.

The Task Manager

The Task Manager provides a quick and easy way of displaying your local system performance. This feature shows the current status of key items such as CPU and memory usage, as well as a recent history of usage.

To invoke the Task Manager, right-click the taskbar, then select Task Manager from the pop-up menu. To display the system performance, select the Performance tab. Note in Figure 8.3 that, in addition to CPU and memory usage, the actual physical

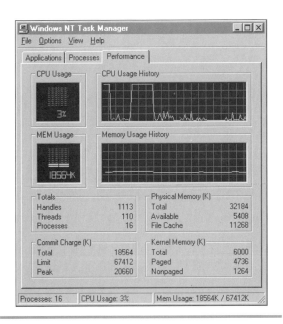

The Task Manager Performance tab.
Figure 8.3

available memory and the amount allocated to the system kernel is also displayed. When the Performance Monitor is running, a small graph is displayed next to the clock on the taskbar. This is a minimized version of the CPU usage graph.

Also of interest when analyzing your system's performance is the Windows NT Task Manager Processes display. This can be used to display the CPU and memory usage of each process currently running. You can stop an individual process from this window simply by highlighting the relevant process and clicking the Stop Process button. Also, by using the View Select Columns window, you can access additional information on the memory usage of each process. The Task Manager Processes display is shown in Figure 8.4.

The base priority of a process can be changed by using the task manager process list. Select the process from the process list and right-click, then select the Set Priority option from the menu.

Windows NT has 31 priority levels, which are divided into four base priority groups: idle, normal, high, and realtime. Once a process is set to run in one of these base priority groups, Windows NT will automatically adjust the process priority level up or

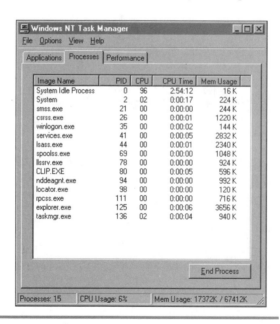

The Task Manager Processes tab.
Figure 8.4

down by two, depending on the actual processes' resource requirements. A more detailed explanation of the Windows NT priority levels is given in Chapter 1.

The Performance Monitor

As we have seen, the Task Manager Performance display gives an overall indication of both the current system load and the CPU time used for each process. Although this is a good starting point and allows the easy discovery of rogue processes, it does not allow you to ascertain the root causes of any performance issues. To do this, you need to use the Performance Monitor.

The Performance Monitor provided with Windows NT is arguably one of the best performance monitoring tools available for any operating system. With it, you can easily monitor all kinds of weird and wonderful operating system performance counters on both local and remote systems. However, the incorrect interpretation of the results presented frequently causes problems; it's quite easy to come to the wrong conclusions—especially if you don't fully understand the results being presented.

Unlike earlier operating systems, which contained many parameters that required tuning to enhance system performance, Windows NT has very few user-configurable parameters. For all intents and purposes, the operating system is self-tuning. This means that you are using the Performance Monitor purely to isolate the relevant hardware components that are causing the performance bottlenecks.

 The ultimate reference on all performance-related issues within Windows NT has to be the Windows NT Resource Kit by Microsoft Press. This book is clearly the best place to start your quest in understanding and interpreting Windows NT performance issues.

The Performance Monitor can present the monitoring information in several formats: line chart, histogram, or statistics counter screen. In addition, the monitored information can be obtained from numerous systems. An example Performance Monitor line chart is shown in Figure 8.5. This chart shows information gathered from both a local and a remote host.

A very useful feature of the Performance Monitor is the Alert function. This is used to trigger an alert message to a predefined set of users or to start a management program when certain conditions are met—for example, you might want to be informed when a certain disk has less than 10 percent disk space free.

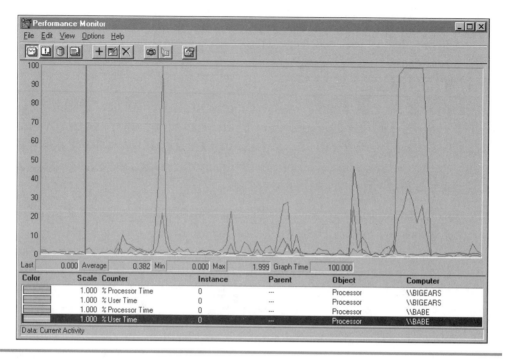

A Performance Monitor line chart.
Figure 8.5

When using the Alert feature on systems, the Performance Monitor can be run as a system service by using additional software available in the Windows NT Resource Kit. You can also set the Performance Monitor to automatically run at startup.

The list of available objects that can be monitored by the Performance Monitor depends on which system components are installed. Virtually all the Windows NT operating system components contain some type of counters that the Performance Monitor can use. The key common components available on all Windows NT systems are memory-, disk-, and processor-based counters. In addition, numerous network-based counters are also available, depending on which networking components have been installed. An overview of some of the key objects and their counters is shown in Table 8.4.

The object selection window for the line chart display of the Performance Monitor is shown in Figure 8.6. This window is displayed when you have used the Add To button.

When you select an object, you can then select the counters associated with the object and add them to the Performance Monitor, as required. As you add objects and

Object	Counter	Description
Processor	% Processor time	Time that the processor is devoting to doing something useful in relation to the CPU idle time.
	% User time	Percentage of total processor time devoted to user activities.
Memory	Available bytes	Total memory available for use; expressed in bytes.
	Page faults/sec	Number of virtual memory pages that weren't located in main memory.
Logical Disk	% Free space	Free disk space available for use in relation to total logical disk size.
	Avg. disk queue length	Number of disk reads and writes queued to the disk.

Table 8.4 Key performance objects and counters.

counters, a legend bar at the bottom of the window displays information about each line on the chart or bar of the histogram. The same objects shown in the Figure 8.5 line chart can be seen in histogram format in Figure 8.7.

You will need to enable the disk performance counters before any data can be collected for use with the Performance Monitor. The default is for disk performance counters to be disabled because of the small additional overhead required to maintain them. To enable and disable the counters at the Windows NT command prompt, use

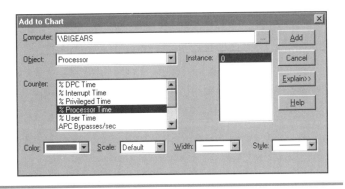

The Add to Chart window.
Figure 8.6

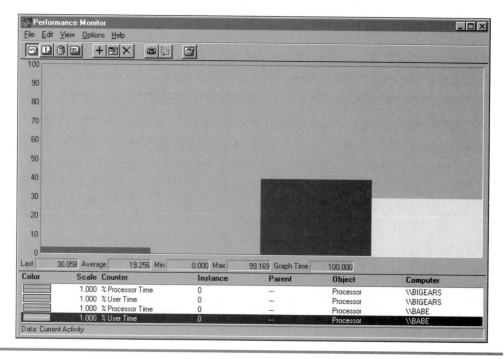

A histogram performance display.

Figure 8.7

diskperf -y for enable and **diskperf -n** for disable. You'll need to reboot for the changes to take effect.

It is often desirable to produce log data over a long period of time for the Performance Monitor to analyze at a later date. This is also useful in analyzing the changing pattern of usage that occurs on all servers. Configuring the Performance Monitor to log data is done by using the Log View menu. One advantage of using logged data is that you don't have to view the data in realtime, but can go straight to the areas you're interested in. Keep in mind that when you add objects to logs, only the entire object can be added and not individual counters.

If you can't achieve the view or obtain the information by using the views available in the Performance Monitor, an Export Data function is available that allows the collected data to be written to either tab-separated or comma-delimited files for analysis by additional spreadsheet tools.

The Network Monitor And Monitoring Agent

The Network Monitor that's shipped with Windows NT Server can be used to determine network load and performance statistics. The Network Monitor is the same product that is shipped with the Server Management Software (SMS), although the Windows NT Server version does have several functions disabled. The functions only available with SMS are Find Routers and Resolve Addresses From Names. Also, only traffic sent to and from the local system may be captured.

The Network Monitor window initially consists of four display areas. These are used to display a graph of network utilization, total network statistics, session statistics, and station statistics. The display areas can be configured as required. The initial Network Monitor display is shown in Figure 8.8.

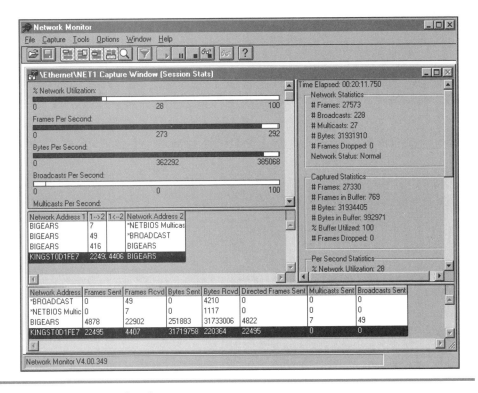

The Network Monitor display.

Figure 8.8

Practical

Guide To

Event And

System

Monitoring

The following section provides real-world examples on configuring, viewing, and interpreting the system event logs, as well as using the monitoring tools.

Locating And Examining Unsuccessful Logon Attempts

After an external audit of your company's security, the security team recommends that a weekly report of all unsuccessful logon attempts be produced for review by senior managers. (Like you haven't got enough work to do already; it's bound to be the senior managers who can't log on.)

Well, as the saying goes, you just work here. If that's what they want, that's what they'll get. The place to start is with the User Manager, because if the Audit policy is not configured to audit logon failures, you're not going to be able to gather the information you need to write your report.

1. Select Start|Programs|Administrative Tools|User Manager.

2. In the Policies menu, choose Audit. The Audit Policy window will be displayed. If it isn't already selected, choose Audit These Events.

3. Select the Logon and Logoff Success and Failure options, as shown in Figure 8.9. Click OK, and close the User Manager.

If you're wondering why you would select the Success option when you're only interested in Failure, remember that any figure for logon failures will be quite meaningless without the number of successful logons to compare it to. By selecting both options, you can present the actual percentage of logon failures.

Now, auditing is enabled. All user logon failures will generate a security audit event, which will be recorded in the security event log. So, at required intervals, you can check this log and see who can't remember their password:

1. Click Start|Programs|Administrative Tools|Event Viewer.

2. The Event Viewer title bar will display the name of the log currently viewed. If it doesn't read "Security Log," choose Security in the Log menu.

3. Logon failures will have the Padlock icon displayed next to them, and the category will be described as Logon/Logoff. Double-clicking an event entry provides you with a detailed view.

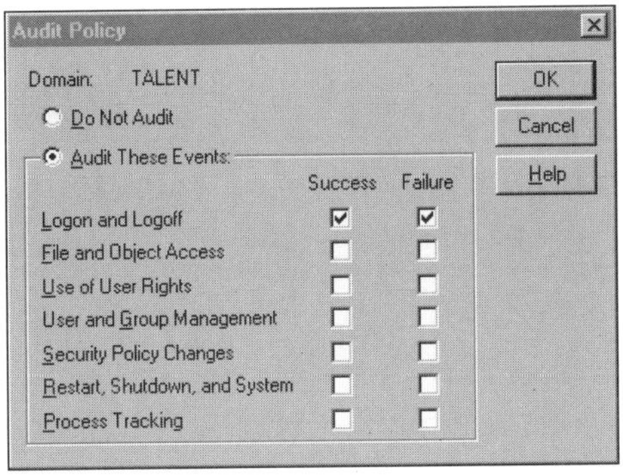

The Audit Policy window.

Figure 8.9

Great. The display shows who failed to logon and when, but there are lots of successful entries and only a few failures, making it a bit difficult to see what's going on. Isn't there a way to simplify the display and locate the failures? Yes, there is. The View Option menu contains a Filter function that can be used to filter out the entries you want to view.

1. In the View menu, choose Filter Events. The Event Filter window will be displayed.

2. In the Source box, choose Security from the drop-down list. In the Category box, choose Logon/Logoff. Make sure only Failure Audit is selected in the Types window.

3. Set the start and finish date to view the time period you are interested in. Click OK. The Security display will now be filtered to show just the logon failures between the specific dates and times. It's that simple.

Hey, wait a minute...what about the percentage of success-to-failure logons? Well, that's the trouble with good ideas. You always end up doing more work than you bargained for. You need to save the event log into a text file by using the Event Log Save function. Then, use your favorite spreadsheet to produce your amazing report.

Modifying Event Log Settings

Your company employs a lot of temporary workers on 30-day contracts. You decide that it might be a good idea to keep the security event records for at least 90 days. That way, if anything comes to light after one of these employees has left, you still have a record of what happened on the system. The motto "covering your back" (or other anatomical parts) comes to mind.

Remember, to make any changes to the log settings for either the system, security, or application logs, you must be a member of the Administrator group.

1. Click Start|Programs|Administrative Tools|Event Viewer.

2. In the Log menu, choose Log Settings. The Event Log Settings window will be displayed.

3. In the Change Settings For box, choose Security on the drop-down list.

4. Choose the Overwrite Events Older Than option. In the Days box, set the required number of days—in this case 90, as shown in Figure 8.10.

5. Click OK, and exit the Event Viewer.

All security events will now be logged in the security event log before getting overwritten.

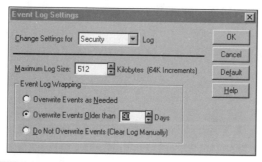

Configuring event logs.
Figure 8.10

Local System Performance Problems

You return from lunch only to find your workstation performance has taken a nose-dive. You have an urgent job to do—still trying to balance your bank account—and you want to know what's going on with your system. Well, a quick and easy way to check what's going on is to use the Task Manager Performance and Process displays.

1. Right-click the taskbar.

2. Choose Task Manager on the pop-up menu.

3. Click the Performance tab; the CPU and Memory Usage monitors will be displayed. You'll probably see your CPU time stuck at 100 percent, indicating you have a runaway process.

4. Click the Processes tab; the list of currently running processes will be displayed. Your runaway process should have its CPU usage time increasing at Warp Factor 9.

5. If the process is an application, you can use the End Process button to terminate the process. Click the process in question, then click End Process. You will receive a warning about the possible loss of data from terminating processes abruptly, as shown in Figure 8.11, but hey, the thing's broken. If the process is an actual system process, you will be denied access, so hit Reboot.

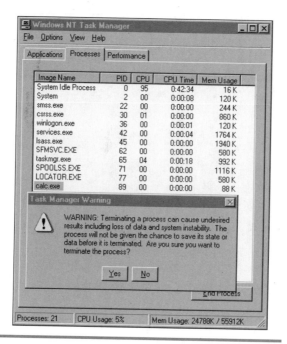

Terminating a process.
Figure 8.11

Changing A Process's Priority

Your Windows NT Server is just generating the end-of-month management reports. One particular management meeting has been scheduled earlier than usual, and the management team is hanging around your desk waiting for their reports to appear.

Now, as much as you like management, you do have several urgent and personal phone calls to make. So, increasing the priority of the report these guys are waiting for will get rid of them even quicker.

1. Right-click the taskbar.

2. Choose Task Manager on the pop-up menu.

3. Click the Process tab; the list of currently running processes will be displayed.

4. Select the process you wish to boost from the process list and right-click. From the pop-up menu select Set Priority. The four base priority groups are displayed in a pop-up menu, and the current process priority will have a check next to it. Select the required process priority from the menu.

In addition to increasing the base priority of the process you want to boost, decreasing the performance of the other reports being generated might be a good idea.

 It is not advisable to increase the priority of an application to run as a realtime process. The Windows NT internal software runs at the realtime priority, and a rogue application run at the same priority could create a resource conflict within Windows NT.

Monitoring System Performance

You have just received the minutes from the last management meeting, and the performance of one of the servers has been criticized as not being up to snuff. Although no one has mentioned it to you, you know this will end up being a political hot potato at the next management meeting. You'd better start gathering the information for your defense now.

The performance of a server can be both a subjective and emotive item. The users will always swear up and down that as soon as you leave the room, the server slows down. Your only recourse is to start logging the performance of the server in question and perhaps run a comparison with another.

1. Click Start|Programs|Administrative Tools|Performance Monitor.

2. In the Edit menu, choose Add To Chart, or use the Add To Chart button on the toolbar.

3. In the Computer box, select the system you want to monitor.

4. In the Object box, select Processor from the drop-down list. In the Counter list, click % Processor Time, and then click the Add button. Now, click % User Time in the Counter list, and then click the Add button again.

5. In the Object box, choose Memory from the drop-down list. Choose Available Bytes from the Counter list, and click the Add button. From the Counter list, choose Page Faults/Second. Click the Add button and then the Done button.

The Performance Monitor, shown in Figure 8.12, now displays a good selection of basic performance counters. If you want to run a comparison with another server, just click the Add To Chart button again and set the computer name to the required server. Now add the same counters, and you will have your comparison.

This simple performance test might not reveal the performance problem you have, but it's a good start. If a problem isn't shown, it might be worth adding the disk object to the chart and seeing if one particular disk is causing a performance bottleneck. This situation often occurs when several heavily used applications are located on the same disk.

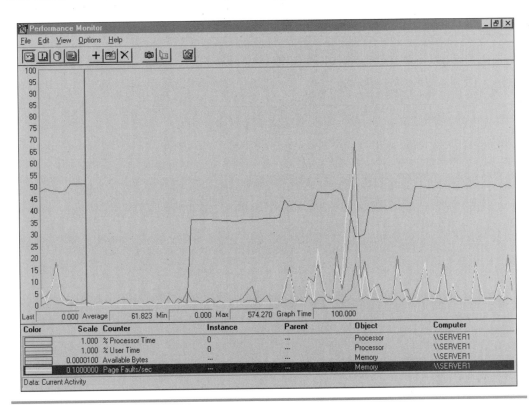

The Performance Monitor.
Figure 8.12

Logging And Viewing Performance Data

Although the performance data can be logged and viewed in realtime, as in the Monitoring System Performance example, sitting and watching the Performance Monitor all day is not the most productive use of anyone's time. Instead, the data can be logged and viewed at a later date:

1. Click Start|Programs|Administrative Tools|Performance Monitor.

2. In the View menu, choose Log, or use the Log button on the toolbar.

3. In the Edit menu, choose Add To Log. The Add To Log window will be displayed.

4. From the Add To Log window, choose the required computer name, and then the objects to log—for instance, Memory and Processor. Click the Done button. When logging performance data, only objects can be selected, not individual counters.

5. In the Options menu, choose Log. The Log Options window will be displayed. Select the required path and file name for the data to be logged to.

6. Click the Start button. The Performance Monitor will now start to log the selected objects. The Status box on the Performance Monitor will show the status of the object collection.

7. When enough data has been captured to give an overview of the system performance, choose Options|Log. In the Log window, click the Stop Log button.

The data that has been captured can now be displayed in whatever way suits your needs. For example, to display the captured data or any previously captured data in chart format, do the following:

1. Click Start|Programs|Administrative Tools|Performance Monitor.

2. In the View menu, choose Chart, or use the Chart button on the toolbar.

3. In the Options menu, choose Data From. The Data From window will be displayed.

4. Choose the Log File option. In the Input Log box, select the performance data file containing the logged data. Click OK. The file in use will be displayed at the bottom of the window.

5. In the Edit menu, choose Add To Chart. The computers and objects that have been logged will be shown. Select the counters that you are interested in, and add them to the chart.

Configuring System Alerts

The accounts department keeps running out of disk space on their main accounts disk. Once they get rid of all the garbage contained on the disk, they have plenty of spare capacity. However, they never clean it out until you shout at them, and by that time, they have already run out of room.

Now, you are not usually all that concerned about whether users can do their work if they are causing their own problems. However, the accounts department is a special case. After all, if they're not working, who's going to pay the vending company to fill up the vending machines? A fate worse than death: no coffee. It's a well-known fact that system administrators have to maintain a 50 percent coffee-to-blood ratio.

An early warning system is needed to issue a warning when the accounts disk has less than 10 percent of its disk space free. You can do this by configuring alerts in Performance Monitor.

1. Click Start|Programs|Administrative Tools|Performance Monitor.

2. In the View menu, choose Alert, or use the Alert button on the toolbar.

3. In the File menu, choose New Alert Settings.

4. In the Edit menu, choose Add To Alert. An Add To Alert window will be displayed, as shown in Figure 8.13.

5. In the Computer box, select the name of the computer system you use to monitor.

6. In the Object box, select Logical Disk from the drop-down list. In the Counter list, choose % Free Space.

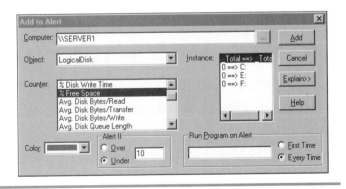

Adding alerts.
Figure 8.13

7. In the Alert If pane, select Under, and type in "10". Click the Add button, and then click the Done button.

8. In the Options menu, choose Alert. The Alert window will be displayed.

9. Click the network alert pane Send Message To Option, and in the dialog box, type in the name of the computer you want notified when the alert is tripped. This system must have the Messenger Service running to receive the alerts. Click OK, and the alert will be functional immediately.

The designated host will now receive notification each time the alert is tripped.

Network Monitoring

The users from one segment connecting to your server are losing connection from your application server. You decide to use the Network Monitor to try and track down the problem.

The Network Monitor is available with Windows NT Server, but not with Workstation. The monitor allows network utilization and errors, as well as captured network data, to be displayed and logged. If the Network Monitor hasn't been installed on your server, you will need to install it as follows:

1. Click Start|Settings|Control Panel.

2. Double-click the Network icon. Click the Services tab. Click the Add button, and select Network Monitor Agent and Tools from the network services list.

3. Click OK, and confirm the location of the Windows NT source software. The relevant software components will be added. Click the close button. The computer will need to be restarted before the Network Monitoring tool can be used.

To track down the problem using the Network Monitor, do the following:

1. Click StartPrograms|Administrative Tools|Network Monitor.

2. The Network Monitor window will be displayed. To start the monitor, click the Start Capture button. The current network utilization will be displayed, as shown in Figure 8.14.

3. To view the captured data, click the Stop And View Capture button. The Capture Data Summary window will be displayed. Double-click an entry for a more detailed view. The captured data can be saved with the Save As option in the File menu.

If any network errors are detected, they will be logged at the bottom of the total statistics pane.

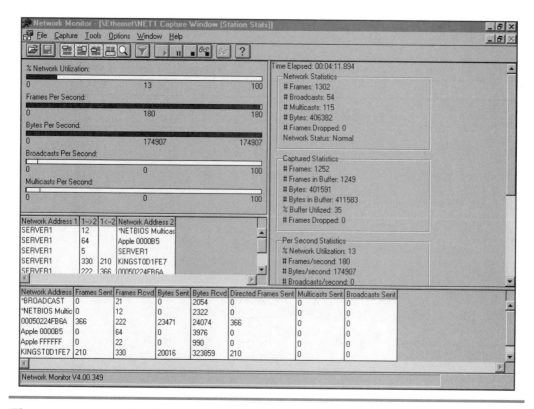

The current network utilization.

Figure 8.14

Quick Reference Specifications

The following are the bare-bones facts and figures.

- *All Event logs can only be cleared by an administrator.*

- *Event logs can be archived in three formats: native event format, plain text, and comma delimited plain text.*

- *Windows NT has 31 priorities, which are represented by one of four priority groups: idle, normal, high, and realtime.*

- *Disk performance counters are disabled by default. To collect the counter information, issue the **diskperf -y** command at the Windows NT command prompt.*

Utilities To Use

The utilities used in this chapter and their functions are listed in this section. Consider this section to be a memory aid for the busy system administrator.

Event Viewer

- *View system, security, and application logs.*
- *Set event log size and event retention time.*

Task Manager

- *Monitor local system performance.*
- *Boost process base priority.*
- *Terminate a process.*

Performance Monitor

- *Monitor local and remote system performance.*
- *View logged performance data.*
- *Define system alerts.*

Network Monitor

- *Monitor network utilization.*
- *Capture data packets.*
- *Monitor network errors.*

User Manager Or User Manager For Domains

- *Define the events to be audited.*

Chapter 9

Trouble-shooting

Administrator's Notes...

Chapter 9

Troubleshooting an operating system is one of those tasks you hope to avoid; when you are called upon to perform such tasks, your skills are often rusty. This chapter hopes to point you in the right direction concerning common troubleshooting techniques.

In addition to this chapter, you should refer to Chapter 8, which includes details on using the Event Viewer. This utility can often provide vital clues when you are trying to resolve a problem. Also, Chapter 3 provides details on the system startup process, which may help resolve boot problems.

Windows NT Diagnostics

Windows NT Diagnostics, contained in the Administrative Tools program group, can be used to display the current hardware and software configurations of both local and remote systems. The configuration information displayed by Windows NT Diagnostics is, in most cases, obtained from the Registry, but Diagnostics provides a much more user-friendly way of displaying the configuration data.

The Windows NT Diagnostics sheet has nine information pages available: Version, System, Display, Drives, Memory, Services, Resources, Environment, and Network. The System page is shown in Figure 9.1.

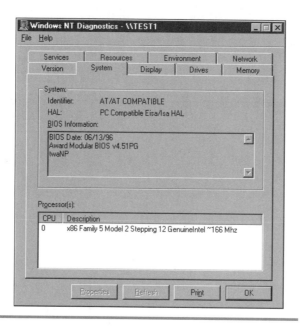

The System page in Windows NT Diagnostics.
Figure 9.1

Windows NT Boot Problems

As far as users are concerned, one of the most visible problems is a completely un-available system—in other words, the system doesn't start. If the system in question is a critical server, the pressure to return the server to service quickly mounts. Table 9.1 provides the most common boot problems and the fixes for them.

A boot floppy can be used to correct many boot problems quickly and efficiently. In fact, you can start the system by using the boot floppy, allowing you to resolve the boot problem at a more convenient time. (The Practical Guide in this chapter pro-vides full details on how to create a boot floppy.) The boot information detailed in this chapter applies to Windows NT systems running x86-based computers; RISC systems rely on onboard firmware to configure the initial boot process. Details on the RISC boot process can be obtained from the manufacturer of your RISC system.

Windows NT Boot Floppy

One of the most useful tools that system administrators can create is a Windows NT boot floppy. Although this floppy can't hold the entire Windows NT operating system, it

Boot Errors	Possible Causes and Fixes
NTDETECT failed.	NTDETECT.COM in the root folder of the boot drive is corrupt or missing. Try booting from a boot floppy. If this starts Windows NT successfully, copy NTDETECT from the boot floppy to the Windows NT boot disk root folder. Alternatively, you can boot using the Windows NT setup disk and repair the system using the emergency repair disk.
A kernel file is missing from the disk.	NTLDR in the root folder of the boot drive is missing. This problem can also be fixed by using either the boot floppy or the emergency repair disk to copy NTLDR into the root folder of the boot drive.
Windows NT could not start because of a computer disk hardware configuration problem. Could not read from the selected boot disk. Check boot path and disk hardware.	The path and device boot line in BOOT.INI could be incorrect. Refer to Chapter 3 for more on the structure of the boot command line.
No error message displayed, but the system starts Windows NT without displaying the operating system selection menu and waiting for the boot time-out period.	The BOOT.INI file is missing from the root folder of the boot drive. Once the system has started, log on to Windows NT and copy BOOT.INI from the boot floppy to the root folder of the boot disk.
Windows NT could not start because the following file is missing or corrupt: <WINNT ROO>\SYSTEM32\NTOSKRNL.EXE. Please re-install a copy of the above file.	The reason and resolution given could be the correct action to take; however, if the BOOT.INI file is pointing toward the wrong partition, this error can occur. Try booting using the boot floppy. If this works, check or replace the BOOT.INI file. If the boot floppy displays the same error message, use the Windows NT setup disk and the emergency repair disk to resolve the problem.

Table 9.1   Common boot problems.

can contain the key boot files that can be used to diagnose and repair boot problems. The boot floppy is the only way to start a Windows NT system with a failed primary mirror member system disk. (Further details are given in the Practical Guide.)

The Windows NT boot floppy is a generic boot disk. In other words, if the hardware configuration of your Windows NT systems are all the same, with Windows NT located on the same disk partitions, a single boot floppy can be used to support them.

Emergency Repair Disk

The emergency repair disk provides methods for both fixing problems with the Windows NT system partition and restoring the Windows NT configuration. The emergency repair disk cannot be used to directly start the system—in other words, it is not bootable—but it can be used in conjunction with the Windows NT setup disks.

The biggest problem with the emergency repair disk is that one emergency repair disk is required per computer, so 300 computers require 300 emergency repair disks. For this reason, corporate users often do not use emergency repair disks for Windows NT workstations. If they experience a serious problem with a workstation, they will wipe the current installation of Windows NT and install a new copy. (This, of course, means that local data storage is forbidden.)

A description of the files copied to the emergency repair disk is given in Table 9.2.

Failed Mirror Set Members

Windows NT Server can be configured to use disk mirroring to provide disk fault tolerance. (Details on disk mirroring and other disk fault-tolerant techniques can be found in Chapter 4.) The steps required to replace a failed mirror member are relatively straightforward:

1. Break the mirror set. This will assign separate drive IDs to the mirror set members.

2. Either select a new drive with the required free space or replace the fault drive and create a new mirror set using the good former mirror set member.

When a system disk (the boot drive from which Windows NT starts) is part of a mirror set, and the shadow, or secondary, member of the shadow set fails, the procedure to resolve the failure is the same as that we have just seen. However, if the primary boot disk—the one the computer physically accesses when starting from the hard drive, known as C:—fails, the system will, of course, continue running if the failure

File Name	Description
AUTOEXEC.NT	Used in the initialization of the virtual MS-DOS environment.
CONFIG.NT	Used in the initialization of the virtual MS-DOS environment.
DEFAULT._	Compressed copy of the HKEY_USERS\DEFAULT Registry key.
NTUSER.DA_	Compressed copy of the default user profile, NTUSER.DAT.
SAM._	Compressed copy of the HKEY_LOCAL_MACHINE\SAM Registry key.
SECURITY._	Compressed copy of the HKEY_LOCAL_MACHINE\SECURITY Registry key.
SETUP	Contains log of which files were installed and a checksum for each file, which can be used to detect and repair file corruption.
SOFTWARE._	Compressed copy of the HKEY_LOCAL_MACHINE\SOFTWARE Registry key.
SYSTEM	Contains the disk configuration information. This file will only exist if you have saved the disk configuration information to the emergency repair disk by using the Configuration Save utility in the Disk Administrator. The data contained in this file is also included in the SYSTEM ._ file.
SYSTEM._	Compressed copy of the HKEY_LOCAL_MACHINE\SYSTEM Registry key.

Table 9.2   Contents of the emergency repair disk.

occurs while Windows NT is in use. The actual replacement and mirroring of the replacement drive does present some difficulties, however. In the Windows NT Server Resource Kit, Microsoft provides two ways to recover the failed primary disk. The first method includes the following steps:

1. Break the mirror set, and remove the failed drive.

2. Replace the failed drive with the shadow drive.

3. Install a new drive as a replacement for the shadow drive.

4. Restart the system, and reestablish the mirror relationship.

The second method is to:

1. Break the mirror set.

2. Back up the entire shadow disk, including the Registry.

3. Replace the failed drive, install a new copy of Windows NT onto the replacement drive, and then restore the backup of the shadow disk onto the replacement drive.

4. Restart the system, delete the shadow disk partition, and then reestablish the mirror relationship.

Both methods have limitations and are not straightforward. A third method for recovering the primary disk is given in the practical guide of the chapter. Try testing all three methods to see which one best suits your hardware configuration.

NT Backup

Both Windows NT Workstation and Server are provided with a file backup utility, as shown in Figure 9.2. This utility is located in the Administrative Tools program group and can be used to back up both files and folders (this is not a disk-backup product). The Backup utility can be used with any of the supported Windows NT file systems.

The Backup utility can perform various types of backups, including incremental backups. However, because no scheduling capabilities exist within the Backup utility, backups must either be performed manually or scheduled using the AT command line utility.

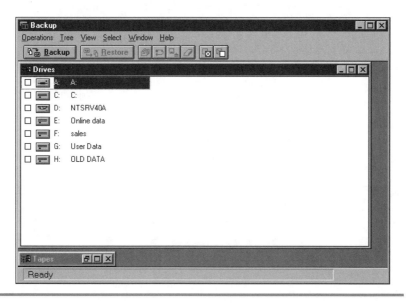

The Windows NT Backup utility.
Figure 9.2

(Details of this utility can be found in Chapter 11.) Both options are less than ideal, leading to a range of third-party backup solutions being developed for Windows NT that provide not only backup scheduling, but many other features as well.

Service Update Packs

Service update packs are issued by Microsoft to resolve problems and provide enhancements to Windows NT. These packs are cumulative—you only have to install the latest service pack to gain all the fixes and functions of all the service packs for the particular version of the operating system. This means that the service packs are quite large. For example, Service Pack 4 for Windows NT 3.51 reached 10 MB.

Service packs are language-specific, so you need to obtain the correct language version for the operating system you are using. The US service pack, however, is used for most English-speaking countries, such as the United Kingdom.

Practical

Guide To

Troubleshooting

The following section provides real-life examples and step-by-step instructions on how to troubleshoot key areas of Windows NT. To avoid politician-speak—that is, saying a lot but not actually telling you anything—I describe the recovery techniques I use with my particular hardware. The techniques you use could be slightly different. However, you can use the steps described in this section as templates to implement your own recovery methods.

Creating A Boot Floppy

Being the sensible person you are, you decide to create a boot floppy to help with any future system fault-finding you might have to do. You have, of course, been prompted to do this after a less-experienced system administrator accidentally removed the NTLDR file from one of the remote servers.

As you discovered, the absence of NTLDR did not affect Windows NT while it was running. However, the next time the server was rebooted, it failed to restart, causing you to gain at least three gray hairs.

1. Insert a blank floppy disk into your computer's floppy disk drive. Double click the My Computer icon to access the My Computer window, as shown in Figure 9.3.

2. Select the floppy disk drive icon where you inserted the blank floppy disk. From the My Computer menu, choose File|Format to access the Format dialog box, as shown in Figure 9.4.

3. Choose Start to format the floppy disk. A Format warning dialog box appears. Click OK to start the disk format. The status bar at the bottom of the dialog box indicates how far the format operation has progressed.

4. When the format is finished, click OK and then Close.

The My Computer window.
Figure 9.3

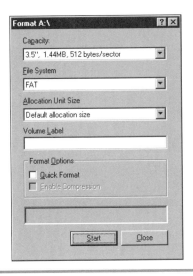

The Format dialog box.

Figure 9.4

5. Choose Start|Programs|Windows NT Explorer. The Windows NT Explorer window appears.

6. Some of the files required for the boot floppy are hidden. To display hidden files in Windows NT Explorer, choose View|Options. The Options window appears, as shown in Figure 9.5. Choose the Show All Files option in the Hidden Files pane, and click OK. You are returned to the Windows NT Explorer window.

7. Select the root folder of the boot disk—for example, the C: icon in the left-hand pane of Windows NT Explorer.

8. Select the following files in the root folder of the boot disk: NTLDR, BOOT, and NTDETECT. While holding down the right mouse button, drag and drop the files onto the floppy disk in the left-hand pane. When you release the right mouse button, a pop-up menu appears. From this menu, choose Copy Here. The selected files are copied to the boot floppy.

Depending on the configuration of your system, you might need to copy two extra files onto the boot disk: BOOTSECT.DOS, which is used if your system is configured for a dual boot (e.g., MS-DOS or Windows NT), and if your system boots from a SCSI disk drive, NTBOOTDD.SYS. If these files don't exist in the root folder of your computer's boot hard disk drive, you do not require them.

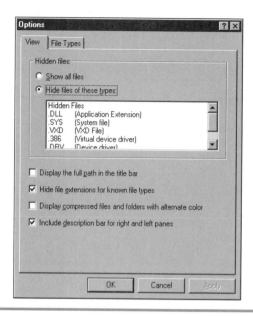

The Windows NT Explorer Options window.

Figure 9.5

9.   While the boot floppy is in the floppy disk drive, restart the computer to verify that the boot floppy functions correctly.

It's a good idea to reformat the floppy disk you intend to use as your Windows NT boot floppy before copying the required boot files to it. The floppy needs to be reformatted under Windows NT, because the FAT structure used by NT is different than the structure created when a floppy disk is formatted under MS-DOS.

Creating A Fault-Tolerant Boot Floppy

Now that all your Windows NT servers are using disk mirroring on their system disks, you decide it's about time you created a fault-tolerant boot floppy. Although the procedure detailed in this section starts from scratch, you could modify a normal Windows NT boot floppy by adding the correct boot line, as described in Steps 9 through 11 of this example.

1. Insert a blank floppy disk into your computer's floppy disk drive. Double click the My Computer icon to access the My Computer window.

2. Select the floppy disk drive icon where you inserted the blank floppy disk, and from the My Computer menu, choose File|Format. The Format dialog box appears.

3. Click Start to format the floppy disk. A Format warning dialog box appears. Click OK to start the disk format. The status bar at the bottom of the dialog box indicates how far the format operation has progressed.

4. When the format is finished, click OK and then Close.

5. Choose Start|Programs|Windows NT Explorer. The Windows NT Explorer window appears.

6. Some of the files required for the boot floppy are hidden. To display hidden files in Windows NT Explorer, choose View|Options. The Options window appears. In the Hidden Files pane, choose the Show All Files option, and click OK. You are returned to the Windows NT Explorer window.

7. Select the root folder of the boot disk—for example, the C: icon in the left-hand pane of Windows NT Explorer.

8. Select the following files in the root folder of the boot disk: NTLDR, BOOT, and NTDETECT. While holding down the right mouse button, drag and drop the files onto the floppy disk in the left-hand pane. When you release the right mouse button, a pop-up menu appears. From this menu, choose Copy Here. The selected files are copied to the boot floppy.

9. In the left-hand pane of Windows NT Explorer, double click the floppy disk icon. Right click the BOOT.INI file that you just copied to the floppy. From the pop-up menu that appears, select Properties.

10. In the File Properties dialog box that appears, clear the Read-only attribute box, and click OK. You are returned to the Windows NT Explorer window.

11. Double click BOOT.INI. Notepad is started, and the BOOT.INI file opened. As the last line to this file, append the path information required to boot the shadow set member. (Chapter 3 gives details on the format of the BOOT.INI boot line structure.) In this example, the shadow set member is attached to the same disk controller but has drive ID 1; a complete BOOT.INI file of this configuration is shown in Figure 9.6. Exit Notepad, saving the file back to the floppy.

12. Verify that the fault-tolerant boot floppy has been created correctly by starting the system with the floppy. If all is well and the system disk is in fact a mirror set, the system should begin the Windows NT Startup and crash shortly after displaying the blue screen. This is expected behavior, indicating that the fault-tolerant boot disk is starting the system from the shadow disk.

A fault-tolerant BOOT.INI file.
Figure 9.6

Recovering From A Failed Primary Mirror Member System Disk

"This is not a drill, repeat, not a drill." These are the words that strike terror in the heart of any system administrator. You have lost your primary mirror member system disk, which means your system is no longer directly bootable and, of course, it will be your PDC. (PDCs are described in Chapter 7, but you will recognize the importance of them when users start beating you over the head with their keyboards.)

Well, thinking they were safe with mirrored disks, they laughed at you when you said you wanted to test your recovery techniques. But *you* knew that one day you would be proven right.

1. If the system is up and running when the primary mirror member system disk failure occurs, Windows NT will continue to function by using the shadow mirror member, and you can proceed to Step 2. If the system is currently down and cannot be started—in other words, the primary system disk has failed during the power-on and start sequence, Windows NT will not be directly bootable. Insert the fault-tolerant boot floppy, and start Windows NT from this by using the shadow disk. (Details on creating a fault-tolerant boot floppy are given in the previous tutorial.)

2. It is recommend practice to take a full backup of the remaining system disk mirror member in case the recovery of the mirror set fails for any reason. The steps required to do this depend on the backup utility you use. Once the backup is finished, you can continue with the recovery as follows. Choose Start|Programs|Administrative Tools|Disk Administrator. The Disk Administrator window appears. Figure 9.7 shows a system disk mirror set when the primary mirror member has failed.

3. Select the mirror set by clicking either of the mirror set members. Choose Fault Tolerance|Break Mirror. A dialog box appears. Click Yes to confirm that the mirror set should be broken. Because this is a system disk mirror set, the system needs to be restarted. Click Yes to continue. The mirror set is marked to be broken, and Disk Administrator now displays the mirror set members as two different volumes, as shown in Figure 9.8.

4. Choose Partition|Commit Changes Now. Click OK to acknowledge the Emergency Repair Disk informational dialog box that appears. Click OK again to restart the system.

5. When the system shuts down, but before it restarts, power-off the system and replace the failed drive. Start the system using the fault-tolerant boot floppy, remembering to select the shadow member to boot from.

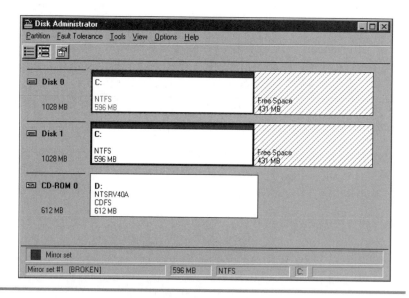

Disk Administrator with a failed mirror set member.
Figure 9.7

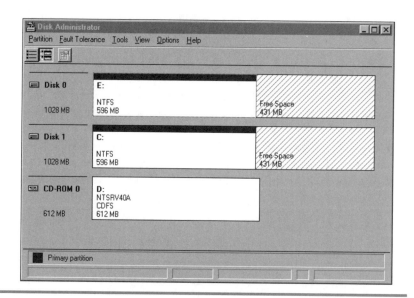

Disk Administrator with the mirror relationship broken.
Figure 9.8

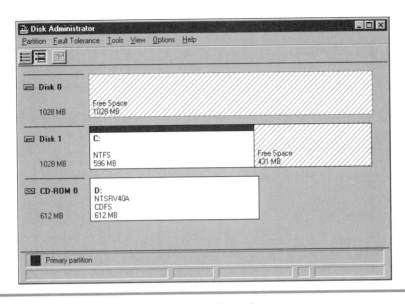

Disk Administrator with the failed drive replaced.

Figure 9.9

6. Choose Start|Programs|Administrative Tools|Disk Administrator. Figure 9.9 shows the Disk Administrator view of both the newly installed disk and the former shadow member, which is being used as a single-volume system disk.

7. A new mirror set can now be established. Select the current system disk, hold down the CTRL key, and select the new disk. Choose Fault Tolerance|Establish Mirror. A Disk Administrator informational dialog box appears regarding the creation of a fault-tolerant boot floppy. Click OK. The Disk Administrator displays the mirror set.

8. Choose Partition|Commit Changes Now. Click Yes to confirm the save changes operation. Click Yes again to confirm that the system can be restarted.

9. Click OK to acknowledge the informational dialog box regarding the emergency repair disk. Click OK to initiate the system shutdown. The system restarts and will once again start using the fault-tolerant boot floppy and selecting the shadow disk to start from.

10. Choose Start|Programs|Administrative Tools|Disk Administrator. The mirror set is indicated as initializing, as shown in Figure 9.10.

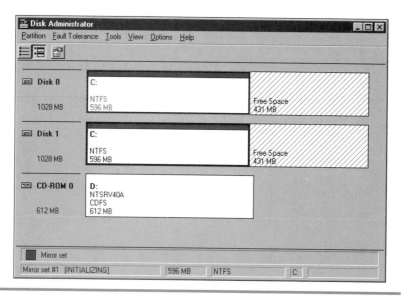

The mirror set initializing.
Figure 9.10

11. Once the initializing is finished, the mirror set is shown as healthy. You must wait until this occurs before proceeding. (The Disk Administrator display is static; press F5 to refresh the display.) Restart the system, and let the startup sequence boot from the mirror set; in other words, don't use the fault-tolerant boot floppy. If the new drive is functioning correctly and the mirror operation was successful, the system will attempt to start Windows NT but will crash and display the blue crash screen. This is expected behavior that verifies the new disk is functioning correctly.

12. The mirror partition contained on the shadow disk now needs to be removed (the shadow disk is the original shadow disk, not the new disk that has just been installed). There are two ways to delete the shadow partition. The first is to boot an MS-DOS boot disk and use FDISK to remove the partition. The second method uses the Windows NT setup disks to start the operating system installation procedure, a portion of which allows you to create and delete partitions. (Full details of this procedure can be found in Chapter 10.) Whichever method you use, make sure that the correct partition is removed.

13. Once you have removed the shadow disk partition, restart the system and allow Windows NT to start up in the normal way from the newly installed system disk—in other words, don't use the fault-tolerant boot floppy. The system should now start successfully. Once the system has started, log on and continue.

14. Choose Start|Programs|Administrative Tools|Disk Administrator. The system disk mirror set will now have a status of broken, because one-half of the mirror is no longer available. Choose Fault Tolerance|Break Mirror, and confirm you want to break the mirror set by clicking the Yes button. Click Yes again to confirm the system restart requirement.

15. Choose Partition|Commit Changes Now. Click OK to acknowledge the informational dialog box regarding the emergency repair disk. Click OK to initiate the system restart. Allow the system to restart normally.

16. Choose Start|Programs|Administrative Tools|Disk Administrator. Select the system disk, and while holding down the CTRL key, select the disk where you want to recreate the shadow partition. Release the CTRL key. Choose Fault Tolerance|Establish Mirror. Click OK to acknowledge the informational dialog box that appears regarding the fault-tolerant boot floppy.

17. Choose Partition|Commit Changes Now. Click Yes to confirm the changes. Click Yes again to confirm the system restart requirement. Click OK to acknowledge the informational dialog box that appears regarding the emergency repair disk. Click OK to initiate the system restart. Allow the system to restart in the normal way. The mirror set is created, and fault tolerance is once again provided for the system disk on this computer.

This example shows the recovery of the system disk primary mirror member. Some hardware configurations might require a different technique to perform the recovery; however, this example can be used as a template to assist in your own techniques. Always attempt a trial recovery of your system before the system is in use. A real failure is not the time to test your recovery technique.

Creating An Emergency Repair Disk

Although emergency repair disks are often not created for workstations, they are always needed for servers. In your rush to get Windows NT running, you haven't yet created one. Do it now! You won't be able to when the system is broken.

1. Choose Start|Programs|Windows NT Explorer. The Windows NT Explorer window appears.

2. Locate and double click the RDISK utility located in the SYSTEM32 subfolder.

3. The Repair Disk Utility dialog box appears, as shown in Figure 9.11. Click Create Repair Disk. A Repair Disk Utility warning message appears, advising that the floppy disk will be reformatted. Click OK.

The floppy disk is now formatted, and the Setup data files are copied to the disk.

In this example, an emergency repair disk was created using the information contained in the %SYSTEMROOT%\REPAIR folder. This folder is not automatically updated when changes are made to the operating system. To update this information and create a new emergency repair disk containing this information, choose Update Repair Info when using the Repair Disk utility.

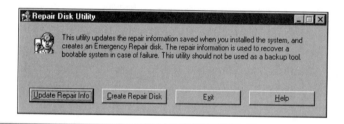

The Repair Disk Utility dialog box.
Figure 9.11

Restoring The Administrator Password

You've gone and done it, haven't you? You forgot the Administrator password and, of course, you don't have another Administrator account to use. Well, it had to happen, so I'm glad it has happened to you instead of me. Here's how to restore the password by using the emergency repair disk. (Let's hope you can remember what the password was when you created the emergency repair disk. If you can't, you'll need to reinstall Windows NT.)

1. Start the computer using Setup disk 1 of the Windows NT source software. You will be prompted when you should insert Setup disk 2.

2. The Welcome To Setup screen appears, with various options. The option required for this example is Repair; press R to select this.

3. You can now set the repair options. By default, all options are set, indicated by an X in the adjacent checkboxes. Available repair options include:

   - Inspect Registry Files

   - Inspect Startup Environment

   - Verify Windows NT System Files

   - Inspect Boot Sector

4. We're only interested in restoring the Administrator password, so deselect all of these options except Inspect Registry Files. (The Security Account Manager, which holds the Administrator password, is managed via the Registry). Select Continue, and press Enter. The Mass Storage Detection screen appears.

5. Press Enter to continue. You are prompted to insert Setup disk 3 and press Enter when ready. The mass storage devices are detected. If the detected device list is correct and you do not have any device support disks, press Enter. Alternatively, if the list is incorrect or you have device support disks from the manufacturer, press S. For this example, we'll assume the list is correct, so we will press Enter. The device and file system device drivers are loaded.

6. The Setup screen inquires if you have the emergency repair disk for this system; press Enter to confirm that you do. You are prompted to insert the emergency repair disk and press Enter when ready.

7. The Windows NT boot hard disk is checked, and the Windows NT Restore Registry screen appears, allowing the following Registry components to be restored:

- SYSTEM (system configuration)

- SOFTWARE (software configuration)

- DEFAULT (default user profile)

- NTUSER.DAT (new user profile)

- SECURITY (security policy)

- SAM (user account database)

8. Select the Security option by highlighting it and pressing Enter. An X is placed in the checkbox adjacent to the selected option. Now, press Continue and then Enter. The Registry security components are restored.

9. You are prompted to remove the emergency repair disk from the floppy disk drive and press Enter to restart the computer. Once the computer has restarted Windows NT, you will be able to log on using the Administrator account and password as it was set when the emergency repair disk was created.

When you restore the Security Account Manager database, only the Administrator and Guest accounts will be restored—in other words, the built-in accounts. All other accounts will be lost and must be either re-created or restored from your backups. This is why you should only use the emergency repair disk to restore the Administrator password as the last resort.

Fixing A Corrupt Operating System

You have had a power failure, and now, Windows NT seems to contain some corrupt system files. The emergency repair disk contains a checksum for each file that was generated when the file was installed. This checksum can be used to determine where the problem is.

1. Start the computer using Setup disk 1 of the Windows NT source software. You will be prompted when you should insert Setup disk 2.

2. The Welcome To Setup screen appears, with various options. The option required for this example is the Repair facility; press R to select this.

3. You can now set the repair options. By default, all options are set, as indicated by an X in the adjacent checkboxes. Available Repair options include:

    - Inspect Registry Files

    - Inspect Startup Environment

    - Verify Windows NT System Files

    - Inspect Boot Sector

4. We are attempting to fix a suspected corruption, so leave all of these options selected, and press Continue.

5. The Mass Storage Detection screen appears. Press Enter to continue. You are prompted to insert Setup disk 3 and press Enter when ready. The mass storage devices are detected. If the detected device list is correct and you do not have any device support disks, press Enter. Alternatively, if the list is incorrect or you have device support disks from the manufacturer, press S. For this example, we'll assume the list is correct, so press Enter. The device and file system device drivers are loaded.

6. The Setup screen inquires if you have the emergency repair disk for this system. Press Enter to confirm that you do. You are prompted to insert the emergency repair disk and press Enter when ready. You will be prompted to insert the Windows NT source software into your CD-ROM drive if it isn't already in the drive.

7. The Windows NT boot hard disk is checked, and the Windows NT Restore Registry screen appears, which allows the following Registry components to be restored:

    - SYSTEM (system configuration)

    - SOFTWARE (software configuration)

- DEFAULT (default user profile)
- NTUSER.DAT (new user profile)
- SECURITY (security policy)
- SAM (user account database)

8. Because we don't want to change the system configuration (in other words, replace the Registry), press Enter to continue.

9. Any files that have been discovered to be different from the original files that Setup copied during the Windows NT installation are displayed. You are given the following options:

- To skip this file, press ESC. The file will not be repaired.
- To repair this file, press Enter.
- To repair this file and all other non-original files, press A.
- To exit Setup, press F3.

10. We want to repair the files that are corrupt, so press Enter. The file is repaired. The Setup program continues to examine the files on the hard disk; any other files not matching the originals are displayed and can be repaired in the same way. When finished, press Enter to restart your computer.

Any files that have been updated by either the installation of a program or the installation of a service update pack will be flagged as being different from the original files. This does not necessarily mean the files are corrupt; you will have to use you own judgment in each individual case. Any service pack updates should be reapplied to the system once the repair process is over.

Saving The Disk Configuration Information

You have just created some disk stripe sets on one of your systems. You know if you ever have to reinstall Windows NT on this system, these disk stripe sets will be unavailable if you don't have a copy of the disk configuration information. With thinking like this, you could go far (well, at least to the other end of the office).

1. Choose Start|Programs|Administrative Tools|Disk Administrator. The Disk Administrator window appears.

2. Choose Partition|Configuration|Save. The Insert Disk dialog box appears, prompting you to insert a formatted floppy disk. The disk configuration information will be saved onto this disk. Click OK when ready. Click OK to acknowledge the successful saving of the disk configuration information.

 The emergency repair disk contains a copy of the disk configuration information. This copy is held within the Registry data. Often, system administrators store a separate copy of the disk configuration information on the emergency repair disk by using the technique shown in this example. This is done to both simplify the restore process if the data is required and to enable drives to be moved between different Windows NT systems without having to restore Registry data. If you do store the data on the emergency repair disk, remember that each time the emergency repair disk is updated, the data contained on it is deleted.

Restoring The Disk Configuration Information

You have been having a few unusual problems with your system of late that you can't quite put your finger on. To try and resolve these problems, your hardware maintainer has sent along an engineer to run some diagnostics on your system.

You can tell by the panicked look on the engineer's face that she hasn't used a Windows NT system before, but she does offer to run a diagnostic test on your system, which you gratefully accept. Once the diagnostics start to run, she mentions something about disk corruption and says she will repair it for you. Just as her finger hits the Enter key, you scream, "No!" But, it's too late. Expecting a FAT partition, her diagnostics have totally destroyed your NTFS system partition. (You didn't want to leave early tonight anyway, did you?)

1. Figure 9.12 shows the disk configuration of your system before the system partition was mangled. Because the system is now no longer bootable, you'll need to use the Windows NT setup disks to reinstall Windows NT. Full details on the Windows NT installation process are given in Chapter 10. Take care not to delete or overwrite any partitions other than the system partition when doing this.

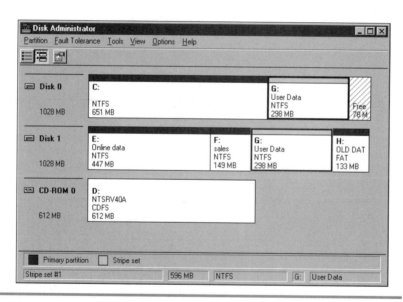

The Disk Administrator view of the disk configuration.
Figure 9.12

2. Once Windows NT is reinstalled, choose Start|Programs|Administrative Tools|Disk Administrator. The Disk Administrator window appears. The disk configuration after the reinstallation of Windows NT is shown in Figure 9.13. Note that the drive letter assignments have changed and that access to the disk stripe set has been lost completely. If you have stored the disk configuration information onto a floppy disk, as described in the previous tutorial, you only need to perform Step 3. If you haven't, and you are using the emergency repair disk, you need to perform the rest of the steps.

3. Choose Partition|Configuration|Restore. A dialog box appears, warning that the drive configuration information will be changed to match the previously saved configuration data. Click Yes to continue. The Insert Disk dialog box is displayed, prompting you to insert the disk that contains the saved disk configuration information. Click OK to continue. The configuration data is restored, and a system restart is required. Click OK to restart the system.

4. Start the computer using Setup disk 1 of the Windows NT source software. You will be prompted when you should insert Setup disk 2.

5. The Welcome To Setup screen appears, with various options. The option required for this example is Repair, so press R to select this facility.

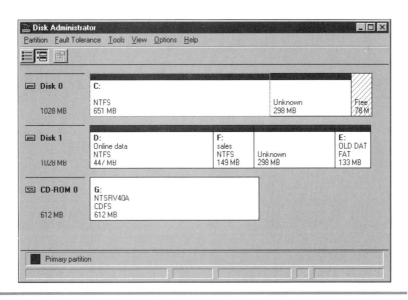

The Disk Administrator view of the disk configuration after installation.
Figure 9.13

6. You can now set the repair options. By default, all options are set, as indicated by an X in the adjacent checkboxes. Repair options available include:

    •   Inspect Registry Files

    •   Inspect Startup Environment

    •   Verify Windows NT System Files

    •   Inspect Boot Sector

7. Because we're only interested in restoring the disk configuration information, deselect all of these options except Inspect Registry Files (the disk configuration information is held as part of the Registry). Select Continue, and press Enter.

8. The Mass Storage Detection screen appears. Press Enter to continue. You are prompted to insert Setup disk 3 and press Enter when ready. The mass storage devices are detected. If the detected device list is correct and you do not have any device support disks, press Enter. Alternatively, if the list is incorrect or you have device support disks from the manufacturer, press S. In this example, we'll assume the list is correct, so we'll press Enter. The device and file system device drivers are loaded.

9. The Setup screen inquires if you have the emergency repair disk for this system. Press Enter to confirm that you do. You are prompted to insert the emergency repair disk and press Enter when ready.

10. The Windows NT boot hard disk is checked, and the Windows NT Restore Registry screen appears. This allows the following Registry components to be restored:

    •   SYSTEM (system configuration)

    •   SOFTWARE (software configuration)

    •   DEFAULT (default user profile)

- NTUSER.DAT (new user profile)

- SECURITY (security policy)

- SAM (user account database)

11. Select the System option by highlighting it and pressing Enter. An X is placed in the checkbox adjacent to the selected option. Now, select Continue, and press Enter. The disk configuration information is restored. You are prompted to remove the emergency repair disk from the floppy disk drive and press Enter to restart the computer. Figure 9.14 shows the disk configuration as shown by the Disk Administrator once the system has started.

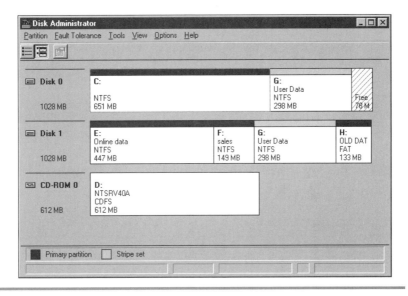

The Disk Administrator view of the disk configuration once restored.

Figure 9.14

Clearing Stuck Print Jobs

You find that you have a buildup of print jobs that just aren't coming out on the print device. Everything looks OK, but it just doesn't work. A gentle kick might help (that is, a *software* kick, so don't try reshaping the server case with your shoe).

1. Choose Start|Settings|Control Panel. The Control Panel appears.

2. Double click the Service icon. The Service window appears.

3. Select the Spooler from the Service list, and choose Stop. The Services confirmation box appears, as shown in Figure 9.15. Click Yes to stop the spooler service.

4. With the spooler service still selected in the service list, press Start. The spooler service is restarted.

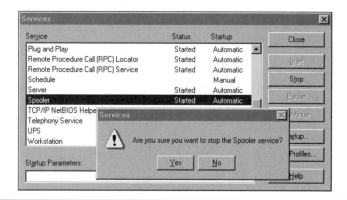

The Services confirmation dialog box with the spooler service highlighted.

Figure 9.15

Diagnosing RAS Connection Problems

You are trying to join the worldwide revolution known as the Internet. Unfortunately, you are having a tough time connecting to your Internet service provider. Although these guys probably use Windows NT in the infrastructure, when you tell them you want to connect to them using NT, they repeat the chant, "Windows 3.1 and 95 only." At best, they will provide you with the bare minimum of details on how to connect to them; after that, you're on your own. Enabling logging for the RAS connections might be a good idea. At least you can see what's going on.

1. Choose Start|Run. The Run dialog box appears.

2. Click the Browse button, and use the Browse dialog box to select the Registry Editor REGEDT32 located in the SYSTEM32 subfolder. Click OK. The Registry Editor appears.

3. Select HKEY_LOCAL_MACHINE\SYSTEM\CurrentControlSet\Services\RasMan\ Parameters. This subkey contains the logging data value. By default, this will be set to 0.

4. Double click the logging value. The DWORD Editor appears, as shown in Figure 9.16. Change the data value to 1, and click OK.

5. You'll need to stop and restart the remote access service (RAS) for this change to take effect. To do this, choose Start|Settings|Control Panel. The Control Panel appears.

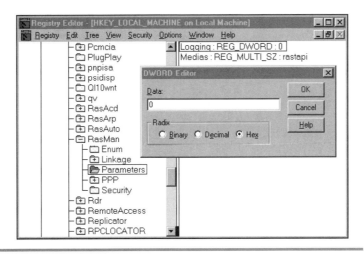

The Registry DWORD Editor dialog box.
Figure 9.16

6. Double click the Services icon to access the Services window. Select the Remote Access Server service in the Service list, and click the Stop button. A Service warning dialog box appears. Click Yes to stop the service. Once the service has stopped, make sure the service is still selected, and click the Start button. The RAS service restarts.

The next time the RAS is used, a log file will be created in the SYSTEM32\RAS subfolder. This log file (DEVICE.LOG) will show the connection sequence used when RAS communicates with the modem and performs the logon operation.

Diagnosing Problems With PPP Connections

Well, your quest to become the fastest surfer on the planet is stalled at the moment. You've finally managed to get a connection going to your Internet service provider, but now the PPP (point-to-point protocol) connection seems to be failing. OK, let's turn that logging value on.

1. Choose Start|Run. The Run dialog box appears.

2. Click the Browse button, and use the Browse dialog box to select the Registry Editor REGEDT32 located in the SYSTEM32 subfolder. Click OK. The Registry Editor appears.

3. Select HKEY_LOCAL_MACHINE\SYSTEM\CurrentControlSet\Services\RasMan\ PPP\Logging, as shown in Figure 9.17.

4. Double click the logging value, which by default is set to 0. The DWORD Editor is displayed. Change the data value from 0 to 1, and click OK.

5. You'll need to stop and restart the RAS for this change to take effect. To do this, choose Start|Settings|Control Panel. The Control Panel appears.

6. Double click the Services icon to access the Services window. Select Remote Access Server in the Service list, and click the Stop button. A Service warning dialog box

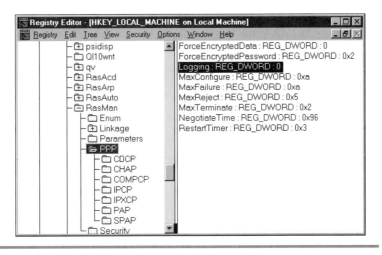

The PPP logging Registry value entry.
Figure 9.17

appears. Click Yes to stop the service. Once the service has stopped, make sure the service is still selected, and click the Start button. The RAS service will restart.

The PPP.LOG file is created in the SYSTEM32\RAS subfolder and will log the PPP connection information.

Configuring System Recovery

You need to think about configuring system recovery now before you have a problem. The debugging information generated by the system recovery could be used by a Windows NT specialist to diagnose the reason for the system failure.

1. Choose Start|Settings|Control Panel. The Control Panel appears.

2. Double click the System icon to access the System Properties sheet.

3. Click the Startup/Shutdown tab. The Startup/Shutdown page appears, as shown in Figure 9.18. The following system recovery options can be defined on this page:

   - Write An Event To The System Log

   - Send An Administrative Alert

   - Write Debugging Information To

   - Overwrite Any Existing File

   - Automatically Reboot

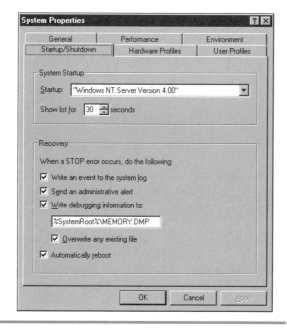

The Startup/Shutdown page in System Properties.

Figure 9.18

The options you set obviously depend on your particular requirements. As a minimum, Write An Event To The System Log should be set. If the system in question is a Windows NT Server, you might well want it to automatically reboot so the system won't be down if it stops overnight.

Generating A Diagnostic Report

You have been given the task of gathering the hardware configuration of several workstations. The Windows NT Diagnostic tool can be used to generate a report for this purpose. This example produces a summary report. A more detailed report can be generated if required.

1. Choose Start|Programs|Administrative Tools|Windows NT Diagnostics. The Windows NT Diagnostics sheet appears.

2. Choose File|Save Report. The Create Report dialog box appears.

3. Select the report parameters you require—whether the report should be produced for all tabs or just the current tab and how detailed it should be. Use the Destination pane to define the output location of the report. Figure 9.19 shows the output for a summary report generated for the Display tab.

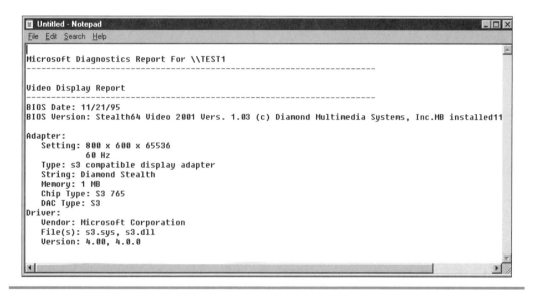

A Windows NT Diagnostics summary report.
Figure 9.19

Displaying IRQs In Use

You need to install an additional disk controller on your system, and you don't want to pull all of the other boards out of the computer to discover how they are already configured. You did, of course, have a record of the hardware configuration of this system, but it was misplaced during the last office reorganization.

1. Choose Start|Programs|Administrative Tools|Windows NT Diagnostics. The Windows NT Diagnostics sheet appears.

2. Click the Resources tab. The IRQs currently in use appear on the page, as shown in Figure 9.20.

The Resources page in Windows NT Diagnostics.
Figure 9.20

3. To display the properties of a particular IRQ, select the IRQ from the Resources page by clicking on it, and then choose the Properties button. The IRQ Properties window appears, as shown in Figure 9.21.

4. You can view the I/O ports by using the I/O Port button on the Resources page. To obtain a hard copy of this information, click the Print button.

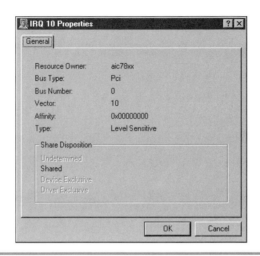

The IRQ Properties window.
Figure 9.21

Resolving Device Detection Problems

The system is causing some problems on startup that seem to be device-related. What you really need is a way of seeing what devices are detected and what their configurations are.

1. Choose Start|Programs|Windows NT Explorer. Windows NT Explorer appears.

2. In the left-hand pane, select the root folder of the boot drive. Because NTDETECT.COM is a hidden, read-only file, you need to change the file attributes before you can rename the file.

3. Choose View|Options. The Options window appears. In the Hidden Files pane of the View sheet, select the Show All Files option, and click OK.

4. You are returned to Windows NT Explorer. Right click NTDETECT.COM in the right-hand pane and from the pop-up menu that appears, select Properties. The Properties window appears, as shown in Figure 9.22. Clear the Read-only checkbox, and click OK.

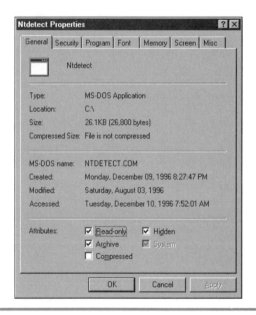

The Ntdetect Properties window.
Figure 9.22

5. You are returned to the Windows NT Explorer window. Right click NTDETECT.COM again, and from the pop-up menu, select Rename. Type the temporary name you want to assign to the current version of NTDETECT.COM, and press Enter. When the confirmation box appears, confirm the file rename operation by pressing Enter again.

6. Insert the Windows NT Source CD-ROM into your CD-ROM drive. In the left-hand pane of Explorer, click the CD-ROM drive containing the Source CD-ROM. Locate and select NTDETECT.CHK, which is located in the \SUPPORT\DEBUG\i386 subfolder. Right click the NTDETECT.CHK file, and while holding down the right mouse button, drag and drop the file into the root folder of the boot disk. Release the right mouse button and from the pop-up menu that appears, select Copy Here.

7. Right click the NTDETECT.CHK file that is now in the root folder of the boot drive, and select Rename from the pop-up menu that appears. Rename the file as NTDETECT.COM.

Now when the system restarts, the detected devices are displayed and any problems will be shown. Once the device detection has finished, press any key to display the hardware configuration information. This configuration information will show a detailed view on each detected device. Press any key to view each detected device. When all devices have been viewed, the startup procedure will continue.

 When you have finished using the check version of NTDETECT, do not forget to reinstate the original version. If you don't, each time your computer restarts, you will be taken into the device detection screens, and the system will not automatically reboot.

Running The Hardware Detection Tool

You have installed a new I/O board into your Windows NT workstation, and now the system won't successfully start Windows NT. You have consulted the documentation that came with the I/O board, and it hasn't been much help. Before you return the I/O board as being DOA, it might be worth running the Hardware Detection Tool, just in case you have a device clash.

1. Insert a blank formatted floppy disk into your floppy disk drive and the Windows NT CD-ROM into the CD-ROM drive.

2. Choose Start|Programs|Windows NT Explorer. Select the CD-ROM drive and locate the \SUPPORT\HQTOOL folder. Within this folder, double click the MAKEDISK file to create the device detection floppy.

3. Start the computer using the device detection floppy you are having hardware problems with. Now, use the Hardware Detection Tool to scan and save your hardware configuration. Figure 9.23 shows a sample of the output file produced by running this tool.

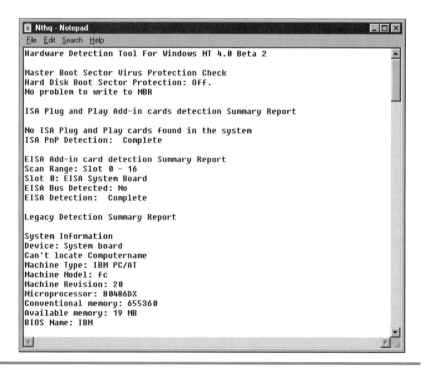

A sample output from the Hardware Detection Tool.
Figure 9.23

Chapter 9: Practical Guide

Installing A Service Update Pack

You have been running Windows NT for a while, and it seems to be pretty stable. There have been one or two minor problems, though, and you decide to install the latest service pack to see if it will resolve the problems.

1. Choose Start|Programs|Windows NT Explorer. The Windows NT Explorer window appears.

2. Locate and double click the service update pack—for example, NT4_SPL1.EXE, which is a self-extracting update file containing documentation.

3. Double click the README text file to review which problems this update fixes and any additional installation steps that might be required for your configuration.

4. Double click the UPDATE file. The update procedure begins, and the Windows NT Setup screen appears. The Setup Message dialog box appears. Click OK to confirm the update operation. After the update runs, a reboot is required for the updated system to be used. Click the Restart Computer button when the update is finished.

Checking Disks For Errors

As part of your weekly checks, you decide to scan all disks on your server for disk errors. (Haven't you learned yet that turning over stones often gives you a nasty surprise?) Your heart's in the right place, though. Finding and correcting problems before the users notice them is the efficient way to work.

1. Choose Start|Programs|Windows NT Explorer. The Windows NT Explorer window appears.

2. In the left-hand pane, right click the disk drive you want to check. From the pop-up menu that appears, select Properties.

3. The Drive Properties sheet is displayed. Click the Tools tab to access the Tools page. Select the Check Now button in the Error-checking pane. The Check Disk dialog box appears, as shown in Figure 9.24.

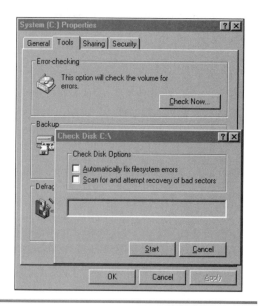

The Check Disk dialog box.
Figure 9.24

4. Two options can be set in the Check Disk dialog box:

    • Automatically fix filesystem errors

    • Scan for and attempt recovery of bad sectors

To perform the automatic fix option, the Check Disk utility must be able to gain exclusive access to the disk. If the disk you are checking is the Windows NT system disk, this will be impossible because files are permanently open on this disk. To overcome this problem and allow the system disk to be checked, the Check Disk utility will display an option box that allows the disk to be marked for checking the next time Windows NT is started. This will cause the boot-time version of the utility to run.

Quick Reference Specifications

The following are the bare-bones facts and figures.

- *The emergency repair disk can be used to restore the Administrator password, the Registry, and the disk configuration.*

- *System fixes and updates are provided via service update packs.*

- *Crash dumps can be written to a file for later analysis.*

Utilities To Use

The utilities used in this chapter and their functions are listed in this section. Consider this a memory aid for the busy system administrator.

My Computer Icon

- Formatting floppy disks.

Disk Administrator

- Saving and restoring disk configurations.

RDISK

- Creating and updating emergency repair disks.

REGEDT32

- Enabling logging for RAS and PPP connections.

Services Icon

- Stopping and starting the spooler service.

System Icon

- Configuring the recovery options after a system failure.

Windows NT Setup Disks

- Restoring data from the emergency repair disk.
- Checking for system disk corruption.

Windows NT Diagnostics

- Generating diagnostic reports.
- Displaying assigned IRQs.

NTDETECT.CHK

➤ *Displaying hardware devices as they are detected.*

Windows NT Explorer

➤ *Creating Windows NT boot floppies.*

➤ *Performing disk error checking.*

Chapter 10

Installation And Basic Configuration

Administrator's Notes...

Chapter 10

Windows NT has certain hardware criteria that must be met before the operating system can be installed. The system resource requirements are outlined in this chapter. In addition, you should check the hardware compatibility list (HCL) provided with the Windows NT distribution to ensure that the hardware you are going to install Windows NT on is supported. The HCL lists all hardware that has passed compatibility testing with Windows NT.

System Requirements

The system resource requirement for both Windows NT Workstation and Server are given in this section.

Windows NT Workstation

- 32-bit x86-based computer system, 486/25 MHz minimum, or a system based on a supported RISC processor, such as MIPS, Alpha, or PowerPC.

- VGA or higher resolution display adapter.

- 12 MB of memory minimum with x86-based system; 16 MB of memory recommended. 16 MB of memory required with RISC system.

- CD-ROM drive or access to a CD-ROM across the network.

- 117 MB minimum free disk space on x86-based systems: 148 MB with RISC systems.

- Mouse or other pointing device.

- 3.5-inch disk drive with x86-based systems.

Windows NT Server

- 32-bit x86-based computer system, 486/25 MHz minimum, or a system based on a supported RISC processor, such as MIPS, Alpha, or PowerPC.

- VGA or higher resolution display adapter.

- 16 MB of memory.

- CD-ROM drive.

- 125 MB minimum free disk space on x86-based systems; 160 MB with RISC systems.

- Mouse or other pointing device.

- 3.5-inch disk drive with x86-based systems.

Licensing Modes

Two different licensing modes are used with Windows NT: per server and per seat. During the installation of Windows NT, you will be prompted to choose one of these modes. The following section provides details on both modes to help you make your choice.

If you are unsure of which method to choose, select the per server licensing mode; this mode allows you a one-way conversion to per seat licensing, if per server turns out to be unsuitable for your needs. The licensing agreement prohibits a per seat licensing mode to be changed to a per server.

Per Server

Each client access license is assigned to a particular server and allows only one connection to that server for basic network services. If you select per server licensing, you must specify the number of client access licenses you have purchased. Per server is often more economical for networks in which clients connect to only one server.

Per Seat

When using the per seat licensing mode, each computer that accesses a Windows NT server for basic network services requires a client access license. Once a client computer is licensed, it may be connected to any number of Windows NT servers. The per seat licensing mode is often more economical in networks where the clients connect to several Windows NT servers.

 Basic network services is defined as accessing file or print services—in other words, connecting to folder and printer shares.

Practical

Guide To

Installation

And Basic

Configuration

The following section provides real-life examples and step-by-step instructions on how to install and configure Windows NT.

Installing Windows NT Workstation

Okay, this is it, the moment you have been waiting for. The management has agreed that a single Windows NT workstation can be installed for evaluation, with the plan to eventually switch to Windows NT. Get this right, and the world (okay, the desktop) is yours.

1. Start the computer with the Windows NT Workstation Setup disk 1 in the floppy drive. The Windows NT Setup program starts. You are prompted to insert Workstation Setup disk 2 at the appropriate time.

2. The installation continues. The Welcome To Setup screen appears, with four options:

    *   To learn more about Windows NT Setup before continuing, press F1.

    *   To set up Windows NT now, press Enter.

    *   To repair a damaged Windows NT version 4.0 installation, press R.

    *   To quit Setup without installing Windows NT, press F3.

3. Press Enter. The Windows NT Setup mass storage device detection screen appears. This is used to either automatically detect or manually define the mass storage devices available on this system. Two options are available:

    *   To continue, press Enter. Setup will attempt to detect mass storage devices in your computer.

    *   To skip mass storage device detection, press S. Setup will allow you to manually select SCSI adapters, CD-ROM drives, and special disk controllers for installation.

Certain types of mass storage devices can't be automatically detected. In fact, the detection attempt can cause the computer to lock up. If this happens, reboot and use the manual detection method.

4. Press Enter, and the device scan is performed. You are prompted to insert Workstation Setup disk 3. Press Enter. The device detection continues, and relevant device drivers are loaded. A list of detected mass storage devices is displayed, along with the following two options:

    *   To specify additional SCSI adapters, CD-ROM drives, or special disk controllers for use with Windows NT, including those for which you have a device support disk from a mass storage device manufacturer, press S.

- If you do not have any more device support disks from a mass storage device manufacturer, or you do not want to specify additional mass storage devices for use with Windows NT, press Enter.

5. Press Enter. The necessary device and file system drivers are loaded, and you are prompted to insert the Windows NT CD-ROM. The Windows NT licensing agreement is displayed. Press Page Down to read the whole agreement. When you reach the bottom of the agreement, press F8 to accept the terms and conditions of the agreement or press Esc if you do not accept them. If you press Esc, the installation will terminate.

6. Press F8. Setup scans your computer and prepares a hardware list, which includes the computer type, display, keyboard type, keyboard layout, and the pointing device. Any of these items can be manually changed if they don't match your requirements. To change an item, use the up or down arrow key to highlight the item you want to change, and then press Enter. The alternatives for that item are then displayed. When all items are correct, press Enter.

7. Windows NT Setup displays a list of available disk partitions. Use the up or down arrow keys to highlight a partition in the list. The following options are available:

   - To install Windows NT on the highlighted partition or unpartitioned space, press Enter.

   - To create a partition in the unpartitioned space, press C.

   - To delete the highlighted partition, press D.

   Because Workstation is being installed on a new computer with blank disks, the partitions need to be created.

8. Press C. The Setup program displays the Create New Partition screen, which provides two options:

   - To create the new partition, enter a size, and press Enter.

   - To return to the previous screen without creating the partition, press Esc.

9. The minimum and maximum size of the partition that can be created is displayed. Set the partition size, and press Enter. You are returned to the partition screen, and the newly created partition is shown in the partition list.

10. Press Enter, and the highlighted partition is selected. Because the partition is newly created, it needs to be formatted. Two file systems are available: FAT or NTFS. (Details of

each can be found in Chapter 4.) For this example, we'll use NTFS. Select the required file system, and press Enter. The partition is formatted, and a progress bar is displayed to show the status of the operation. You are then required to indicate the folder where you want Windows NT installed. The default folder is \WINNT. Press Enter.

11. Setup now examines your hard disk for corruption. This is a two-stage test. The first is a mandatory basic test. The second is a more exhaustive test, which can take some time on large-capacity disks. The following two options are available:

    • To allow Setup to perform an exhaustive secondary examination on your hard disk(s), press Enter.

    • To skip the exhaustive examination, press Esc.

12. Because this is a new system, it's a good idea to run the secondary examination, so press Enter. You are prompted to insert the Windows NT Workstation CD-ROM into your CD-ROM drive and press Enter when ready. Setup copies the required files to your hard disk. A progress bar shows the status of the copy operation. The initial portion of Setup is now completed. You are prompted to remove any floppy disks and compact disks from your computer. Press Enter, and your computer restarts.

13. The setup process marks the partition you have selected to be converted to NTFS. The system is restarted and the partition converted.

 This conversion step is required because the initial setup procedure only understands the FAT file system. Therefore, the partition is created as a FAT partition, the initial Windows NT system files are copied to this partition, and once the setup procedure actually starts running Windows NT, the partition is converted to NTFS.

14. You are prompted to insert the Windows NT Workstation CD-ROM into your CD-ROM drive. Click OK. Setup continues copying files from the CD-ROM to the newly created disk partition. The Windows NT Setup Wizard is displayed, which will guide you through the rest of the setup procedure. The next three parts of Setup are described by Windows NT as:

    • Gathering information about your computer.

    • Installing Windows NT Networking.

    • Finishing Setup.

15. Click Next. The Windows NT Workstation Setup Wizard then provides you with four different setup options. The options and their descriptions are shown in Table 10.1.

Setup Options	Description
Typical	Recommended for most computers.
Portable	Options useful for portable computers are installed during Setup.
Compact	To save disk space, none of the optional components are installed.
Custom	For advanced users. All available setup options may be customized.

Table 10.1   Setup installation options.

16. Select Typical, and click Next. The Name And Organization dialog box appears. Enter your full name and the name of your company in the relevant boxes. This information will be used to personalize your installation of Windows NT.

17. Click Next. The Registration dialog box appears. Enter the 10-digit CD key, located on a yellow sticker on the back of your CD case. Click Next. The Computer Name dialog box appears. The computer name must be unique on your network and can be up to 15 characters. Enter the name in the box, and click Next.

18. You now need to set the Administrator Account password. This password can be up to 14 characters. Enter and confirm the password in the box, and click Next.

19. The Emergency Repair Disk dialog box appears. (The use of this disk is discussed in Chapter 9.) Two options are available:

    • Yes, create an emergency repair disk (recommended).

    • No, do not create an emergency repair disk.

    Yes will be selected by default.

20. Click Next. The Windows NT Components dialog box appears. This can be used to select the software components to be installed. Two options are available:

    • Install the most common components (recommended).

    • Show me the list of components so I can choose.

    The Install option will be selected by default. The software components that aren't installed at this point can be installed later by using the Control Panel utilities.

21. Click Next. The second part of this portion of the setup is now highlighted on the setup screen: Installing Windows NT Networking. Click Next. The Windows NT Workstation Setup dialog box appears, with two options:

- Do not connect this computer to a network at this time.

- This computer will participate on a network.

22. Participating on a network is the default. This option has two sub-options:

- Wired to the network. Your computer is connected to the network by an ISDN adapter or network adapter.

- Remote access to the network. Your computer uses a modem to remotely connect to the network.

Wired to the network is the default.

23. Click Next. Setup displays the Search For A Network Adapter dialog box. Click the Start Search button. The computer is scanned for a network adapter. If your adapter is not found, choose Select From List to manually select the correct adapter. From the Select Network Adapter dialog box, select the adapter, and click OK.

24. Click Next. The Network Protocols dialog box appears. Three protocols are available: TCP/IP, NWLink, and NetBEUI. (Details of each of these protocols can be found in Chapter 7.) TCP/IP is the default. Click Next. Setup is now ready to install the components you have selected. Individual software components may display dialog boxes to obtain more information.

25. Click Next. Depending on the type of network adapter installed, a Network Card Setup dialog box may be displayed. This is used to enter the hardware configuration details for the network adapter. Click Continue. The TCP/IP installation begins. A TCP/IP Setup dialog box appears, asking whether you want to use a DHCP server. A DHCP server can be used to dynamically provide an IP address. (Further details on DHCP servers can be

found in Chapter 7.) Click No to refuse the DHCP server. The TCP/IP Properties sheet appears. Enter the IP address and the subnet mask. Click OK. Setup is now ready to start the network software.

25. Click Next. The Workgroup Or Domain Configuration dialog box appears. Select either the Workgroup or Domain option, and enter the relevant domain or workgroup name. Click Next.

26. Click Finish. The Date/Time Properties sheet appears. Select the required time zone and whether the system should automatically adjust the clock for daylight saving changes. Click the Date & Time tab. Set the correct date and time.

27. Click Close. The Display Properties dialog box and the detected display adapter type are displayed. Click OK. Use the Display Properties dialog box to select the required display settings. Select Test. A display test pattern is displayed for 5 seconds. The Testing Mode dialog box appears. Click Yes if the display test was successful. Otherwise, click No, and change the display settings before repeating the test. Click OK to save the display settings.

28. Setup continues copying the Windows NT source files and configuring the installed software components. The default NTFS security is also set. You are prompted to insert a floppy disk into drive A, which will be used to create the emergency repair disk. Click OK. The floppy disk is formatted, and the configuration files are copied to the disk. The setup is now complete. You are prompted to remove all disks from the floppy and CD-ROM drives.

29. Click Restart Computer. The computer system restarts, and the installation is complete.

Installing Windows NT Server

Well, the Windows NT Workstation trial went so well that they've decided to try out Windows NT Server.

1. Insert the Windows NT Server Setup disk 1 into the floppy disk drive, and start your computer. Windows NT Setup is started. You are prompted to insert Server Setup disk 2.

2. Press Enter. The installation continues. The Welcome To Setup screen is displayed, with four options:

    *   To learn more about Windows NT Setup before continuing, press F1.

    *   To set up Windows NT now, press Enter.

    *   To repair a damaged Windows NT version 4.0 installation, press R.

    *   To quit Setup without installing Windows NT, press F3.

3. Press Enter. The Windows NT Server Setup Mass Storage Device Detection screen appears. This is used to either automatically detect or manually define the mass storage devices available on this system. Two options are available:

    *   To continue, press Enter. Setup will attempt to detect mass storage devices in your computer.

    *   To skip mass storage device detection, press S. Setup will allow you to manually select SCSI adapters, CD-ROM drives, and special disk controllers for installation.

 Certain types of mass storage devices can't be automatically detected. In fact, the detection attempt can cause the computer to lock up. If this happens, reboot and use the manual detection method.

4. Press Enter. You are prompted to insert Server Setup disk 3. Press Enter when ready. The device detection continues, and the relevant device drivers are loaded. A list of detected mass storage devices is displayed, with the following two options:

    *   To specify additional SCSI adapters, CD-ROM drives, or special disk controllers for use with Windows NT, including those for which you have a device support disk from a mass storage device manufacturer, press S.

    *   If you do not have any more device support disks from a mass storage device manufacturer, or you do not want to specify additional mass storage devices for use with Windows NT, press Enter.

5. Press Enter. The device and file system drivers are loaded. You are prompted to insert the Windows NT Server compact disk into the CD-ROM drive. Press Enter when ready. The Windows NT licensing agreement is displayed. Press Page Down to read the whole agreement. When you reach the bottom of the agreement, press F8 to accept the terms and conditions of the agreement, or press Esc if you do not accept them. If you press Esc, the installation will terminate.

6. Press F8. Setup scans your computer and prepares a hardware list, which includes the computer type, display, keyboard type, keyboard layout, and pointing device. Any of these items can be manually changed if they don't match your requirements. To change an item, use the up or down key to highlight the item you want to change. Then press Enter. The alternatives for that item are then displayed. When all items are correct, press Enter.

7. Windows NT Setup displays a list of available disk partitions. Use the up or down arrow keys to highlight a partition in the list. The following options are available:

   • To install Windows NT on the highlighted partition or unpartitioned space, press Enter.

   • To create a partition in the unpartitioned space, press C.

   • To delete the highlighted partition, press D.

   Because Server is being installed on a new computer with blank disks, the partitions need to be created.

8. Press C. The Setup program displays the Create New Partition screen, which provides two options:

   • To create the new partition, enter a size, and press Enter.

   • To return to the previous screen without creating the partition, press Esc.

9. The minimum and maximum size of the partition that can be created is displayed. Set the partition size, and press Enter. You are returned to the partition screen, and the newly created partition is shown in the partition list. The following three installation options are available:

   • To install Windows NT on the highlighted partition or unpartitioned space, press Enter.

   • To create a partition in the unpartitioned space, press C.

   • To delete the highlighted partition, press D.

10. Press Enter. The highlighted partition is selected. Because the partition is newly created, it needs to be formatted. Two file systems are available: FAT or NTFS. (Details of each can be found in Chapter 4.) For this example, we'll use NTFS. Select the required file system, and press Enter. The partition is formatted, and a progress bar is displayed to show the status of the operation. You are then required to indicate the folder where you want Windows NT installed. The default folder is \WINNT.

11. Press Enter. Setup now examines your hard disk for corruption. This is a two-stage test. The first is a mandatory basic test. The second is a more exhaustive test, which can take some time on large-capacity disks. The following two options are available:

    • To allow Setup to perform an exhaustive secondary examination of your hard disk(s), press Enter.

    • To skip the exhaustive examination, press Esc.

12. Because this is a new system, it's a good idea to run the secondary examination, so press Enter. You are prompted to insert the Windows NT Server CD-ROM into your CD-ROM drive and press Enter when ready. Setup copies the required files to your hard disk. A progress bar shows the status of the copy operation. The initial portion of Setup is now completed. You are prompted to remove any floppy disks and compact disks from your computer. Press Enter, and your computer restarts.

13. The setup process sets the partition you have selected to be converted to NTFS. The system is restarted and the partition converted.

 This conversion step is required because the initial setup procedure only understands the FAT file system. Therefore, the partition is created as a FAT partition, the initial Windows NT system files are copied to this partition, and once the setup procedure actually starts running Windows NT, the partition is converted to NTFS.

14. Setup continues. You are prompted to insert the Windows NT Server CD-ROM into your CD-ROM drive. Click OK. Setup continues copying files from the CD-ROM to the newly created disk partition. The Windows NT Setup Wizard is displayed, which will guide you through the rest of the setup procedure. The next three parts of Setup are described by Windows NT as:

    • Gathering information about your computer.

    • Installing Windows NT Networking.

    • Finishing Setup.

15. Click Next. The Name And Organization dialog box appears. Enter your full name and the name of your organization.

16. Click Next. The Registration dialog box appears. Enter the 10-digit CD key (located on the back of the CD-ROM case on a yellow sticker).

17. Click Next. The Licensing Mode dialog box appears. Two client licensing modes are available with Windows NT Server:

    • Per server. Used for concurrent connections. Each concurrent connection to this server requires a separate client access license.

    • Per seat. Each computer that accesses Windows NT Server requires a separate client access license.

    Use License Manager (located in the Administrative Tools program group) to record the number of client access licenses purchased to avoid violation of the licensing agreement.

18. Select the required licensing type, and click Next. The Computer Name dialog box appears. Enter a computer name of up to 15 characters. This name must be unique on your network.

19. Click Next. The Server Type dialog box appears. Three different types of Windows NT Server are available: primary domain controller (PDC), backup domain controller (BDC), and standalone server. (Chapter 7 gives more detail on each type.) Choose one of the three types. For this example, we'll choose the PDC option, which is the default.

20. Click Next. The Administrator Account dialog box appears. Enter and confirm a password of up to 14 characters for the built-in Administrator account.

21. Click Next. The Emergency Repair Disk dialog box appears, with the following options:

    • Yes, create an emergency repair disk (recommended).

    • No, do not create an emergency repair disk.

    The default is Yes. Click Next. The Windows NT Server Setup dialog box appears. This can be used to remove or add software components from the setup procedure, or the default can be accepted. Click Next to accept the default settings.

22. You are now ready to install Windows NT Networking. Click Next. Two options are given for how the computer will participate on a network:

- • Wired to the network. Your computer is connected to the network by an ISDN adapter or a network adapter.

- • Remote access to the network. Your computer uses a modem to remotely connect to the network.

Wired to the network is the default.

23. Click Next. The Microsoft Internet Information Server can be installed at this point. The default is for the server to be installed, so clear the checkbox to bypass the server installation.

24. Click Next. Setup displays the Network Adapter dialog box, which is used to define and configure the network adapters. Click the StartSearch button to scan for network adapters. If your network adapter isn't found, click Select From List and manually select the correct adapter. Click OK. The network adapter is added to the Network Adapter list.

25. Click Next. The Network Protocols dialog box appears. Three protocols are available: TCP/IP, NWLink, and NetBEUI. (Chapter 7 details each of these protocols.) TCP/IP and NWLink are the default.

26. Click Next. The Network Services dialog box appears, which lists the network services that will be installed by the setup procedure. You can add additional services by choosing Select From List. Click Next. Setup is now ready to install the networking components. Click Next again. Depending on the type of network adapter installed, a Network Card Setup dialog box may appear. This is where you enter the network adapter hardware configuration details, if required.

27. The TCP/IP Setup dialog box appears, asking whether you want to use a DHCP server. A DHCP server can be used to dynamically provide an IP address. (Further details

about DHCP servers can be found in Chapter 7.) Click No to refuse the DHCP server. The setup continues.

28. The TCP/IP Properties sheet appears. Enter the IP address and subnet mask of the computer you are installing NT on. Click OK. The Show Bindings dialog box appears. This can be used to disable network bindings or rearrange the order of the bindings. Click Next. The networking portion of the setup is now complete.

29. Click Next. Because this installation has been specified as a primary domain controller, you'll need to provide the name of the domain that this PDC will manage. Enter the domain name, and click Next. Click Finish to continue.

30. The Date And Time Properties sheet appears. Select the correct time zone, and select the Date & Time tab. Set the correct date and time.

31. Click Close. The Display Properties dialog box appears. The auto-detected display details are shown. Click OK. Set the required display settings, and select Test. Click OK. The display test pattern is displayed for 5 seconds. Confirm whether the display test was successful. If it wasn't, change the display settings, and try the test again. Confirm the display setting by clicking OK. Now, click OK on the Display Properties box to continue the setup.

32. The default security is set on the Windows NT NTFS partition. You are then prompted to insert the floppy disk you want to use as the emergency repair disk into drive A. Click OK.

33. The Windows NT 4.0 installation is now complete. Remove the disk from the floppy drive and compact disk from the CD-ROM drive. Click the Restart Computer button.

Upgrading Windows NT

Now that your company is committed to Windows NT, users are coming out of the woodwork all over the company with Windows NT systems they had actually been using for some time. They have asked you to upgrade their systems to the latest version of Windows NT.

1. Start the computer with the Windows NT Workstation Setup disk 1 in the floppy drive. The Windows NT Setup program begins. You are prompted to insert Workstation Setup disk 2 at the appropriate time.

2. The installation continues. The Welcome To Setup screen appears, with four options:

   • To learn more about Windows NT Setup before continuing, press F1.

   • To set up Windows NT now, press Enter.

   • To repair a damaged Windows NT version 4.0 installation, press R.

   • To quit Setup without installing Windows NT, press F3.

3. Press Enter. The Windows NT Setup mass storage device detection screen appears. This is used to either automatically detect or manually define the mass storage devices available on this system. Two options are available:

   • To continue, press Enter. Setup will attempt to detect mass storage devices in your computer.

   • To skip mass storage device detection, press S. Setup will allow you to manually select SCSI adapters, CD-ROM drives, and special disk controllers for installation.

 Certain types of mass storage devices can't be automatically detected. In fact, the detection attempt can cause the computer to lock up. If this happens, reboot and use the manual detection method.

4. Press Enter, and the device scan is performed. You are prompted to insert Workstation Setup disk 3. Press Enter. The device detection continues, and the relevant device drivers are loaded. A list of detected mass storage devices are displayed, along with the following two options:

   • To specify additional SCSI adapters, CD-ROM drives, or special disk controllers for use with Windows NT, including those for which you have a device support disk from a mass storage device manufacturer, press S.

- If you do not have any more device support disks from a mass storage device manufacturer, or you do not want to specify additional mass storage devices for use with Windows NT, press Enter.

5. Press Enter. The necessary device and file system drivers are loaded. You are prompted to insert the Windows NT Workstation CD-ROM into your CD-ROM drive. Press Enter when ready. The Windows NT licensing agreement is displayed. Press Page Down to read the whole agreement. When you reach the bottom of the agreement, press F8 to accept the terms and conditions of the agreement, or press Esc if you do not accept them. If you press Esc, the installation terminates.

6. Setup automatically detects that a previous version of Windows NT is installed on this computer and displays a screen telling you to press Enter to upgrade Windows NT. Press Enter. Setup now examines your hard disk for corruption. This is a two-stage test. The first is a basic mandatory test. The second is a more exhaustive test, which can take some time on large-capacity disks. The following two options are presented:

   - To allow Setup to perform an exhaustive secondary examination on your hard disk(s), press Enter.

   - To skip the exhaustive examination, press Esc.

7. Press Enter. The test is performed, and the upgrade continues. When this part of the setup is finished, you are prompted to remove the floppy disks and CD-ROM from your drives. Press Enter, and the computer restarts.

8. You are prompted to insert the Windows NT Workstation CD-ROM into the CD-ROM drive. Click OK. The Windows NT Workstation Upgrade dialog box appears. Click Next. Enter the 10-digit CD key located on the back of the CD case into the CD Key dialog box.

9. Click Next. The Optional Components dialog box appears. Click Next to accept the default components. The Upgrading Windows NT Network Services Setup window appears, and depending on the network services installed, additional dialog boxes may be displayed.

10. Click Finish. You are prompted to insert a floppy disk into drive A to create the emergency repair disk. Insert the disk, and click OK. The floppy disk is formatted and the configuration files are copied to the disk. The setup is now complete. You are prompted to remove all disks from the floppy and CD-ROM drives. Click the Restart Computer button. The computer system restarts, and the upgrade is complete.

Changing The Licensing Type

Because you have had a reasonably small Windows NT network, you have been using the per server licensing mode. As the network grows, it becomes clear that switching to the per seat mode will be more economical for further licensing.

1. Choose Start|Settings|Control Panel. The Control Panel appears.

2. Double click the Licensing icon. The Choose Licensing Mode dialog box appears, as shown in Figure 10.1.

3. Click the Per Server option to change from per seat to per server licensing mode.

4. Choose Add Licenses. The New Client Access License dialog box appears, as shown in Figure 10.2. Enter the number of licenses you have purchased in the Quantity pane.

5. Click OK. The per server licensing agreement appears. Select the "I agree that..." option box to accept the license, and click OK. You are returned to the Choose Licensing Mode dialog box. Click OK.

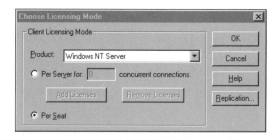

The Choose Licensing Mode dialog box.
Figure 10.1

The New Client Access License dialog box.
Figure 10.2

Regenerating The Windows NT Setup Floppy Disks

Big, big trouble. Your new puppy has just eaten your Windows NT setup disks. (Don't worry, the vet says he'll be okay.) Your problem is your new boss starts today and has already said that she wants to see how you install Windows NT onto a new system. As the old "dog ate my homework" excuse never worked very well at school, I'm sure your new boss is not going to fall for it. Not to worry. As long as you are able to salvage the Windows NT compact disk by wiping the dog slobber off, we should be able to save your job.

1. Insert the Windows NT Source Software compact disk into the CD-ROM drive. Choose Start|Programs|Command Prompt. The Command Prompt window appears.

2. Change the path to the CD-ROM and the correct subfolder for your processor type—for instance, D:\I386.

3. Enter "WINNT32 /OX" at the command prompt. Press Enter. The Windows NT 4.00 Upgrade/Installation dialog box appears, as shown in Figure 10.3.

4. Click Continue. The Windows NT 4.00 Workstation Installation/Upgrade dialog box prompts you to insert the three new setup disks in turn, as shown in Figure 10.4. Insert the first of three blank formatted disks you want to become the new Setup disk 3, and click OK. Repeat the process for both disk 2 and disk 1. Disk 1 is also known as the Windows NT Setup boot disk. When the regeneration of the three setup disks is complete, you are returned to the Windows NT Command Prompt window.

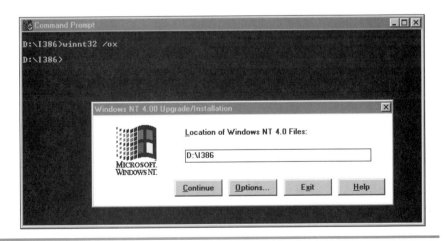

The Windows NT 4.00 Upgrade/Installation window.
Figure 10.3

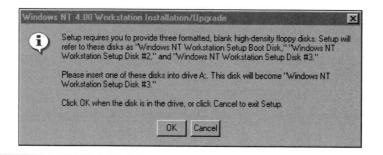

Instructions for creating new setup disks.
Figure 10.4

Quick Reference Specifications

The following are bare-bones facts and figures.

- *Per server licensing mode is often more economical in networks where clients connect to a single server.*

- *Per seat licensing mode is often more economical in networks where clients connect to several servers.*

Utilities To Use

The utilities used in this chapter and their functions are listed in this section. Consider this as a memory aid for the busy system administrator.

Licensing Icon

➤ *Change from per server licensing method to per seat.*

WINNT32

➤ *Create setup disks.*

Chapter 11

Hints And Tips

Administrator's Notes...

Chapter

11

This chapter does not focus on one particular area but, instead contains a mixed bag of hints and tips that don't neatly fit into the other chapters. Many of the points covered in this chapter are provided to make the day-to-day workload a little easier for the system administrator.

Scheduling

One area of weakness in the current release of Windows NT is scheduling. A basic scheduling utility is provided, managed via the **AT** command, that enables commands and programs to be scheduled to run at a specified date and time. However, no dependencies can be set (for example, setting the system to run Job 3 only after Job 1 and Job 2 have successfully been run). Such dependencies are often required for complex scheduling tasks.

The **AT** command is used from the Windows NT command prompt and is not the most user-friendly administration tool. In fact, incorrect **AT** commands are often entered, which then fail at the specified time. This can be very frustrating, because little information is usually given regarding the cause of the problem. It's worth checking the System Event log if you have problems with failing jobs.

The Schedule service needs to be running before you can use the **AT** command. Help can be obtained by adding a ? switch to the command, for instance, **AT /?.**

Shortcuts

To increase productivity and make frequently used programs and applications easier to locate, you can create a shortcut to the object from the Windows NT desktop. A shortcut can be configured on any object, including folders, disk drives, computers, and printers. When created, a shortcut appears as an icon with a small arrow in its left-hand corner. In addition, shortcuts can be placed in the Startup program group to automatically start the object upon logon.

Multiple shortcuts can be configured on the same object, and different security can be configured on each one. The deletion of a shortcut doesn't affect the original object.

Finding Resources

Locating computers in a large network by using the browser tools—for example, Network Neighborhood—can get increasingly difficult as the network expands, especially when the computer names are similar. For example, many companies employ a computer naming scheme that indicates where a computer is located in the organization, such as BL1A6 for Building 1, Area 6. Although this is useful for physically locating computers, it is less than ideal when using the browser tools. Locating files and folders can be just as troublesome, especially if you're not sure of the full name of the object you want to locate.

The Find utility, shown in Figure 11.1, is a handy alternative. In addition to locating computers, Find can be used to locate files and folders. Various search options are available with Find, including searching for files that contain a particular text string.

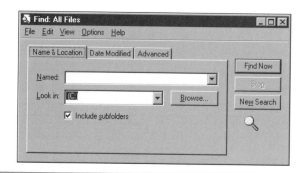

The Find utility dialog box.
Figure 11.1

Windows Messaging

Windows Messaging is a term used to describe user communication. For example, email and faxing are both parts of Windows Messaging. Windows NT is shipped with a client version of Microsoft Exchange, which can be used to connect to both Microsoft mail post offices and Internet mail services, and provide email facilities. These facilities are accessed via the Inbox icon on the desktop. The Practical Guide for this chapter contains an example of configuring Windows Messaging for use with Internet mail.

Practical

Guide To

Hints And Tips

The following section provides real-life hints and tips in step-by-step format.

Disabling The CD-ROM Autorun

Whenever you're in a hurry, which, of course, is all the time, the slightest holdup can send your blood pressure climbing. One feature of Windows NT that adds to your problems (at least, it does to mine) is the Autorun facility. Autorun brings up the Windows NT CD-ROM dialog box, as shown in Figure 11.2, each time you insert any application CD into your CD-ROM drive. Although the Autorun feature can be handy, especially when browsing a new CD-ROM, it's a pain to have to close this dialog box every time you load the Windows NT source software to be used by an administration tool.

Don't worry. You can use the Registry to disable this feature and keep your blood pressure from going off the scale.

1. Choose Start|Run. The Run dialog box appears.

The Windows NT CD-ROM dialog box.
Figure 11.2

2. Click Browse, and use the Browse dialog box to select the Registry Editor REGEDT32, located in the SYSTEM32 subfolder. Click OK. The Registry Editor window appears.

3. Select the HKEY_LOCAL_MACHINE subtree. Select the SYSTEM\CurrentControlSet\ Services\Cdrom subkey, as shown in Figure 11.3.

4. Double click the Autorun data value in the right-hand pane of the Registry Editor. The DWORD Editor dialog box appears. Change the data entry from 1 to 0, and click OK.

5. Exit the Registry Editor. You'll need to restart the system for the change to take effect.

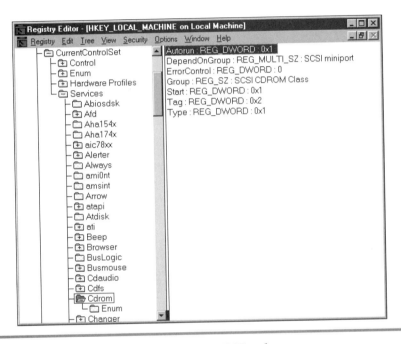

The Registry Editor, HKEY_LOCAL_MACHINE subtree.
Figure 11.3

Using The Recycle Bin To Restore A File

Yes, it happens even to system administrators—especially when they're under pressure. You got to your desk late one morning and found one of the data disks was running low on free disk space. You got a little overzealous pruning old data files from the disk, and the users are now beginning to notice.

Well, you could restore the deleted files from the last backup, but that would take some time. Luckily, the deleted files have only gone as far as the Recycle Bin.

1. Double click the Recycle Bin, displayed on your desktop. The Recycle Bin window appears, as shown in Figure 11.4.

2. Select the file you want to restore from the file list. Choose File|Restore. The file is restored back to its original location.

3. To remove all files from the Recycle Bin—in other words, actually delete them—choose File|Empty Recycle Bin. Then click Yes to confirm the file deletion. The Recycle Bin is emptied, and the display is updated.

note *When files are deleted from the Windows NT command prompt, the files are deleted immediately and are not moved to the Recycle Bin. The Recycle Bin can be completely disabled if required (that is, if you like living dangerously or if your organization's security policy requires it).*

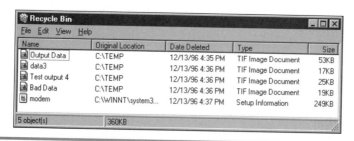

The Recycle Bin window.
Figure 11.4

Configuring The Recycle Bin Properties

The Recycle Bin has proven its usefulness now on more than one occasion. You decide to increase the maximum size of the Recycle Bin, thereby increasing the number of deleted files that are retained.

1. Right click the Recycle Bin, located on your desktop.

2. From the pop-up menu, choose Properties. The Recycle Bin Properties window appears, as shown in Figure 11.5.

3. To make changes affecting all hard disks attached to this system, select the Use One Setting For All Drives option, located on the Global page. To make changes for each individual drive, select Configure Drives Independently.

4. To change the size of the Recycle Bin, move the Maximum Size Of The Recycle Bin slider to the required size. Click OK.

> *The Recycle Bin automatically deletes the oldest files it contains when the bin becomes full.*

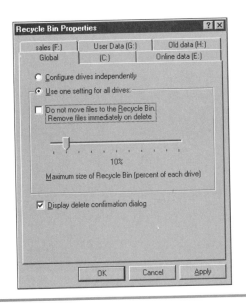

The Recycle Bin Properties window.
Figure 11.5

Changing The Network Bindings Order

You have various network protocols in use on your site. As discussed in Chapter 7, Windows NT is protocol-independent and will function with whichever protocol you decide. Say, for instance, you have multiple protocols installed on the same system, and you need to establish a connection to a network resource. If that network resource isn't known to the system—in other words, there is no existing connection to that resource—Windows NT will first attempt to establish a connection to the resource by using the protocol at the top of the protocol list. If this connection fails, the next protocol in the list is attempted, and so on.

This trial-and-error connection process can introduce a slight delay. Although this delay can't be removed, you can minimize it by making sure the most common protocol is at the top of the protocol list. For example, if your system connects mainly to TCP/IP-based systems and occasionally to both NetBEUI- and IPX-based systems, it makes sense to have TCP/IP as the first protocol in the bindings list.

1. Choose Start|Settings|Control Panel. The Control Panel window appears.

2. Double click the Network icon to access the Network utility sheet.

3. Choose the Bindings tab. The Bindings page appears. Double click the services displayed in the Service pane to expand the list. The protocols are displayed as shown in Figure 11.6.

4. Select the protocol you want to want to move, and select either Move Up or Move Down, as required.

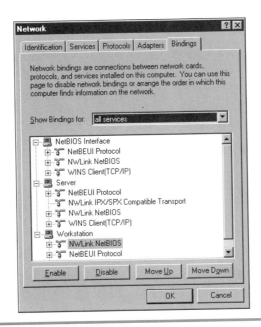

The Bindings page showing protocols.
Figure 11.6

Using The **AT** Command

You have written a command procedure to clear a temporary folder at the end of each day. You don't want to manually run this procedure each night, because your memory isn't what it used to be. Short of buying additional software, using the **AT** command is the only choice you have. It'll be messy, but here goes:

1. Choose Start|Programs|Command Prompt. The Windows NT Command Prompt window appears.

2. Type *AT* in the Command Prompt window, and press Enter. If Windows NT responds that the service has not yet been started, you'll need to start the Schedule service before using the **AT** command. If the Schedule service is already started, skip to Step 6.

3. To start Schedule, choose Start|Settings|Control Panel. The Control Panel window appears.

4. Double click the Services icon to access the Services dialog box. Select the Schedule service from the Services list, and click the Startup button. The Service Startup dialog box appears.

5. In the Startup Type pane, select the Automatic option, and click OK. You are returned to the Services window. With the Schedule service still selected, click the Start button. The service is started. Exit the Services window, and return to the Command Prompt window.

6. Enter the job you want to schedule—for example, **AT 21:30 "C:\sys\purge.exe"**. Figure 11.7 shows both Help for the **AT** command and an actual **AT** command scheduled.

```
Command Prompt                                                    _ □ X
C:\>at /?
The AT command schedules commands and programs to run on a computer at
a specified time and date. The Schedule service must be running to use
the AT command.

AT [\\computername] [ [id] [/DELETE] | /DELETE [/YES]]
AT [\\computername] time [/INTERACTIVE]
    [ /EVERY:date[,...] | /NEXT:date[,...]] "command"

\\computername     Specifies a remote computer. Commands are scheduled on the
                   local computer if this parameter is omitted.
id                 Is an identification number assigned to a scheduled
                   command.
/delete            Cancels a scheduled command. If id is omitted, all the
                   scheduled commands on the computer are canceled.
/yes               Used with cancel all jobs command when no further
                   confirmation is desired.
time               Specifies the time when command is to run.
/interactive       Allows the job to interact with the desktop of the user
                   who is logged on at the time the job runs.
/every:date[,...]  Runs the command on each specified day(s) of the week or
                   month. If date is omitted, the current day of the month
                   is assumed.
/next:date[,...]   Runs the specified command on the next occurrence of the
                   day (for example, next Thursday).  If date is omitted, the
                   current day of the month is assumed.
"command"          Is the Windows NT command, or batch program to be run.

C:\>at
Status ID   Day                    Time          Command Line
------------------------------------------------------------------------
        6   Tomorrow               9:30 PM        c:\winntpurge\clear.exe

C:\>
```

*Help for the **AT** command and a scheduled command.*
Figure 11.7

note

*This example would only run the command once. To achieve our aim of running
the command each day, you can put the **AT** command at the end of the program.
Then, when the program is completed, it will reschedule itself for the next day. Or
use the **every** switch with the **AT** command. Details on the **every** switch are given
in the online help for the **AT** command.*

Creating Shortcuts

Locating and selecting tools used on a day-to-day basis can be a real pain. One item that comes to mind is the Registry Editor REGEDT32, which has been used numerous times throughout this book. You could add an icon for the Registry Editor to the Administration Tools program group, or, as we will do in this example, you can create a shortcut that takes you directly to it from the desktop.

1. Choose Start|Programs|Windows NT Explorer. The Windows NT Explorer window appears.

2. Locate and right click the Registry Editor REGEDT32, contained in the SYSTEM32 subfolder. A pop-up menu appears.

3. From this menu, select Create Shortcut. A shortcut to the REGEDT32 object is created and appended to the subfolder. Right click the shortcut, and while holding down the right mouse button, drag and drop the shortcut onto the desktop.

Now, to access the Registry Editor, just double click the Shortcut icon. The shortcut is treated by Windows NT as an object in its own right, and as such, you can configure security and auditing on it. To change any of the shortcut properties, right click the shortcut, and select Properties from the pop-up menu. The Shortcut Properties window appears, as shown in Figure 11.8.

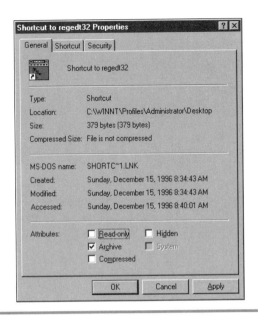

The Shortcut Properties window.
Figure 11.8

Converting FAT Volumes To NTFS

You have noticed that one of the old data volumes attached to your Windows NT server is still using FAT as its file system. (Shame on you! No local security. You will be drummed out of the administrators' secret lodge, and trust me, it's painful.) To spare yourself the humiliation and pain, it's a good idea to convert the file system to NTFS.

1. Choose Start|Programs|Command Prompt. The Windows NT Command Prompt window appears.

2. Enter the **convert** command, along with the drive letter of the drive you want to convert— for example, **convert h: /fs:ntfs**. An example drive conversion is shown in Figure 11.9.

> *If the drive you want to convert is the system drive, a system restart is required for the conversion process to run.*

Converting a FAT volume to NTFS.
Figure 11.9

Changing The Default Installation Device

Ever since you reconfigured your system after the last hardware upgrade, each time you want to use the Windows NT source software to install a new software component or read the online manuals, you have to change the CD-ROM drive ID in the dialog box that appears. This is necessary because the CD-ROM no longer has the same drive ID as it did when you first installed Windows NT.

You can fix this problem in one of three ways: reassign the drive IDs (details on doing this can be found in Chapter 4), change the default installation device stored in the Registry, or never make any changes. For this example, changing the default installation device is probably the most appropriate.

1. Choose Start|Run. The Run dialog box appears.

2. Click Browse, and use the Browse dialog box to select the Registry Editor REGEDT32, located in the SYSTEM32 subfolder. Click OK. The Registry Editor window appears.

3. Select the HKEY_LOCAL_MACHINE subtree. Select the \SOFTWARE\Microsoft\ Windows NT\CurrentVersion subkey. Double click the SourcePath data value in the right-hand pane of the Registry Editor. The String Editor dialog box appears, as shown in Figure 11.10.

4. Enter the required device and path for the Windows NT source software. In other words, specify which is the default installation device—for example, D:\I386. Click OK.

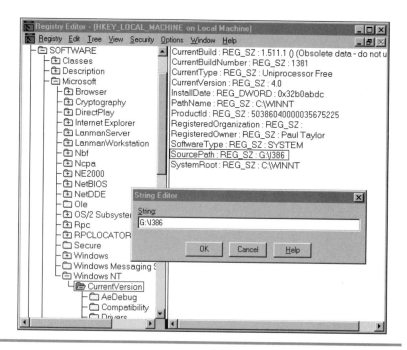

The String Editor dialog box in the Registry Editor.
Figure 11.10

Configuring Automatic Adjustment For Daylight Saving Time

Two time changes a year are just two too many. The adjustment can be easily forgotten, and it makes for very short winter days. (Moving to Arizona where it appears to be permanently summer—no daylight savings time—might not be a bad idea.) You can make the transition a little easier in the workplace, however, by setting Windows NT to automatically adjust for daylight saving time.

1. Choose Start|Settings|Control Panel. The Control Panel window appears.

2. Double click the Date/Time icon. The Date/Time Properties sheet appears. Choose the Time Zone tab to access the Time Zone page, as shown in Figure 11.11.

3. Select the Automatically Adjust Clock For Daylight Saving Changes checkbox. In the Time Zone box, verify that the correct time zone is set for your region, and click OK.

This is at least one clock you won't need to worry about when it comes to the next time change.

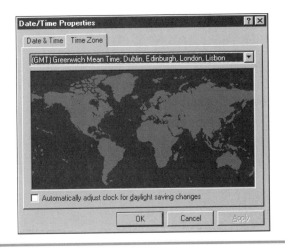

The Time Zone page in Date/Time Properties.
Figure 11.11

Changing The Installed Software Components

When you installed your server, your new boss was watching. This meant you didn't get a chance to install all of the games. The boss has now lost interest in all these boring computer issues, so you can remedy this oversight. (Of course, more mundane software components can be installed the same way.)

1. Choose Start|Settings|Control Panel. The Control Panel window appears.

2. Double click the Add/Remove Programs icon. The Add/Remove Programs Properties sheet appears. Click the Windows NT Setup tab to access the Windows NT Setup page, as shown in Figure 11.12.

3. Select Games from the Components list. Then click the Details button. A dialog box appears showing which games components are installed. Select the additional components you want to install, for example, 3D-Pinball, and click OK. If it's not already in the CD-ROM drive, you will be prompted to install the Windows NT source software and click OK.

Happy gaming! (By the way, playing 3D-Pinball on your server is a great way to slow it down and convince the boss it needs to be upgraded again.)

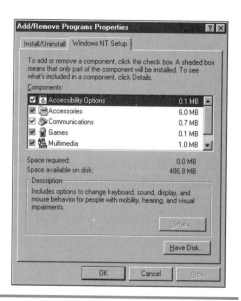

The Windows NT Setup page in Add/Remove Programs Properties.
Figure 11.12

Using The Find Utility To Locate A Computer

You need to locate a computer to check what network resources it is offering, but you have several thousand computers running Windows NT and it's the end of a long day. At about this time of day, computer names do tend to get a bit blurred around the edges. Take it easy, and let Find do the work for you.

1. Choose Start|Find|Computer. The Find: Computer dialog box appears.

2. In the Computer Name selection box, enter the name of the computer you want to find, and click the Find Now button.

3. As shown in Figure 11.13, the lower part of the Find: Computer dialog box displays the computer matching your search criteria.

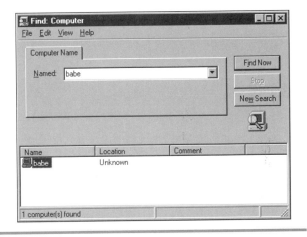

The Find: Computer dialog box.
Figure 11.13

Using The Find Utility To Locate Files And Folders

You came in this morning and found that your server was running low on disk space. This really doesn't make any sense; there was loads of free disk space when you finished work last night. It looks like someone has been eating disk space overnight. To identify the disk hog, you can use Find to display all files created since a certain date and time.

1. Choose Start|Find|Files Or Folders. The Find: All Files dialog box appears.

2. Click the Date Modified tab, and select the Find All Files Created Or Modified option.

3. In this example, we want to list files created over the last day, so select the During The Previous Day option, making sure that the day count is set to 1. Click Find Now. All files created during the previous day are found, as shown in Figure 11.14.

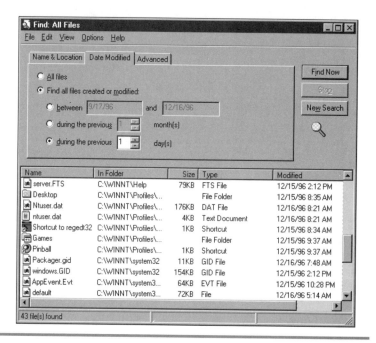

The Find: Files dialog box.
Figure 11.14

Configuring The Inbox For Internet Mail

Your Windows NT rollout is nearly complete, just one or two computers still need Windows NT installed. One of these systems uses a dial-up connection to an Internet service provider to send and receive Internet mail. The package used is MS-DOS based and accesses the communication hardware directly, so it doesn't work under Windows NT. You have at last discovered a use for the Inbox icon on your desktop. The dial-up networking software will need to be configured for connecting to your Internet service provider before you can use the Inbox to send and receive Internet mail. Details on configuring the dial-up software to do just this are given in Chapter 7.

1. Double click the Inbox icon on the Windows NT Desktop. A Microsoft Exchange dialog box will appear. Click Yes to install the Windows Messaging software. The Software will be installed, and you are returned to the desktop.

2. Double click the Inbox icon again, and the Windows Messaging Setup Wizard will appear. While the Inbox is configuring for Internet mail, clear the Microsoft Mail checkbox, and click Next.

3. Click the method to use to connect to the Internet mail server. The two options available are Use Dial-Up Networking and Use A Network Connection To Gain Access To Internet Mail. Select Dial-Up Networking for this example, and click Next.

4. Enter the Internet Mail Server name or IP address of the server that forwards your mail to you. This server is located at your Internet service provider, and they will be able to provide you with this information. Click Next.

5. Select the mail transfer method that suits your requirements. Figure 11.15 shows the two options available. For this example, select Automatic and then click Next.

6. Enter the email address for your mail account. For example, pault@system1. Click Next. Enter the mailbox account name and password for the Internet mail server. This information can be obtained from your Internet service provider. Click Next.

7. Confirm the location of your personal address book. If you don't already have one, a personal address book will be created for you automatically. Click Next.

8. Confirm the location of your personal folder file. If you don't already have one, a personal folder file will be created for you automatically. Click Next. Then click Finish to complete the setup process. The Inbox Windows Messaging window will appear as shown in Figure 11.16. The Inbox will contain a welcome message from Microsoft, which contains instructions on how to use the Windows Messaging system.

The Windows Messaging Setup Wizard mail transfer methods.
Figure 11.15

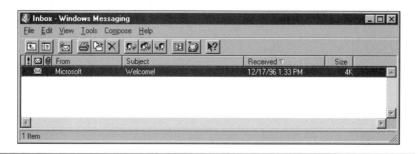

The Inbox Windows Messaging window.
Figure 11.16

Optimizing Server Throughput

One of your Windows NT Servers is used to host a client/server application and, against your better judgment, there are several network shares used on this server. The team using the client/server application has been complaining about the application slowing down at peak times. The following should help you decide how to optimize the server throughput for network applications:

1. Choose Start|Settings|Control Panel. The Windows NT Control panel will be displayed.

2. Double click the Network icon, and the Network utility window will appear. Click the Services tab from the Network Services list displayed on the Services sheet.

3. Select Server, and click Properties. The Server dialog box will be displayed, as shown in Figure 11.17.

4. Select the Maximize Throughput For Network Applications option and then click OK. You are returned to the Services sheet. Click Close. A Network Settings Change dialog box will be displayed. A reboot of the computer will be required for the changes to take effect. Click Yes to restart the computer now.

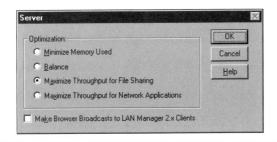

The Server dialog box.
Figure 11.17

Quick Reference Specifications

The following are the bare-bones facts and figures.

➤ *Shortcuts can be used to point to either printers, folders, files, computers, or disk drives.*

➤ *The Scheduler service must be running to use the **AT** command.*

➤ *The Recycle Bin properties can be set on a per-disk or a global basis.*

Utilities To Use

The utilities used in this chapter and their functions are listed in this section. Consider this a memory aid for the busy system administrator.

AT Command

- Scheduling jobs.
- Managing scheduled jobs.

Convert

- Converting FAT volumes to NTFS.

Date/Time Icon

- Configuring automatic adjustment for daylight saving time.

Find

- Locating computers, files, and folders.

Inbox Icon

- Installing, configuring, and using Windows Messaging.

Recycle Bin

- Restoring deleted files.
- Managing properties of file deletion.

REGEDT32

- Disabling the CD-ROM Autorun.

Network Icon

- Changing the order of the network bindings.
- Optimizing the server throughput.

Appendix A   Administrative Tools Reference

This appendix lists the Windows NT Administrative Tools and the functions they perform. Table A.1 lists various system administrative tasks and the tools to use to perform them, as well as each tool's location. For example, if you want to change the pagefile size, but can't remember which tool to use, look up pagefile in Table A.1, and it will show you that the System icon, accessed via the Control Panel, should be used. You will often find that there are several different ways to perform the same task; only the most common are listed in the table.

Add Printer Wizard

- Create printers.
- Connect to network printers.

Command Prompt

- Start processes.
- Schedule programs and commands with the AT command.

Convert

- Convert FAT volumes to NTFS.

Date/Time Icon

- Configure automatic adjustment for daylight saving time.
- Set the system date and time.

DHCP Manager

- Create and manage the leased IP address range.
- View which IP addresses are managed by which host.

Dial-up Networking

- Define phone book entries.
- Connect to remote LANs using RAS.
- Connect to the Internet.

Disk Administrator

- Create and format disk partitions, volumes, and stripe sets.
- Create and format stripe sets with parity.
- Establish and break mirror/duplex sets.
- Assign drive IDs.
- Save and restore disk configuration.

Display Icon

- Set display colors and resolution.
- Configure password-protected screen savers.

DNS Manager

- Manage the DNS Service.

Event Viewer

- View the System, Security, and Application event logs.
- Set event log size and retention time.

File Manager

- Create and manage Macintosh volumes.

Inbox

- Install the Windows messaging system.

- Compose, read, and delete messages.

Licensing Manager

- Change from per server to per seat licensing method.

MacFile

- View, disconnect, and send messages to Macintosh users.

- View and close client connections to Macintosh volumes.

- View and close files opened by Macintosh clients.

My Computer Icon

- Format floppy disks.

- Locate files and folders on your computer.

Network Client Administrator

- Create a network installation disk.

- Install domain management tools on network systems.

Network Icon

- Change domain, workgroup, or computer names.

- Add or remove network services.

- Add, remove, or configure protocols.

- Add, remove, or configure network adapters.

- Change the order of network bindings.

Performance Monitor

- Monitor local and remote system performance.
- View logged performance data.
- Define system alerts.

Printer Properties

- Set printer permissions.
- Set printer auditing.
- Configure separator pages.
- Configure printer scheduling.

RDISK

- Create and update Emergency Repair Disk.

Recycle Bin

- Restore deleted files.
- Manage properties of file deletion.

Registry Editor

- Search the Registry of a particular key.
- Manage the Registry on a remote computer.
- Save Registry keys.
- Modify Registry entries.
- Set Registry permissions and auditing.

Remote Access Administrator

- View and administrate RAS.
- Assign user permissions for dial-up communications.

Server Manager

- Add and remove computers from domain.

- Send messages to domain computers.

- Promote BDC to PDC.

- Synchronize domain controllers.

- Create and manage Macintosh volumes.

- Send messages to Macintosh clients.

- View and disconnect users.

- Configure folder replication.

Services

- Start and stop system services.

- Change service startup types.

System Policy Editor

- Create domain-wide system policies.

- Create domain-wide user policies.

- Create user and system-specific policies.

Task Manager

- Change a process's base priority class.

- Monitor local system performance.

- Terminate a process.

User Manager

- Configure the system audit policy.

- Create, copy, rename, and delete system user accounts.

- Set and change user passwords.

- Set account and user rights policy.

- Define paths for profiles and logon scripts.

User Manager For Domains

- Configure the domain audit policy.

- Create, copy, rename, and delete domain user accounts.

- Set and change user passwords.

- Set account and user rights policy.

- Define paths for profiles and logon scripts.

- Set account logon restrictions.

- Establish domain trusts.

Windows NT Diagnostics

- Generate diagnostics reports.

- Display assigned IRQs.

Windows NT Explorer

- Manage files and folders.

- View and set object permissions.

- Create, copy, move, and delete files and folders.

- Configure auditing on files and folders.

- Take ownership of files and folders.

- Perform disk error checking.

Windows NT Setup Disks

- Restore data from the emergency repair disk.

- Check for system corruption.

WINNT32

- Create setup disks.

- Install and upgrade Windows NT.

WINS Manager

- Manage the WINS server replication functions.

- View registered WINS clients.

- Backup and restore the WINS database.

Task	Tool Used	Accessed Via
Auditing (Configure policy for workgroup)	User Manager	Administrative Tools
Auditing (Configure policy for domain)	User Manager for Domains	Administrative Tools
Audit Logs (Viewing and configuring)	Event Viewer	Administrative Tools
Disk Volumes (Administrative functions)	Disk Administrator	Administrative Tools
Domains (Add and remove computers from domain)	Server Icon	Control Panel
Domains (Establishing and managing trusts)	User Manager For Domains	Administrative Tools
Files and Folders (Administrating)	Windows NT Explorer	Programs Group
Format hard disks	Disk Administrators	Administrative Tools
Format floppy disks	My Computer	Desktop
Manage Macintosh clients	MacFile	Control Panel
Messaging (Installation, use, and configuration)	Inbox	Desktop

continued

Table A.1   System administrative tasks.

(continued)

Task	Tool Used	Accessed Via
Network Resources (Using and managing)	Windows NT Explorer	Programs Group
Network Configuration (Protocols and services)	Network Icon	Control Panel
Pagefile (Change and create)	System Icon	Control Panel
Printers (Create and connect to)	Add Printers Wizard	Settings Group
Printers (Delete and manage)	Printer Properties	Settings Group
Process (Changing priorities)	Task Manager	Task Bar
Process (Starting)	Command Prompt	Programs Group
Process (Terminating)	Task Manager	Task Bar
Scheduling	Command Prompt	Programs Group

Table A.1   System administrative tasks.

Appendix B

Windows NT Changes And Enhancements

This appendix details the major differences between Windows NT 3.51 and 4.0. As this book is aimed at system administrators, the changes to the application programming interfaces have been omitted.

Windows NT Common Features

Common features of both Windows NT Workstation and Server are detailed in this section.

The User Interface

The most notable change introduced with Windows NT 4.0 is the inclusion of the Windows 95-style graphical user interface. This replaces the Windows 3.1-style GUI previously used with Windows NT. If you are not familiar with the Windows 95 GUI, Windows NT 4.0 can, at first glance, appear to be a totally new operating system, and it can take some time getting used to. However, once you delve beneath the surface, you will find the same core operating system.

With the introduction of the Windows 95-style GUI, several administrative tools have also been replaced. The most important tool changes are the File Manager, which has been replaced by the Windows NT Explorer, and the Print Manager, which has been replaced by the Printer window. Most of the other system administration tools are unchanged, although they do have the Windows 95-style windows.

Another less obvious, but no less important, change to the graphical user interface is that Microsoft has changed the system architecture of Windows NT by moving the GUI from User mode to Kernel mode. By placing the GUI in Kernel mode, the GUI gains direct access to the computer hardware. This provides a performance improvement, as the GUI is now less dependent on other software components to perform its tasks. However, as the GUI now has direct hardware access, any problems within the GUI could cause Windows NT to crash.

High Performance File System

The High Performance File System (HPFS) is the native OS/2 file system. Until Windows NT 4.0, HPFS volumes could be accessed and used by Windows NT. However, certain native Windows NT facilities, such as local file security and disk compression, couldn't be used with HPFS volumes. It has never been possible to format Windows NT with HPFS, as support was only provided to assist with the migration to Windows NT.

All support for HPFS volumes has been dropped with Windows NT 4.0. If you have a Windows NT 3.51 system with HPFS volumes attached, you will need to convert them to NTFS by using the conversion utility before upgrading to Windows NT 4.0.

Internet Explorer

Internet Explorer is an integrated Web browser that can be used to access data on the Internet, as well as corporate intranets. Internet Explorer is not only included with Windows NT 4.0, but is automatically installed on your desktop, thus encouraging its use.

When dial-up networking has been configured, Internet Explorer can automatically dial up your Internet service provider to access Internet-based resources.

Microsoft Exchange

A client version of Microsoft Exchange is provided with Windows NT 4.0 and provides Windows messaging services. The Exchange client can be accessed from the desktop via the Inbox icon. The Inbox is referred to as the Universal Inbox, as it can be interfaced with not only Microsoft Mail, but with the Internet and other online mail services, as well.

Hardware Profiles

Hardware profiles can be used to configure Windows NT for different hardware configurations—for example, a laptop computer could be used with or without a docking station, thus having two completely different hardware configurations. By creating profiles for each configuration, Windows NT can be started with the correct software components for each configuration. This stops the software service failure messages that would usually be displayed, for example, when starting an undocked laptop if the network adapter is not present.

Netware Client

The Netware Client shipped with Windows NT is now NDS aware; in other words, the client is compatible with the NDS structure used by Netware 4. Prior to Windows NT 4.0, the Netware client could only be use with Netware 4 servers in bindery emulation mode.

Netware user passwords can now be automatically synchronized with the Windows NT user passwords. With NT 3.51, when the user changed her Windows NT user password, the Netware user password had to be changed manually. This is no longer the case. However, this is only a one-way synchronization process. If a user manually changes her Netware 4 password, her Windows NT password will not change automatically to match it.

Point-To-Point Tunneling Protocol

The Point-to-Point Tunneling Protocol (PPTP) enables the creation of a virtual network across the Internet. This allows native Windows NT file and print services to be accessed via the Internet. The Point-to-Point Tunneling protocol creates a virtual network by encapsulating any of the supported RAS protocols before routing them across the Internet.

Administrative Wizards

A number of administrative wizards are now available to guide the system administrator through the basic administrative tasks. However, they can become quite tedious, as you will be led through the administrative task step-by-step.

Telephony Application Program Interface

The telephony application program interface (TAPI) enables Windows NT to store your modem configuration details. When a new TAPI-enabled communication package is installed, the application can obtain the modem configuration details for your modem from Windows NT, saving you from having to enter these details each time you install communication software.

Enhancements To Windows NT Server

This section details the enhancements that apply only to Windows NT Server; these are in addition to the common features already discussed.

Internet Information Server

The Internet Information Server (IIS) is a fully functional Web server (a Web server makes available files and applications by using the Hypertext Transport Protocol, or HTTP). The IIS is now fully integrated with the Windows NT source software CD-ROM and installation process. Previously, IIS was available as a separate product.

A version of IIS is also supplied with Windows NT Workstation, but it is referred to as Peer Web Services.

FrontPage

To help the user create Web pages, a copy of FrontPage is now included with Windows NT Server. FrontPage is a Web authoring and management tool that includes various configuration and management wizards to assist in the creation of Web sites.

Domain Name System

The Domain Name System (DNS) provides an IP-to-host name look-up function. Previously, the DNS server software was only available as part of the unsupported software shipped with the Windows NT resource kit.

Network Monitor

A cut-down version of the Network Monitor shipped with Microsoft's System Management Server (SMS) is included with Windows NT Server. This version of the Network Monitor is limited to capturing network data packets sent to and from the server that the monitor is running on. With the full SMS version, all data packets on the network can be captured.

# *Appendix*

Windows NT User Rights

Table C.1 provides a complete list of Windows NT user rights and the rights that are defined as advanced are indicated with an X.

Right	Advanced Right	Description
Access this computer	–	Allows users to log on or establish network connections to this computer.
Act as part of the operating system	X	Operations can be performed as part of the operating system. Currently used by some of the Windows NT subsystems.
Add workstations to domain	–	Permits non-Administrator accounts to add workstations to the domain. This right is not currently implemented.
Back up files and directories	–	Permits users to back up files and folders that they don't have direct access to (overrides the file and folder permissions).
Bypass traverse checking	X	Allows users to access files and folders contained in a parent folder that they have been denied access to. This right needs to be removed from users who require POSIX compliance.

continued

Table C.1 The Windows NT user rights.

(continued)

Right	Advanced Right	Description
Change the system time	–	Allows the time of the Windows NT computer to be changed.
Create a pagefile	X	Allows a pagefile to be created. This right is not currently implemented.
Create a permanent shared object	X	Used internally with Windows NT to create special permanent objects.
Create a token object	X	Used by the Local Security Authority to create the user Security Access Token on logon.
Debug programs	X	Permits the user to debug low-level objects.
Force shutdown from a remote system	–	Permits computer to be shut down from a remote system. This right is not currently implemented.
Generate security audits	X	Permits security audit log entries to be generated.
Increase quotas	X	Allows object quotas to be increased. This right is not currently implemented.
Increase scheduling priority	X	Permits the scheduling priority of a process to be increased.
Load and unload device drivers	–	Permits device drivers to be installed and removed.
Lock pages in memory	X	Permits pages to be locked into memory. Locked pages will not be paged out from main memory to the pagefile.
Log on as a batch job	X	Permits jobs to be logged on as batch processes. This right is not currently implemented.
Log on as a service	X	Permits a process to be run as a service.

continued

Table C.1 The Windows NT user rights.

(continued)

Right	Advanced Right	Description
Log on locally	–	Permits local logon using the workstation keyboard.
Manage auditing and security log	–	Permits the events that are to be audited on an object to be defined. Also allows the security event log to be managed.
Modify firmware environment values	X	Allows the modification of system variables contained in nonvolatile RAM. Only used with computers with necessary hardware.
Profile single process	X	Permits the performance sampling of a single process.
Profile system performance	X	Permits the performance sampling of the system.
Replace a process level token	X	A right used only by the operating system to modify a process' security access token.
Restore files and directories	–	Permits users to restore files and folders that they do not have direct access to.
Shut down the system	–	Permits the system to be shut down.
Take ownership of files or other objects	–	Permits ownership of objects to be taken, overriding the assigned permissions.

Table C.1 The Windows NT user rights.

Appendix D

Networking Technologies

As the number of Windows NT administrators increases in direct proportion to the number of Windows NT installations, these new administrators might not have an appropriate background. If these administrators don't understand NT's basic networking concepts, they can be at a disadvantage when it comes to supporting Windows NT. This appendix is aimed at providing a grounding in networking technology, and the information contained in it will stand you in good stead, regardless of which future network operating system you support.

LANs And WANs

LANs (Local Area Networks) and WANs (Wide Area Networks) are two of the most common network acronyms. The widespread use of networking means that most organizations now have a mixture of both.

A LAN can be defined as the network you are locally attached to, whereas the WAN provides connectivity between remote locations, for example, connecting the Boston branch office to the New York head office. The line defining a LAN and a WAN often becomes blurred—in fact, the term ELAN is sometimes used to describe an Extended Local Area Network.

Ethernet

The development of Ethernet can be traced back to the 1970s, when a radio-wave-based network named ALOHANET was developed by the University of Hawaii for inter-island data communications. From this basic network concept, the Xerox Corporation developed the Ethernet network technology to run over coaxial cable. Xerox later was joined in the development of Ethernet by Intel and Digital Equipment Corporation (DEC).

Networking computers with Ethernet has become relatively inexpensive; however, in large installations, the actual installation costs of the coaxial cable are the major expense, especially in old buildings that were never designed to take network cables. There are three types of coaxial cable that can be used with Ethernet networks: thick wire, thin wire, and unshielded twisted pair (UTP). Ethernet networks can, and often do, consist of a mixture of all three cable types.

The thick wire coaxial cable is the oldest form of cabling used to connect computers together via Ethernet, and it is both difficult to install and expensive. Attaching new nodes to a thick wire segment involves drilling through the shielding and attaching a transceiver to the cable. Care has to be taken when performing this operation, as causing the shielding of the coaxial cable to touch the inner core of the cable will halt all network traffic. Thick wire coaxial is very robust and can be used in segment lengths of up to 500 meters without any additional hardware.

Thin wire coaxial cable is both considerably cheaper and easier to install than thick wire. However, it is not as robust as thick wire cable and is often damaged—especially when offices are being refurbished. The attachment of nodes to thin wire is achieved by attaching "T" pieces to the cable, which then connect to your computer. However, if there isn't a free "T" piece available on your thin wire segment, an additional piece of cable will need to be added with an additional "T" piece. The network traffic will also need to be interrupted when the "T" piece is added. (Buildings can be wired with special thin wire connection plates, known as make-before-break connectors. These allow computers to be added to the thin wire segment without interrupting the network traffic.) Thin wire segments can be up 185 meters in length without any additional hardware being required.

Both thick and thin wire coaxial cables need to be terminated at both ends of the segment with Ethernet terminators. The terminators place a 50 ohms impedance at the end of the cable. Because these terminators are connected in a parallel fashion, if the impedance is measured on the segment using a multi-meter, the impedance will be 25 ohms. This is a quick and easy check to verify that a segment is terminated properly. If a terminator is removed for the segment or if the coaxial cable is cut, all network traffic on the segment will be interrupted—this could put a whole department out of action.

The third type of cabling that can be used is unshielded twisted pair (UTP), which provides point-to-point network connections combined into a single network via a network device known as a hub. As the cables are connected point-to-point, damaging a single cable will only affect the network node attached to it. In other words, a single user will be out of action instead of a whole department. New buildings are often cabled with UTP during the construction stage, using a technique known as flood wiring. This technique calls for UTP cables to be installed in every location within the building—these can then be used as required. Unshielded Twisted Pair segments can be up to 100 meters in length.

CSMA/CD

Carrier Sense Multi Access, Collision Detect (CSMA/CD) is the technique used with Ethernet networks to transmit the data onto the network. Only one node may transmit at a time. When a network node wants to transmit data onto the network, that node will first "listen" to the network to see if another node is currently transmitting. This is the Carrier Sense. Multi Access means all network nodes are equal and have the same rights to access the network. Collision Detect is used to detect when there are two network nodes transmitting at the same time. For example, if two network nodes both want to send data across the network, they first check to see if the network is free (no one else is currently transmitting data). If they decide the network is free, they both may send their data at the same time—this would cause a network collision. Both network nodes would recognize that a collision has occurred and will stop transmitting. They will both then wait a random amount of time before attempting to transmit the data again. Collisions are expected to occur in an Ethernet network and, as long as the number of collisions is not excessive, they won't cause a problem.

Ethernet network nodes are identified by unique hardware addresses assigned to the network adapters. Ethernet data is sent across the network in data packets. These packets contain both the destination address and source address, the actual data, and a data check sum.

Bridges, Routers, And Repeaters

As we have already discussed, each type of cable used with Ethernet networks has different characteristics. For example, the maximum thin wire single segment length is 185 meters. To extend your network over this length, additional hardware is required. Bridges, routers, and repeaters can all be used to extend you network.

Repeaters can be used to extend a network by regenerating the data packets. The repeater functions at the lowest level and does not understand the packets it is regenerating. All data is passed through a repeater—no filtering is performed.

Bridges can be used to not only extend network segments, but also to filter network traffic, so only the packets needed on a particular network segment will be passed by the bridge, thereby reducing the overall network load.

Routers are used to logically split networks into different areas. Data packets are directed by the routers across the network to reach their destinations. Not all network protocols can be routed. For example, NetBEUI is a nonrouteable protocol. Routers are not always separate hardware devices—sometimes a host computer will act as a router to route packets through two separate network adapters. More details on network protocols are given in Chapter 7.

Token Ring

Token ring networks are an alternative to Ethernet technology that have been developed by IBM. Token rings use what is called a twin ring topology, which has the advantage that if the primary network cable is broken, the network can automatically be switched over to the fallback ring, so no network disruption will occur.

Token ring network nodes are only allowed to transmit data on the network when they hold the token, the token being a data packet that is passed from node to node on the network. This means that only one node at a time will be transmitting, so no collisions will be created.

Like Ethernet, several different types of cable can be used to construct a token ring network, and each cable type has a different maximum length.

ATM, FDDI, And Fast Ethernet

As networks have increased in size and the applications that run across them have become more complex, the available network bandwidth has become a performance bottleneck. To counter this problem, new network technologies have been developed—namely ATM, FDDI, and Fast Ethernet—that increase the speed of the network from the 10 MB per second for Ethernet and the 16 MB per second for Token Ring up to 100 MB per second.

Index

A

Access masks, 34
Account Information
  dialog box, 150
Account policies.
  See also user accounts.
  deleting, 177
  domain-wide, creating, 174-175
  groups
    default, 138-139
    definition, 137-140
    global, 140
    local, 140
    renaming not allowed, 140
  permissions, default, 138-139
  user-specific
    adding, 176
    deleting, 177
Account Policy dialog box, 137
ACEs (access control entries), 33
ACLs (access control lists), 33
Add User dialog box, 176
Add Users and Groups
  dialog box, 208
Add Value dialog box, 45
Administrative accounts, 34-35
Administrator Wizard, 120
Alert function, 307-308

Alert messages
  configuring, 323-324
  triggering, 307-308
Alerter system service, 65
AppleTalk
  definition, 233
  password security risk, 243-244
Application logs
  clearing, 301
  viewing, 301-305
ARC (Advanced RISC Computer)
  naming convention, 62, 64
Architecture, 3-4
arp, TCP/IP command, 238
AT command
  definition, 407
  example, 418-419
Auditing
  event types, 304
  events, 104-105
  files, 125-126
  folders, 125-126
  network servers, 252-253
  printers, 209-210
  Registry change failures, 48-49
  servers, 252-253
  unsuccessful logon
    attempts, 314-315
Autorun facility, disabling, 412-413

B

Backing up data, 336-337
Banner pages.
   See print separator files.
/BASEVIDEO configuration
   switch, 63
BDC (backup domain controllers)
   definition, 227-228
   finding, 276
   promoting to PDC, 277-279
Boot disk. *See* boot floppy.
Boot floppy
   creating, 340-342
   definition, 332, 334
   dual boot requirements, 341
   fault-tolerance, 343-344
   reformatting, 342
   SCSI boot requirements, 341
Boot formats, 62-63
Boot partitions, 92
Boot problems, 332-334
BOOT.INI startup file, 61-63
BOOTSECT.DOS startup file, 61
Browser service, 230
Burst pages.
   See print separator files.

C

C2 security, 36-37
Case sensitivity
   file names, 97
   passwords, 149
   usernames, 149
CDFS (compact disk file system), 98
CD-ROM, disabling Autorun,
   412-413

Check Disk dialog box, 374
Choose Licensing Mode
   dialog box, 400
Commands
   network
      list of, 245
      running on remote host, 238
   TCP/IP, 238
Computer Browser system
   service, 65
Computers, finding on a
   network, 427
Configuration switches, 63
Copy To dialog box, 171
CPU usage, displaying, 305-307

D

Data, distributing over multiple
   disks, 93-94, 118-119
Data compression
   example, 127
   maximum cluster size, 105
   with Windows NT Explorer, 105
Data types, Registry, 6
Daylight savings time,
   adjusting for, 425
DECPSMAN.DLL print monitor, 187
Default operating system,
   setting, 71
Desktop configuration, saving, 141
Device conflicts, 372
Device detection, 370-373
Device drivers, displaying at
   startup, 63
DHCP (dynamic host
   configuration), 236
   clients, tracing, 268

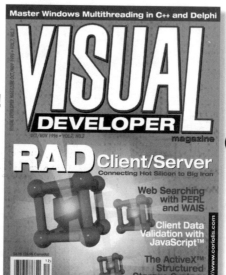